Key Themes in Interpersonal Communication: Culture, Identities and Performance

Key Themes in Interpersonal Communication: Culture, Identities and Performance

Anne Hill, James Watson, Danny Rivers and Mark Joyce

Open University Press

Open University Press
McGraw-Hill Education
McGraw-Hill House
Shoppenhangers Road
Maidenhead
Berkshire
England
SL6 2QL

email: enquiries@openup.co.uk
world wide web: www.openup.co.uk

and Two Penn Plaza, New York, NY 10121–2289, USA

First published 2007

A catalogue record of this book is available from the British Library

ISBN-13: 9780 335 220533 (pb) 978 0335 220540 (hb)

ISBN-10: 0335 220533 (pb) 0335 220541 (hb)

Library of Congress Cataloguing-in-Publication Data
CIP data applied for

Typeset by YHT Ltd, London
Printed in Poland by OzGraf S.A.
www.polskabook.pl

The **McGraw·Hill** Companies

Contents

Acknowledgements

We would like to thank the following for their contribution and support: Angela Bell, Phil Hawks, Marion Kember and our interviewees; and at OU Press/McGraw-Hill – Chris Cudmore, Suzanne Panayiodou and Jack Fray.

The authors and the publishers would like to thank the following for permission to use copyright material:

Figure 1.1, Shannon and Weaver model from *The Mathematical Theory of Communication* copyright 1949, 1998 by Board of Trustees of the University of Illinois. Reproduced with permission of the University of Illinois Press.

Figures 1.2 and 1.3, Osgood and Schramm model and Wilbur Schramm model reproduced with the kind permission of Mary Schramm Coberly.

Figure 1.5, Jakobsen's model from Thomas Sebeok (ed.) *Style in Language* (US: MIT Press) 1960. Reproduced with permission of MIT Press.

Figure 1.10, Becker's mosaic model from *Proceedings of the University of Minnesota Spring Symposium in Speech Communication* 1968, reproduced with the kind permission of The University of Minnesota.

Figure 1.18, Noelle-Neumann's Spiral of Silence from Brown's *Group Processes* (Oxford: Blackwell) 2001.

Table 3.1, Belbin's nine team roles from Belbin *The Coming Shape of Organization* (London: Butterworth Heinemann) 1996.

Every effort has been made to trace the copyright holders but if any have been inadvertently overlooked the publisher will be pleased to make the necessary arrangement at the first opportunity.

List of figures and tables

Introduction

Our aim is to provide you, the reader, with an introduction to the study of interpersonal communication; an introduction that focuses on an exploration of the sociocultural 'surround' in which interpersonal communication takes place and the interplay between this surround and the construction and display of identities through our everyday communicative performances. Many of the messages carried in everyday social interaction can be seen to carry the raw materials out of which identities are explored, displayed and constructed.

We have taken as our starting point Anthony Giddens's argument that in an age of globalization, social fragmentation and change, self-identity has to be forged 'amid a puzzling diversity of options and possibilities' (1991: 3). Research located in a range of sociological, psychological and linguistic perspectives is used to illustrate the potential of everyday communication to contribute to the challenge of forging a sense of identity. We embrace recognition of the possibility that self-identity may be composed of a 'multiplicity of selves' (Eisenberg 2001).

Given the mediated nature of much of modern life in Western countries, this exploration extends to a consideration of the interface between interpersonal and mass communication. Advertising and other forms of media culture, arguably, contain many messages with the potential to impact on the development of self- and social identities.

The growth of cultural diversity within Western societies, as a result of post-war immigration, has not only presented new possibilities and dilemmas for the construction of self- and social identity but also highlighted the need for individuals to be aware of the mosaic of factors impacting upon co-cultural and intercultural communication – indeed such awareness can be seen as a key ingredient of effective interpersonal communication in contemporary Western societies.

It may be useful to share with you at this point some preliminary thoughts about the relationship between **culture** and **communication**. The communication process is an integral part of the culture in which it takes place. The signs, symbols and codes that are the building blocks of the interpersonal communication process are located in cultures. The meanings they convey rely to a considerable extent upon shared cultural understanding. Culture, like the communication process, is *dynamic* and thus so is the nature of the relationship between them. Cultures both identify and differentiate human societies and are woven from many complex factors. The main elements that compose the culture of a society are its history, language(s), traditions, customs, arts, climate, geography, social, political and economic norms, religion(s) and values.

Culture is transmitted through the process of **socialization**, one by which the behaviour of new members of society, for example children or immigrants, is shaped in accordance with the expectations of its culture. This process is sometimes referred to as enculturation. Socialization is often subtle in nature and we may take for granted the cultural expectations of the society into which we have been born and spent many of our formative years. It is when we encounter other cultural expectations that we often become most aware of our own cultural assumptions. Today there are many reasons why we may become aware of other cultural expectations: through travel, for business or leisure, and as a consequence of the forces of immigration and emigration, for example. We are also exposed to a considerable amount of information about other cultures through the mass media.

The process of **enculturation** is arguably most fraught for those who have been socialized into one societal culture but then find themselves having to adapt, for an extended period of time or permanently, to another. The greater the contrast between the cultural assumptions and expectations, the more problematic the process of adapting to the requirements of the new culture is likely to be and, arguably, the more significant the consequences for an individual's communicative competence.

The process of enculturation, however, is very complex and multi-faceted for within cultures are to be found **subcultures** and co-cultures and the processes of socialization found within them interact with those of the main societal culture. Subcultures can be viewed as alternatives to the dominant culture within a society, for they generate their own norms, traditions, values, and beliefs while sharing some of those of the dominant culture. They may also use non-verbal communication and language to establish and maintain boundaries between the subculture and the dominant culture as well as to express **subcultural identity.** Subcultures embody the reactions of a social group to its experiences within society and its members are often those to whom society awards low, subordinate and/or dependent status: youth, for instance. Some subcultures and their members may even be labelled as deviant: eco-warriors might be an example here.

The term **co-culture** is also employed to refer to those groups that generate significantly different patterns of behaviour to those found in the dominant culture. The term, arguably, does not carry the suggestion that these patterns of behaviour are less worthy than those of the main culture and reflects the aspirations of multicultural, pluralistic societies in which respect for individual rights and lifestyle choices is professed and, to some extent, protected in law. However, a counter-argument might be that the term co-culture can mask the real differences in power, influence, status, norms, values and beliefs that may exist between groups, and may underplay the gap that can also exist between tolerance and acceptance.

Some theorists point to the decline of subcultures, and the certainties found within them, and the rise of **post-subcultures**, reflecting, perhaps, a post-modern world. Post-subcultures reflect the, 'fragmentation, flux and fluidity' of contemporary experience in the Western world, particularly among the young (Muggleton and Weinzierl 2004: 3). Allegiance to post-subcultures is viewed as less permanent than that to subcultures: allegiances may shift over time. In the case of youth culture, for example, allegiances may be based more on tastes in music and fashion than on socio-economic position. It is argued that the influence of immigration, travel and global media (the Internet in particular) have produced an array of cultural hybrids and diversity of styles, tastes and political causes that call into question the degree to which youth culture today displays the solidity traditionally associated with youth subcultures.

Whatever the term adopted it should be acknowledged that the wider social groups that individuals belong to can be important **sociocultural variables**, that impact on communicative behaviour. Further, sociocultural differences can be a source of resentment, antagonism, conflict, misconceptions, misunderstandings, stereotypes and prejudice and as such have considerable potential to create barriers to successful interpersonal communication.

The **postmodernist** perspective is that much of contemporary Western culture, like contemporary Western societies, is fluid, fragmented and transitory in nature. Thus it challenges the notion of a clearly defined dominant culture and thus subcultures. Denis McQuail argues that from this perspective, 'Postmodern culture is volatile, illogical, kaleidoscopic and hedonistic' (2005: 131). It is highly commercialized and driven by the mass media. However, postmodernist thinkers differ in their view of the degree to which this is the case. The apparent superficial nature of culture presented here, although capturing perhaps the nature of popular media culture, seems to question the existence of the more solid social structures, roots and relationships from which everyday culture develops. However as Samovar and Porter (2004) and McQuail (2005), among others, point out, there remain robust underpinning social, political and economic structures and movements with the potential to exert a powerful influence on everyday life and how it may be lived.

About this book

We have worked as a team and what you read here has been the result of much discussion between us. However, individual members have taken responsibility for particular chapters: James Watson for 'Communication by design'; Anne Hill for 'Explorations of the nature of identity', 'Groups, roles and identities', 'Social identities' and 'Cross-cultural communication'; Mark Joyce for 'Non-verbal communication, culture and consumption'; and Danny Rivers for 'Identity, culture and outsiders'.

We start with an examination of some of the key models designed to capture the complexities of the communication process. These models provide frameworks of explanation of how the elements of the process may fit together. They also help us to conceptualize the points of contact between the process of interpersonal communication and the negotiation of self-identity. While points of contact are suggested by the authors, as you read through the book you should be able to make many more for yourself. Models covered range from that of Lasswell to Eisenberg's model of communication and identity. Transactional analysis, though not a model, is also considered given its potential to explain the dynamics of interaction.

We move on in Chapter 2 to explore a number of theories that seek to explain the nature of the self and self-identity and the implications for the role of social interaction in shaping a sense of self-identity are raised. A key theme in this chapter is that the construction of identities is problematic in contemporary Western societies. Individuals typically undertake a great deal of their interaction within groups and Chapter 3 examines the relationship between group roles, identity and communicative behaviour. Aspects considered in this chapter include the nature of groups, roles and personas, impression management, interaction analysis, status differentiation and leadership in groups, conformity, group performance, inter-group conflict and cross-cultural differences in communication within groups.

The use of language and non-verbal communication to construct and perform social identities is explored in Chapter 4. The focus is on four key social identities: ethnicity, social class, gender and sexual identities. Topics covered include British Black English, multicultural London English, dialect, accent, gender differences in communicative styles and competences, performivity, metrosexuality, queer theory and queer linguistics.

Chapter 5 examines the elements of non-verbal communication – elements thought to be universal. However the rules for display of non-verbal communication and the meanings attributed to the various non-verbal signs often vary across cultures. It moves on to explore the potential for non-verbal signs for expressing aspects of identity – subcultural identity, for example. This exploration extends to a consideration of the signalling properties of consumer goods and their potential contribution to the construction and display of identity.

Chapter 6 looks at cross-cultural communication and the main cultural variables that can impact on this process are discussed e.g. individualism and collectivism, high and low context communication, and monochronic/ polychronic time patterns. A number of case studies from advertising and business contexts are examined to illustrate the impact such variables can have on cross-cultural communication. Common barriers to intercultural communication such as ethnocentrism, stereotyping and prejudice are discussed, as is a model for transcultural communicative competence.

Chapter 7 explores marginalized identities – individuals and groups labelled as 'outsiders'. Starting with classic theories like that of Becker (1966) the chapter moves on to explore contemporary examples of individuals, groups and subcultures viewed as 'outside' the mainstream. The interplay and transition between the 'outsider' and the 'dominant' or 'mainstream' status and the process by which individuals may move from 'outsider' to 'insider' identity as they adapt to a new culture is explored – the focus here is on the role of interpersonal communication in this process.

Each chapter contains exercises that invite you, the reader, to explore and apply some of the ideas discussed. An introduction to concepts and theories relevant to exploring the themes of culture, identities and performance within interpersonal communication can only provide a taste of what is on offer and we hope that you will feel curious enough to explore further using as a starting point the books and articles in the reference section.

We hope that this book will be of relevance to students studying on a range of higher education courses that have as a part of their curriculum the study of interpersonal communication.

1 Communication by Design: How Models Contribute to our Understanding of Interpersonal Communication

Words to describe things often seem inadequate and inappropriate; they also mean different things to different people. It's an instinct to try communicating in other ways – marks resembling animals on a cave wall, for example – full of meaning at least for those who created the images and for whom they were created. The study of communication has itself often switched into a language of lines, boxes, circles, triangles and spirals, assembled into models of concept and process. These do not stand alone. They supplement text. They do not say everything, but what they do say, they fix, and they are memorable and useful. This chapter looks at how models have been used as devices of analysis and aids to understanding, and notes that the evolution of models progresses alongside, and contributes to, the evolution of the study of communication.

Introduction

The word 'model' has many meanings. It suggests an ideal: something to measure oneself against. We talk of 'role models' whose conduct is in some way an inspiration to us all. We also make models, simplified versions of the real – a model aeroplane. In the study of communication, models aspire to the ideal but are also simplifications of reality. They are about identifying the elements of a process and then suggesting how, through connection, they work in a generalized way.

The evolution of models matches the development of the study of communication; or one might say that the study of communication has often worked through the development of models. Both have a fairly specific history, tending to have been born out of a number of related disciplines – sociology, psychology, linguistics, rhetoric (ancient and modern) and telecommunications, to name but a few.

It is risky to claim exactly when a study took on sufficient substance to be worthy of attention. We could go back as far as 450 BC when Aspasia founded a school of philosophy and rhetoric, and among the key figures of the history of communication would be Socrates, Plato, Aristotle, Cicero, Quintillian and St Augustine of Hippo. However, for the purpose of this chapter, let us ear-mark the late 1940s and 1950s, a period when the world still reeled from the effects of the Second World War.

The propagandist frame

What in particular attracted the twentieth century pioneers of communica-tion and media studies was the apparent success of the Nazi propaganda machine in preparing the German people to embrace Aryan mythology, racial superiority and of course, hatred of those peoples, especially Jews but also including the gypsy population of Europe, who did not match, physically, the Aryan type.

How did a people with a long history of magnificent culture fall for the Nazi myth? This was a question posed by one of the first communication model-makers, Harold Lasswell. Arising out of his musings, researches and observations, he posed, in 1948, a model in question form which has been added to, tinkered with, but remained of value ever since:

Who
Says **What**
In which **Channel**
To **Whom**
With what **Effect?**

The model seems to us now fairly obvious, even simplistic, but let us give credit where it is due: Lasswell identifies five key areas of study, which, by and large, have proved the bedrock structure of the study of communication ever since.

'Who' alerts us to the communicator or communicators. It invites us to ask the questions, just who are the communicators in any situation; what motivates them, what makes them tick; what's special or singular about them and what is their intention?

We are set upon a course of identification, beginning with an identifi-cation parade: are these, as it were, 'the usual suspects'; where are they coming from, with what intellectual, cultural or ideological baggage; and in being communicators, professional or otherwise, what are the constraints that impact on their work; what are the pressures that influence them from day to day?

In turn, 'What?' is about the text, the comment, the content, the dis-course, the message, and we are free to note that What presupposes Not-

What, that is what is not there in the content; what has been selected out of a media presentation or an interpersonal encounter. As for 'Channel', we turn our focus upon the *means* of communication, and that includes the whole panoply of transmission, from body language to TV news and press headlines.

Finally, Lasswell reminds us that communication to a perceived receiver through a channel is one thing, but the actual nature of reception is another. What is sent is not necessarily received in the manner expected by those who construct and transmit messages. There is *response* to be considered. What interested Harold Lasswell in his time was how the public responded to persuasion. Did they swallow propaganda whole; were they selective about it, or did they reject it? Analysts and researchers have been examining the same questions ever since.

Although the Lasswell model is aimed at our approach to the study of mass communication it can equally be used in scrutinizing interpersonal communication. What is the nature of Who, the motivation for expressing a message in a certain way to a certain person, the reason for choosing one form of communication over another? What factors might influence response? If the communicator is seen as a role model, as a **significant other**, their comments will be received in ways different from a stranger expressing the same sentiments, and the response to them might be wholly different.

The noise barrier

Around the same time that Lasswell was posing his key questions, two other American researchers, Claude Shannon and Warren Weaver, were assembling what they termed the 'mathematical' model of communication (see Figure 1.1). This arose out of a very specific task. Shannon and Weaver had been commissioned by the Bell Telephone Company to investigate the nature of telephonic communication. What we are presented with is a *linear* model identifying the actors in the situation and indicating the process. In this case, the information **source** is the communicator, or the **sender** with a **message** to transmit. This is formed into a **signal** through a **transmitter** (the

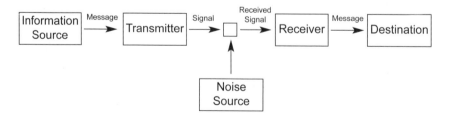

Figure 1.1 Model 1: Shannon and Weaver (1949)

telephone) and heads to its **destination** via the telephone receiver. Now every model worth its salt has one or a number of *salient features*; that is, something of value to our understanding of process.

Noise is the salient feature of the Shannon and Weaver model. It can be used to apply in ordinary face-to-face communication as much as in distanced communication. It means interference: something, or some things, which get in the way of the clarity of the message. It can be physical noise, for example a crackle on the line. It is distraction. Shannon and Weaver in their analysis of the model identify three levels of noise, as relevant to our studies today as when the model was created.

At Level A we experience technical noise. Interestingly, Shannon and Weaver estimated that even if 40 per cent of a telephone conversation were impeded by technical noise, we would still get the gist of the exchange. The authors explain this by noting the **redundancy** built into the language we use. This refers to such features of our exchanges as repetition, the use of familiar phrases, the inclusion of expressions not absolutely essential to the central message.

Redundancy, we realize, is anything but redundant. Pauses, hums and 'aahs' help towards the clarification of messages. On the telephone, they tell the person on the other end of the line that you are listening, paying attention. In face-to-face communication nods, head shakes and other facial and bodily gestures may not be essential to the core of the exchange; but see what happens when they are absent. If we find ourselves in conversation with someone whose face remains mute, the 'poker face', it is not long before we begin to feel uncomfortable. There is no **confirmation**.

Level B of Shannon and Weaver's categorization, semantic noise, occurs when messages are misunderstood, misinterpreted or misconstrued, and arise out of the language being used by one or more of the participants in the communication process. To declare, 'I can't understand a word he/she says' does not mean that literally there is not a single comprehensible word (unless, of course, we are hearing a foreign language we're unfamiliar with). It means we are having difficulty with the 'how' of explanation.

One lunchtime on BBC Radio 4 there was a programme on comedians from the North-East, Newcastle in particular. Though I'd worked for a period in the region, I still found that the accents of the comedians, and the speed at which they delivered their lines, left me nonplussed. Accent, then, proved a noise barrier: whether the problem was semantic or not it was impossible to tell. The sound of the laughter of the audience proved that what is noise for some is quite the opposite for others.

Perhaps really in this case we are talking about Shannon and Weaver's Level C, the effectiveness of the communication as far as the receiver is concerned. The North-East comedians were, within their immediate context of live audiences, effective. Widen the context, continue with the same mode of communication rather than adjusting it to new patterns of reception, and the communication hits noise. It was because of this that the comedians were seen to have been locally popular, but fell short of engaging wider audiences.

Lines give way to circles

Shannon and Weaver make little play with the notion and value of **feedback**. The shortcoming was rectified in later models, and the shape of those models acknowledged feedback as an essential ingredient for successful communication, hence the advent of the circular in preference to linear model. Certainly as far as interpersonal communication is concerned, circularity rather than the linear is more apt as a descriptor of the process.

True, we often go round in circles, but no circle is ever quite the same, for each movement of communication modifies the last. The circular model also suggests that rather than a simple exercise in transmission, the communicative process is one of **transaction** – of assessment, analysis, scrutiny; most of all, of **interpretation**. You say something to me: I interpret it, not only taking note of your words but your non-verbal activity. I respond and you take note of the nature of that response. This is nicely illustrated by Osgood and Schramm's model (see Figure 1.2). Not only is there a degree of circularity between the communicators as messages pass to and fro, there is transaction going on *within* each communicator; a process of internalization, of working out.

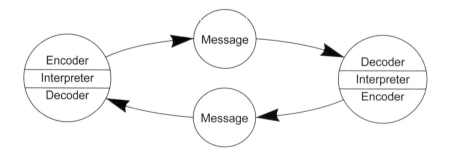

Figure 1.2 Model 2: Osgood and Schramm (1956, originated by Osgood and cited by Schramm 1954)

The circularity of the exchange also suggests that while some sort of signal initiates an act of communication, it never really ends. A comment – a compliment, a harsh word, a generous or unfair judgment, a piece of advice made years ago, may still resonate in our minds; may still cause us a warm glow or bother us, serving to condition our response to the present. As for everyday exchange, who is the initiator – the first person to speak, or the first person to hint by word or sign, 'Yes, I'm willing to enter the circle'?

Reference to **encoder** and **decoder** is an important recognition that the communicators are dealing in **codes** of expression, of language, verbal and non-verbal and, by those means, self-presentation: how a person says something is as important as what he or she says. The encoder in the model is also a decoder in each case; and each is an interpreter.

The focus on encoding/decoding proved an important advance both for models and our ways of scrutinizing communication at every level. It also confirms the complexity of communicative exchange. We decode not only the message but the messenger. The expression 'We was' breaks the rules of the grammatical code, though the message is clear. However, it is likely that a classification, a judgment, has been made about the messenger's communicative knowledge, skill and even background. This might well colour the nature of the communication that follows. It may also affect the nature of the future relationship between sender and receiver.

The importance of common ground

Much research into the nature and process of interpersonal communication has addressed issues of 'like', as in similar, and unlike. Do we communicate better with people who share attitudes, beliefs and values; or do we communicate better with opposites? Evidence seems to suggest that while opposites appeal, communication is most effective where there is a substantial degree of sharing.

Wilbur Schramm (1954) acknowledges this when he gives salience to what in his model of 1956 he calls 'fields of experience' (see Figure 1.3). Here, where the fields of experience of encoder and decoder overlap, there is potential for meaningful communicative interaction, for we can surmise that where there is a sharing of culture, language, values and experience, there is the probability of mutual understanding. Further, shared experience allows participants to 'step into the shoes' of other; that is, to empathize, and thus increase the likelihood of interaction between equals, characterized by a sense of give and take.

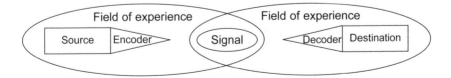

Figure 1.3 Model 3: Schramm (1956)

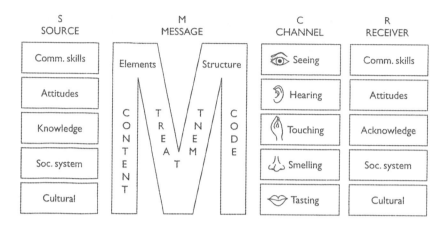

Figure 1.4   Model 4: Berlo (1960)

In *A First Look at Communication*, Em Griffin (2003) lends support to the importance of fields of experience, writing that 'Communication between us begins when there is some shared overlap between two images, and it is effective to the extent that overlap increases'.

The potential for matching or mismatching is neatly illustrated in the SMCR model proposed by David K. Berlo (1960), who studied with Schramm at the University of Illinois (see Figure 1.4)[1]. Here Berlo identifies a number of factors involved in the process of communication between two or more persons. Both source and receiver are prompted and conditioned by their skills, attitudes and knowledge; and their interactivity is influenced by the social and cultural contexts in which communication takes place. The means of communication – the channel – is in turn governed by the senses, obviously by seeing and hearing, but also by touch, smell and even taste.

Berlo prises open the 'Message' impressively into **elements** and **structure**. We have content and that content has to opt for an appropriate means of expression involving the use of a code or language. The suggestion here is that while the model, as it were the starting point, is clear, comprehensive and comprehensible, the actual process of communication once it kicks in, is complicated. Indeed Berlo's model seems to imply that with such complexity all sorts of things could go wrong.

The linguist Roman Jakobson also seeks to identify the vital ingredients of the communication process. He posed a model suggesting a 'fit' between the elements of communication and its **functions** or purposes (see Figure 1.5). 'Addresser' and 'addressee' tend, like 'source' and 'receiver', to be rather clumsy terms, especially now that we have moved away from linear models of transmission. But once we see the functions imposed on the structure of parts, we realize that here is a model that can be usefully applied to real situations.

CONSTITUTIVE FACTORS:

	Context	
Addresser	**Message**	**Addressee**
	Contact	
	Code	

FUNCTIONS:

Referential
(Reality orientation of message)

Emotive	**Poetic**	**Conative**
(Expressive)	**Phatic**	*(Effective of message on Addressee)*

Metalingual

Figure 1.5   Model 5: Jakobson (1958)

The *context* serves a **referential** function: it delineates the communicative situation. It becomes imperative to ask, in terms of simple location, is the interaction taking place on the street, in the home, at the pub; and what is the nature of the exchange?

To employ a tired cliché, we might say, 'I think we have a situation', meaning there's a problem, possibly a crisis. Our understanding of this situation, as either participants or observers, depends on how we 'read' that situation, how much information we have about it, how familiar we are with the context of the interaction; otherwise we might seriously 'get the wrong end of the stick'.

According to Jakobson, the dynamic that occurs between the addresser and addressee serves *emotive, poetic, conative* and *metalingual* functions. Communicator A emotes, expresses, formulating a message that has been put together using a linguistic code; Communicator B **connotes**, that is receives and interprets both the message and the way it has been delivered. *Contact* has made the exchange possible, fulfilling what Jakobson refers to as a *phatic* function, the purpose of which is to open the channel of communication – or as it has picturesquely been put, to oil the wheels of communication.

The ritual dimension of communication

Phatic salutations comprise everyday greeting and exchanges, for example 'Hello!', 'Have a nice day!' or 'What terrible weather!' We realize their importance by their absence, when there is no response to a cheery 'Hello!', a look of indifference in response to a smile. Here we encounter the connative function, the nature of the addressee's response.

If Communicator A wishes to ask a favour of Communicator B, phatic performance can make the difference between a positive or a negative response. To plunge straight in with a request for a favour is less likely to be persuasive than observing the potency of ritual exchange – friendly greeting, ample but not over-effusive non-verbal signals such as smiling, touching and affirmative body language.

The classification of the poetic as a prime function of communication might at first glance seem to be more a desirable than an essential factor, but Jakobson is as right to give it prominence as he is justified in stressing the phatic. Indeed the two are closely linked. The poetic might include a whole range of expressive signs, from our choice of words, the sound of our voices, our intonation, to the ways in which we express ourselves by our looks, dress, ornamentation, movements and gestures.

It is an expression of a number of essential factors – motivation, self-perception and personality, melding into the core element of **self-identity**, as we shall see later in discussing the role of communication in the further-ance of human needs. All the functions listed by Jakobson work towards a metalingual function, 'meta' in this instance meaning larger, grander, involving a 'whole process' of communication, from words to gestures, from silence to self-display within wider, social and cultural contexts.

The dynamics of the triangle

Shapes alter according to the salience of the points the model-maker wishes to emphasize. In 1953 Theodore Newcomb opted for the triangular formation in proposing his famous ABX model (see Figure 1.6). Easy to draw, triangles immediately illustrate two factors: connections and dynamics. Here A, B and X are interconnected in a dynamic situation. The focus is interpersonal communication between A and B, but the militating factor in the commu-nicative exchange, or interaction, between person A and person B is X. This

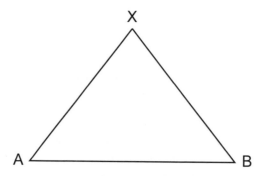

Figure 1.6   Model 6: Newcomb (1953)

can be another person – a friend, a relative, a colleague – or a range of external factors such as attitudes, points of view, issues or events.

What is significant is the **orientation** of A and B to each other with regard to X. Let us take an example of like-dislike. A and B like each another. They agree on X, whatever X is, say a third person. They are, in Newcomb's judgment, in **consonance**; that is they feel at one. There is confirmation. Or let us take the issue of racism as the X-factor. A and B like one another and share a strong antipathy to racism: outcome – consonance.

Things get complicated, however, when A and B like one another, but discover their opinions about racism markedly differ. The outcome now is likely to be **dissonance**; that is A and B find themselves at odds on a deeply-felt matter. They experience unease, emotional discomfort. The stronger the disparity of views on X, the more powerful, goes the theory, the feelings of dissonance.

In contrast, if A dislikes B and discovers they disagree on X, what have we got? Well, here, **expectations** come in to play. If you dislike a person, the probability is that you will disagree on matters of importance, say on values and behaviour. You may say to yourself, 'That's just what you'd expect from B'. Yet if A, disliking B, discovers they agree on X, what then?

According to the theory of consonance/dissonance a feeling of dissonance is likely: person A has encountered the unexpected and will perhaps wonder, 'Have I been wrong about B?' In situations of dissonance, Newcomb argues, there is a 'strain towards symmetry', towards balance. Measures may be taken to restore a sense of equilibrium. In the case of A liking B but disagreeing on X, the participants may simply decide not to discuss X; or there may be a degree of compromise on one side or the other, or both in regard to X. In the case of A disliking B but agreeing on X, the participants, one or both, may reassess their attitude to the other.

Much depends on the strength of feeling A and B have for each other, and how central to their belief system is the X-issue – how much the participants actually *identify* with X. If X symbolizes what a person stands for, if it is a keynote of a person's value system, it could injure relationships and put distance between them.

Newcomb's model is symmetrical. Consonance keeps it that way; dissonance threatens to pull it out of shape. It could be argued, of course, that in the real as contrasted with the theoretical world, conflict is more in evidence than blissful resolution. We should not be surprised about this, or disappointed.[2] As C. David Mortensen says in *Miscommunication* (Mortensen and Ayres 1997), 'Because conflict and confusion are intrinsic features of everyday life, there is no use longing for friction-free conditions'.

Reality, perception and the project of self

Mentioning the 'real' world should remind us that we are actually referring to, acting upon and reacting to our **perceptions** of the real world. Reality may be what we are looking at but perception is what we see; not to mention that our perceptions of reality interact with and sometimes clash with the perceptions of others.

George Gerbner's model of 1956 (see Figure 1.7), exploring the relationship between media messaging and individual reception, emphasizes the difference between **event** (E) and perception of that event (E1) by the communicator (M), leading to a representation of it in one communicative form or another, and in turn perceived by the recipient of the communication (M2). What happens, whether perceived by a media communicator or by an individual is that perception of that event becomes, in Gerbner's term, a *percept*: and it is this which, in the process of communication, as it were, 'does the talking'. Form and content transmit the percept according to criteria of selection, context and availability (of information, for example).

Gerbner highlights the complexity of process, for we can never have a foolproof perception of reality because we cannot know everything about that reality or have a fault-free grasp of context, especially as the communicative

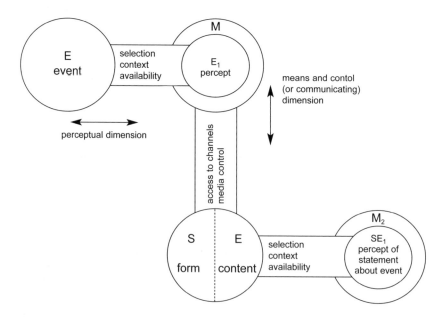

Figure 1.7   Model 7: Gerbner (1956)

act inevitably involves a degree of selection; and this from all participants in the interaction.

It can be said that once E1 comes into play, all is perception. How true or accurate that perception is, how mistaken or biased, fair or prejudiced, will depend upon a complex number of variables. We may for instance be short of skills in the use of communicative forms, or those forms may not be available to us. Our gender, social class, age, ethnicity, education, state of health or wealth may exercise a mediating role in our view of the world and of other people, and how we see ourselves in relation to them.

Not the least of the factors that influence our perceptions and our communicative performance, is experience, past and present. We can no more escape our personal history than our present, though we are not always aware of how the past influences our current perceptions of self and others, and our behaviour, or how far it plays a part in our orientation towards the future.

Both in the study of ourselves and others, at every level of communication, it is essential to consider what Wayne Brochriede (1968) refers to as the **encompassing situation**, what Eric Eisenberg (see later) calls **surround** or what Elizabeth Andersch, Lorin Staats and Robert Bostrom (1969) call the **environment** and which they place in the very centre of their model of 1969 (see Figure 1.8). They see it as the powerhouse that generates the process of interpersonal communication. The environment provides the stimuli that initiate and influence the nature and direction of communication as it proceeds through sending to receiving to sending once more. We can infer that these stimuli come from within ourselves as well as from life outside ourselves.

In the act of initiating an exchange, the source, as the authors point out in *Communication in Everyday Use*, 'is himself a "message"'. Even before he begins to speak, the receiver perceives the message-source; he sees and interprets bodily activity and facial expression; he associates prior impressions he has had of the speaker, conditioning his own responses to the communicator' (Andersch et al. 1969).

In turn, the receiver's behaviour 'will be affected by the environment, his past experiences with the subject to be explored, his biases and interests, his attitudes towards the speaker, and his willingness to participate in this particular communication situation'.

This model contributes other salient features of the process of interpersonal communication. For example, two stages are identified prior to the act of communication – **structuring** and **evaluating**. True, if we are feeling very emotional about something we are likely to blurt out an expression without forethought. On the other hand, past experience might caution us not to voice our opinions or feelings too readily.

We give ourselves pause for thought. We assess how our message might come over to the receiver, and we consider just how best, most effectively,

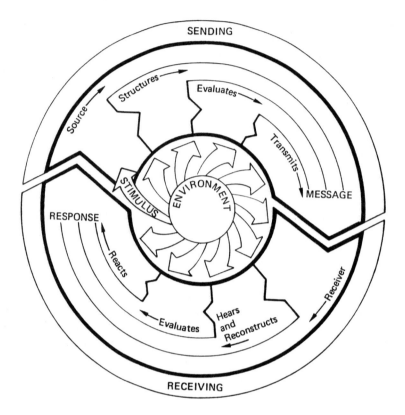

Figure 1.8 Model 8: Andersch, Staats and Bostrom (1969)

that message can be conveyed. We might even decide to say nothing, leaving what we have to say to a look, a smile or a gesture. What we cannot be sure about till it happens is whether there will be a response, and what form this response will take.

In whatever way our communication 'comes over' the receiver will 'hear' and by hearing (that is, paying attention rather than ignoring the receiver's message) will 'reconstruct' the message. This may prove a fair and true reading or a reading varyingly coloured by doubt, uncertainty, prejudice or just plain misunderstanding.

Yet whatever the nature of that reconstruction, a process of evaluation takes place prior to response. It might be said that communication resembles that corny (and with global warming, fast-melting) old metaphor, the iceberg: what appears above the water is the act of communication; below it is the process of 'weighing up' as a prelude to transmission. Once transmission takes place the response is in turn the product of what goes on below the water line.

All the while, self-evaluation is going on, the source interacting 'with his own values, opinions and ideas; in other words, he evaluates his continuing message'. This is a critically important factor for, as Andersch et al. assert, 'it is almost impossible for sources to ignore their own values in any circumstances'. The receiver passes through a matching process except that it is the speaker's message, rather than the environment, which is the receiver's primary stimulus.

From circle to spiral

The Andersch, Staats and Bostrom model is probably the most aesthetically pleasing of all models and the most elegant of circular formats; but could there be a shape better able to represent the more open, the more extempore nature of communication? Another American theorist, Frank Dance, considered there was and he proposed a spiral design as better reflecting the process of communication (see Figure 1.9). In 'A helical model of communication', a chapter published in *Foundations of Communication Theory*, edited by Kenneth K. Sereno and C. David Mortensen (1970)[3], Dance first gives credit to the circular model: 'The circular-communication image does an excellent job of making the point that what and how one communicates has an affect that may alter future communication.' However, Dance goes on,

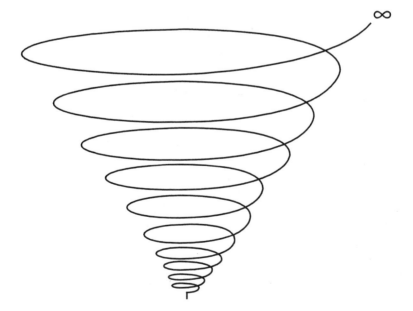

Figure 1.9 Model 9: Dance's helical spiral as a representation of human communication (1967)

'The main shortcoming of this circular model is that if accurately understood it also suggests that communication comes back, full-circle, to exactly the same point from which it started'.

This is 'manifestly erroneous and could be damaging in increasing an understanding of the communication process and in predicting any constraints for a communicative event'. The spiral or helical analogy indicates that, yes, communication is circular but it is dynamic: each twist of the spiral works on the last by revisiting it on a higher level.

Dance compares the spiral model to a 'helically-coiled spring, such as the child's toy that tumbles down staircases by coiling upon itself' which if you 'pull it full out in the vertical position, you can call to your imagination an entirely different kind of communication than that represented by compressing the spring as close as possible upon itself': 'At any and all times, the helix gives geometric testimony to the concept that communication while moving forward is at the same moment coming back upon itself and being affected by its past behaviour, for the coming curve of the helix is fundamentally affected by the curve from which it emerges.'

As Dance points out, the helical model is as applicable to the whole learning process as to the specific scrutiny of communication. In the study of communication the same topics – interpersonal communication, group, organizational and mass communication – are taught at primary, secondary, further and advanced levels, with different and escalating degrees of intensity and difficulty. One level builds on the last, extends it, provides the platform for greater and deeper understanding, hence the way the helical model expands as one loop takes its feed from the one that precedes it.

Dance reminds us 'that in the process of communicative self-emergence and self-identification the interaction with perceived others is essential. As a result, we have two or more helixes interacting and intertwined'.

Denis McQuail and Sven Windahl in *Communication Models for the Study of Mass Communication* (1996) write of Dance's spiral, 'One gets the notion from this model that man, when communicating, is active, creative and able to store information, whereas many other models depict the individual rather as a passive creature'. In *Communication: The Study of Human Communication*, David Mortensen (1972) is equally complimentary about the Dance model, as it illustrates how important it is to 'approach models in a spirit of speculation and intellectual play'.

The intrapersonal dimension

The importance of the connection in communication between our past and present has been stressed. Each is a constant of the other. Similarly it is important to see as constant our inner, or intrapersonal communication: our self-talk. Ultimately it is the source of communication. We could convincingly elaborate on Dance, by designing a double spiral that connects the inner and outer world. As participants in the spiral process we can only guess at what is going on intrapersonally in the heads and hearts of those with whom we communicate.

Indeed it might be said that we are not always certain what is going on in our own heads and hearts. What we do know is that the outside world has a profound influence on our thinking and feeling while our inner world profoundly influences our 'public performance'.

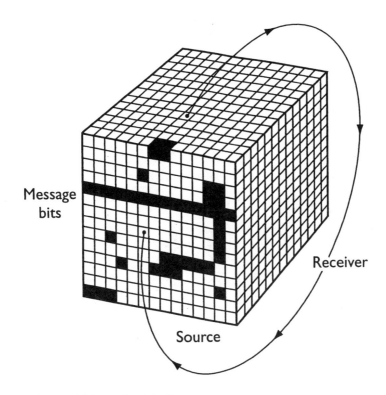

Figure 1.10 Model 10: Becker (1968)

Two models from the 1960s seek to address this situation. Samuel Becker's mosaic or cuboid model (see Figure 1.10) attempts to portray the multidimensional nature of communication, its inner and outer features, and the fact that the inner features run to considerable depths, some of them held back from, or hidden from, public view.

Information, experience, aspects of self-view, perceptions of life and the world are like the tiny cubes of marble or ceramic that make up a mosaic.

These, singly or in association with other 'bits', influence the shape and tenor of the communicative process, prompting, selecting, shaping, censoring.

A darkened bit in the Becker model might be a bad experience from the past, a disappointment, an act of cruelty to which we have been subjected. It is hidden from discourse but it influences it, just as it might influence behaviour. Our communication may be perceived as being defensive, using tactics of closure, to ward off too much attention; of resistance to another person getting close or understanding more than you wish to be understood.

Concealment, therefore, is as much a part of the process as opening up – a scenario made usefully manifest in the Johari Window (see Figure 1.11). This model, like Becker's, suggests an assembly of often competing and over-lapping parts, zones or areas. It is not illustrating a sequence or suggesting a chain of events; rather it identifies crucial features of interpersonal communication that may serve to make for better, or worse, communication. It is really a model about awareness of self and other, suggesting the need for mutuality. Communication, this model nudges us into concluding, is essentially **reciprocal**.

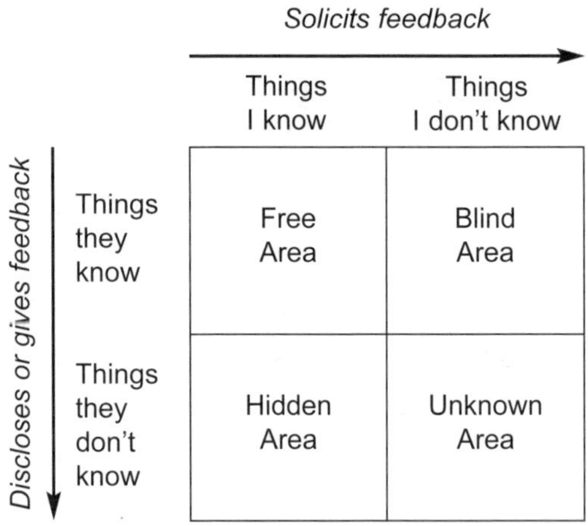

Figure 1.11   Model 11: Johari window (Luft 1969)

The name of the model derives from one created by Joseph Luft and Harrington Ingram, hence 'Jo-hari', in *Of Human Interaction* (Luft 1969). There are things we know about ourselves and others know about us (Free Area); there are things we may be blind to in ourselves, but not to others (Blind Area); there are things we keep to ourselves, of which others are unaware (Hidden Area) and there are things about ourselves that neither we nor others are aware of but which may influence our communication with others (Unknown Area).

To achieve successful communicative interaction we take a route towards **disclosure** or openness. Why do we hold back on disclosure, restrict feedback? Have we been hurt in the past through declaring our thoughts and feelings too freely? The degree to which we open an area or shut it down depends on our previous experience, our past success in opening up, and thus our confidence in the process. It depends essentially on our self-concept. Are we outgoing or introspective? Are we easy with relationships?

It would seem that the ideal would be to expand the Free Area and reduce the other panes in the window, for being secretive about oneself is less likely to improve an interaction than being more open. However, Johari works in different ways for different people at different times and in different situations. In *Miscommunication* (Mortensen and Ayres 1997) David Mortensen writes, 'Sometimes just "letting it all hang out" only makes things worse rather than better' and there are 'countless exceptions to the rule of reciprocity ... Under conditions of threat or stress, one may give in to the counterurge – to cover up rather than uncover'.

On occasion we may reveal things about ourselves to strangers rather than people we know well. The fact that a stranger, a passing acquaintance, knows little or nothing about you might be deemed, in certain circumstances, an advantage because Other has nothing to gain or lose from your openness. Ultimately, though, disclosure depends on the nature of the relationship between the individuals involved and the purpose and nature of their communicative exchange.

Vital cues

At first glance the so-termed **transactional** models of communication (posed as 'pilot models' in 1970 by Dean Barnlund, look formidably complex, which is perhaps appropriate as he refers to 'the complexities of human communication' which 'present an unbelievably difficult challenge to the student of human affairs'. However, as with many models, a few moments of careful viewing assuage anxiety and intrigue with the power of a good crossword.

In the first model (Figure 1.12), communication is an intrapersonal transaction; in the second (Figure 1.13), an interpersonal one, in each case encoding and decoding work in accord with Dance's spiral mode, D and E operating simultaneously.

Before explaining his two models, Barnlund offers us six postulates of communication: it describes the evolution of **meaning**; it is continuous, dynamic, circular, unrepeatable and irreversible. In order to explain the working of his first model, Barnlund takes the example of a man, Mr A (P1) sitting alone in the reception room of a clinic awaiting a doctor's

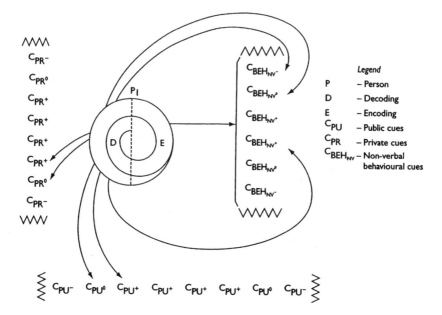

Figure 1.12 Model 12: Barnlund's transactional model (A) (1970)

appointment. As he gazes around the room, Mr A decodes (D) 'or assigns meaning to the various cues available to his perceptual field...'

He transforms these (encodes them) 'so that they are manifest to others in the form of verbal and nonverbal cues ... The spiral line connecting encoding and decoding processes is used to give diagrammatic representation to the 'continuous, unrepeatable and irreversible nature of communication...'

Barnlund differentiates between three different kinds of sign or cue – public, private and behavioural. **Public cues** he subdivides into two, *natural* and *artificial*. Natural cues come from our environment without human intervention. Artificial clues arise from a human's involvement with the outer world, their impact on it, their modification and manipulation of it. Public cues are 'part of, or available to, the perceptual field of all potential communicants' and have been 'created prior to the event under analysis' as well as remaining 'outside the control of the persons under observation'.

Private cues operate intrapersonally, in our own head, part of the lexicon of memory and experience; 'elements or events that are essentially private in nature, that come from sources not automatically available to any other person who enters a communicative field'. If, when private cues are translated into **Behavioural Cues**, speech and non-verbal activity, the decoder of the message (P2, for example) fails to read the cues effectively, the resultant exchange could lead to misperception, confusion and end in defensive communication.

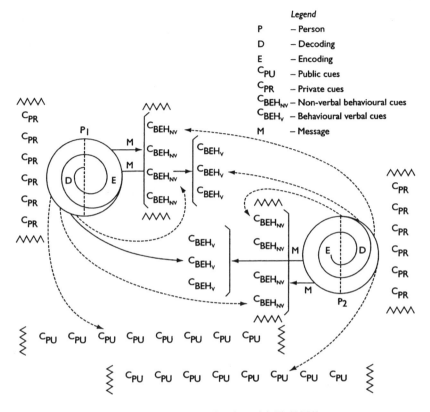

Figure 1.13 Model 13: Barnlund's transactional model (B) (1970)

It may cause dissonance resulting from an inaccurate assessment by P2 of P1; a judgment assembled on too little evidence – too few cues, or indicators, to meaning. Barnlund refers to a process of **transferability**, of public cues becoming private ones, and vice-versa. In other words communication is typified by transactions, one set of cues working on other sets, modifying them and being modified by them. The inner world and the outer world are in a constant process of working on each other.

The use of jagged lines in both models illustrates how 'the number of cues to which meaning may be assigned is probably without limit'. Some cues will carry more meaning, more worth, than others. Barnlund speaks of **valences**, positive, negative or neutral, indicated in the models with (+), (−) or (o). The author echoes Newcomb's notion of consonance-seeking:

> Unless other factors intervene, individuals tend to draw towards cues to which positive valences can be assigned, that is towards cues capable of reinforcing past or emerging interpretations, and away

from cues to which negative valences are attached or those that contradict established opinions and behaviour patterns.

(Barnlund 1970)

If intrapersonal communication, including the relationship of individuals to their environment, were not already complicated, how much more so does the process become when another person enters the scene? Little might be said, but the cues are potentially deafening. One thing is certain: 'there will be a shift in orientation of both individuals.' For example, 'the mere appearance of a second person in an elevator or office will change the character and content of self-to-self communication in both parties'.

Readers may spot the absence of valences (+ − o) in the second model, a decision explained by Barnlund 'because their positive, negative or neutral value would depend on the interpretative decisions' of the communicants. Barnlund concludes by expressing the hope that his pilot models 'will have served a useful purpose if they prompt the search for better ways of representing the inner dynamics of the communication process'.

Transactional analysis

Barnlund's emphasis on the nature of transaction in interpersonal communication has found systematic application as therapy in **transactional analysis (TA)**, developed by Eric Berne in two volumes, *Games People Play* (1964) and *What Do You Say After You've Said Hello?* (1975) and supplemented by Thomas Harris's *I'm OK – You're OK* (1969) with a follow-up, *Staying OK* by Harris and Amy Bjork Harris (1995).

TA is a widely used technique for analysing the process of interpersonal communication and enhancing social skills. The intention is to make us more aware of the way in which our communication can be influenced by our childhood experiences; to enable us to examine the intent behind our communicative acts and to reveal and deal with deceit and dishonesty.

Essentially the framework for analysis rests on 'ego states' out of which, it is claimed, we communicate. A 'transaction' occurs when two people are in conversation during which the ego state of one person addresses the ego state of the other. To distinguish these ego states both in ourselves and others, we need to examine verbal and non-verbal behaviour as it occurs in the context of the encounter.

Berne, in *Games People Play*, identifies three ego states – the **Parent**, the **Adult** and the **Child**, each produced by a playback of our inner *recordings* of past encounters with other people, times, places, events and our reactions to and feelings about them. Many of these recordings belong to our childhood experience. We may be unaware of them though they may continue to affect our communicative acts.

Our Parent state is very much influenced by the behaviour of our own parents and other authority figures encountered in early life. Its area of concern is our responsibilities towards ourselves and others. There are two 'parental voices', that of the critical or **Controlling Parent** and that of the **Nurturing Parent**. The first sets standards of behaviour and can be critical of our own and others' behaviour; the second is caring and protective.

The Adult within us is the voice of reason, rationality and commonsense. It analyses reality, gathering information, drawing conclusions, making judgments, solving problems and making decisions. This voice develops through life and is capable of regulating and overriding the influence of Parent and Child voices.

The ego state of the Child is seen to have three aspects, the **Free** or **Natural Child**, the **Adapted Child** and the **Little Professor**. Creativity, relaxation, the capacity for fun, risk taking and spontaneity characterize the Free Child. The state of the Adapted Child concerns the potential for rebelliousness, compliance or servility when faced with the demands of those in authority. It is argued that our adult responses to authority are conditioned by those we adapted to cope with authority figures when we were children.

The Little Professor signifies the emerging Adult, demonstrating the ability to reason, be creative, solve problems, employ intuition and develop manipulative tactics – that is to use communication and behaviour (like throwing temper tantrums) to obtain what the child wants; tactics that can be carried forward into adulthood.

Transactional states

As we have seen, TA cites three ego states, two of these, the Parent and the Child, further subdivided into Critical or Caring Parent and the Free, Adapted and Little Professor. In turn four transactional states are identified: **complementary**, **angular**, **duplex** and **crossed**, the latter three, according to Eric Berne in *What Do You Say After You've Said Hello?* is where problems of communication occur.

In complementary transactions communication is likely to be even and untroubled, characterized by consonance. People act out of complementary ego states, as in the following example:

> *Doctor:*   I'd like you to take three of these tablets a day for six weeks and this time make sure to remember to take them. (Parent)
> *Patient:*   Right. I always do what I am told. (Child)

To describe a transaction as complementary is not necessarily to say that the responses are always appropriate. You might feel that the patient should have been less servile. Crossed transactions occur when the ego states do not complement each other:

> *Maureen*: Can you help me put the finishing touches to our group presentation? (Adult)
>
> *Sally*: I've done my share and I'm busy. You should not leave everything to the last minute. (Critical Parent)

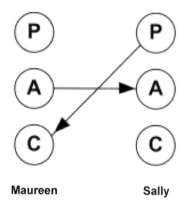

Maureen   **Sally**

An angular transaction occurs when a speaker is covertly addressing one ego state while pretending to address another:

> *Melissa*: *Knowing that Ian would like a romantic relationship with Sally.* I think Sally and Paul are a well-matched couple, don't you? (Adult/Little Professor)
>
> *Ian*: Rubbish! It won't last. (Adapted Child)

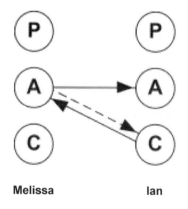

Melissa   **Ian**

In a duplex transaction both communicators are involved in delivering covert as well as overt messages:

> *Arthur:*   I feel I should talk to Jeremy and Robin about this issue. They might benefit from my considerable experience in this area. (Adult/Little Professor)
>
> *Emily:*   Yes. I'm sure they would find it helpful to talk to a much older man. (Adult/Little Professor)

The value of TA is that it may help you spot when and why a conversation is taking a wrong turn, or when you are about to be hooked into giving an inappropriate response; allowing you to keep control and re-balance the transaction. It is important in this respect for the Adult to be in control so that even if other voices are activated, they are used appropriately within the communicative situation.

Games and scripts

Another of Eric Berne's propositions is that we often play games in our interactions with others. He describes a game as 'an ongoing series of complementary ulterior transactions progressing to a well-defined, predictable outcome' (Berne 1964: 44). Games are identified by their hidden motives, their repetitive nature and their promise of psychological gains for the players of the game.

Participants in game playing look, for example, for a known weakness (termed a *gimmick*) of the victim (referred to as the *mark*). Use of the gimmick serves to hook the victim, or mark. The *switch* is the point in the conversation when it takes another direction and the player catches the *mark* out. At this *crossup* point the mark realizes that something has gone wrong with the exchange. They are likely to feel confused and experience dissonance.

The encounter may well begin to fall apart. Successfully hooking, the mark provides the game player with psychological satisfaction. This is the *payoff*. Berne argues that every game, whether played consciously or unconsciously, is a dishonest and defensive form of communication. He identifies many games played in everyday life, such as, 'If it weren't for you ...' or 'See what you've made me do!' If the intended victim is aware of the games people play in interaction and transaction, they will be better prepared to avoid being hooked, and able to deflect the course of exchange on to a more mutually beneficial course.

Scripts are seen by Berne in *What Do You Say After You've Said Hello?* as a type of **psychological narrative** which an individual may act out over lengthy periods of time. These are developed in our early years but can affect our interactions with others throughout our lives. The script contains within it the individual's sense of self and expectations of, and orientation towards, others.

It forms a basis for action. According to Berne, the tendency is for people to seek justification for their scripts. Thus they may act towards others, and interpret the behaviour of others, in line with the expectations set by a script. An example of such a life script might be, 'You can't trust anybody!' suggesting a script characterized by suspicion and a negative view of other people. Again, awareness of the role of scripts emerging from past experience or conditioning can serve to bring about change.

Life positions

Thomas Harris in *I'm OK – You're OK* writes of four life positions that can be employed in TA for exploring an individual's sense of self in relation to others. These, like Berne's Parent/Child/Adult roles are formed in childhood, and they influence the nature and direction of the scripts individuals write for themselves. Life positions are, of course, capable of being modified or changed, though in some cases, Thomas and Amy Harris affirm in *Staying OK*, such changes may require professional help.

I'm OK – You're OK is position one, in which individuals feel confident about their own self-worth as well as that of others. Such a position makes it relatively easier to adopt an open, confident and positive stance when communicating with others. Yet, as Harris argues, considerable effort is required to achieve or maintain this position if, as a result of our childhood experiences, we are left with a feeling of **Not OK**.

More usual is the position **I'm Not OK – You're OK**. Harris points out that through our early lives we are recipients of countless messages, many of them critical, aimed at shaping our behaviour into socially acceptable patterns. The position leaves individuals with a sense of inferiority and this demonstrates itself in defensive communication, of which game playing is an example.

Experience of neglect or abuse in childhood is likely to lead to position three, **I'm OK – You're Not OK**. This reveals itself in communicative modes that are aggressive or hostile, underscored by resentment. Harris' fourth position, **I'm Not OK – You're Not OK** is bleakly negative, characterized by a reined in, despairing attitude that permeates communicative behaviour with others. Readers may well wish to scrutinize their own daily encounters to see how the categorizations made in transactional analysis, game playing and the 'OK' classifications find authenticity in everyday experience.

Reading the signs

It could be said that we live by cues and the stress placed by analysts of communication on the importance of the reading of cues or signs brings us on to communication models of another sort, arising out of the study of signs and sign systems – **semiology** – or as the Americans prefer to term it, semiotics.

At the heart of the semiological approach to communication is the sign. This is the basic element which, assembled through codes into texts, constitutes the primary feature of all forms of communication, from the interpersonal to mass communication.

What we write on paper, or in our computer files, or text message on our mobile phones uses the signs of the alphabet. We encode words, sentences and paragraphs, using (hopefully) the adjunct of another set of signs – punctuation. In our interpersonal speech our words are supplemented by presentational signs – posture, gesture, facial expression, eye contact; the whole panoply of non-verbal communication (NVC).

The goals in operating sign systems may seem pretty straightforward until we realize that different signs have different meanings in different contexts. Decoding signs, in these circumstances, becomes, in the semiological model of communication, far more important and critical than is demonstrated in earlier transmissional models; largely for the reason illustrated in the simplest sign-model (see Figure 1.16). As the figure shows, signs are made up of two parts. The **signifier** is what we can see, touch, hear. It could be a smile, a shrug, a glance away; it could be a comment, the words of which are simple and free of ambiguity. But then there is the **signified**, that which the receiver of the message reads in to the message. Signifier and signified, in a successful exchange, would mean the same thing: what is sent is also what is received. But it need not be so; indeed the reading of the meaning, the **signification** of communication is really what the

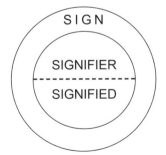

Figure 1.16 Model 16: Sign, signifier, signified

study of signs sets out to do, affirming and confirming Barnland's first postulate.

For example, a person dresses up in the latest style for a party, the hope usually being that what will be signified by costume or suit will favourably impress others at the party. A person may actually wear the signifier but they have little control over the signified, partly because the dress or suit is only one signifier among many.

Other factors – looks, deportment, other people's perception or image of you – contribute to signification. Instead of admiration, the signs may prompt criticism or ridicule. The text of the person, of self, combined with the dress or suit has been **aberrantly decoded**. This does not mean that the decoding of a text is wrong, only that it has not fulfilled the **preferred reading** of the communicator. What Erving Goffman (1959) has referred to as **impression management** has somehow not fulfilled its objective.[4]

The separation of signifier from signified has proved a major step forward in the analysis of communication in all its manifestations. The implication is that meaning is temporal, not fixed, that it is in a constant state of flux; that it is *assigned* in the process of reception.

Meaning is thus eternally contested, subject to eternal scrutiny. Ourselves and others are complex texts in a perpetual state of performance, interacting, interpreting, re-interpreting. We encode ourselves by the minute and the hour, and we decode others who in turn are reading the multiple signs we give off, and decode us.

Roles and narratives

Mention of 'performance' is a reminder of the classification of humankind made by Jaques in Shakespeare's *As You Like It*: 'All the world's a stage/And all the men and women merely players/They have their exits, and their entrances/And one man in his time plays many parts ...'. The **drama-turgical model** of human behaviour and communication identifies the many parts, or roles, we play over time, often simultaneously. We can talk of the script or scripts of self. However, the drama of self differs from theatrical performance in one very important respect: our script is ever-changing and our next act or scene is unpredictable. Even so, once our concept of self has firmed up as teenage years graduate into adulthood, our performance of role steadies, is recognizable by self and others.

A rival generic, or paradigm, model to that of role playing in personal, group, national and international dramas, and overlapping with it, is the concept of **homo narrens** – man and woman as the story-telling animal. We live stories, live in stories, and are authors of our own **narratives**. From gossip to epic novels, stories grip us, entertain us, instruct us, make us bold or cautious, and some stories enter the hearts, minds and nervous systems of whole peoples.

The *homo narrens* model suggests that we not only enjoy stories, telling them and hearing them, we not only learn from them: we *need* them. Equally the dramaturgical model would suggest that human needs play a major part in the role we play. One could venture a step further and say that the history of humanity is also the story of human needs, fulfilled or unfulfilled and of the conflicts that occur when needs and desires clash.

Needs theory

A model of needs, posed by psychologist Abraham Maslow back in the 1950s, has had a long-term impact on our ways of identifying and linking needs to identity as well as the way others – in particular advertisers – have targeted those needs (see Figure 1.17).[5] According to Maslow, needs *motivate*. The salience of his model, however, lies in the way he grades needs into a **hierarchy**, from basic, physiological needs, through the need for safety (security, protection, freedom from danger), upward into love and belonging needs (for friends, companions, family) and esteem needs (respect, admiration, self-confidence, self-worth).

For most of us, desperate hunger or thirst are likely to subvert all other needs. But once we have eaten and drunk our fill, they cease to be a source of motivation. We have time to socialize with our friends. Secure, we are motivated by aspirations and ambitions. We strive to achieve. This gives us self-satisfaction, but it also wins us esteem, arising out of the way others perceive us, and treat us.

If esteem and respect reward our efforts, they continue as motivators. Perhaps we make even greater efforts in order to win more esteem. We appreciate feedback from others and often we rely on it. When that feedback – reward, praise, acknowledgement – is missing, we may experience a loss of motivation. A little of the shine may recede from our self-view. Personal confidence may seep away or drop dramatically.

Jakobson's identification of the phatic function of communication is relevant here. If those seemingly commonplace yet critically important responses to our behaviour – the 'Thanks!', 'Good work!', 'Well done!' – are absent, there is a likelihood that we may cease to be motivated.

At the crest of his hierarchy Maslow places **self-actualizing needs**, the goal of independence and self-fulfilment. It is at the level of self-actualization that, in celebrating our uniqueness, in developing our potential, we also nurture an active vision of the world outside self. Maslow identifies meta-needs such as a person's commitment to truth and justice; and in some cases readiness to sacrifice lower order needs, such as freedom from danger or relief

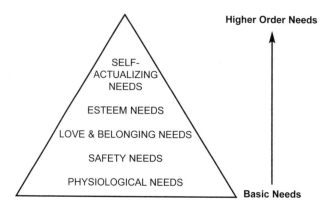

1. PHYSIOLOGICAL NEEDS
    Need for relief from thirst, hunger
    Need for sleep
    Need for sex
    Need for relief from pain, physiological imbalances

2. SAFETY NEEDS
    Need for security
    Need for protection
    Need for freedom from danger
    Need for order
    Need for predictable future

3. LOVE AND BELONGING NEEDS
    Need for friends
    Need for companions
    Need for a family
    Need for identification with a group
    Need for intimacy with opposite sex

4. ESTEEM NEEDS
    Need for respect
    Need for confidence based on good opinions of others
    Need for admiration
    Need for self-confidence
    Need for self-worth
    Need for self-acceptance

5. SELF-ACTUALIZATION NEEDS
    Need to fulfil one's personal capacities
    Need to develop one's potential
    Need to do what one is best suited to do
    Need to grow and expand metaneeds:
        To discover truth; create beauty; produce order; promote justice.

Figure 1.17   Model 17: Maslow's hierarchy of needs (1954)

from pain, in order to fulfil higher needs. Martyrs, whether they be burnt at the stake for their beliefs, or suicide bombers, make the ultimate sacrifice for a belief or a cause. Whether such persons are self-actualizers or simply self-deluded is open to debate.

Maslow sees individuals at the level of self-actualization as being essentially independent in thought and behaviour and not reliant on the esteem of others, which can be a fickle and sometimes misleading phenomenon. Self-actualizers know their worth. They have reached a point of self-fulfilment, self-critical maybe, but confident in their abilities.

Freedom and identity

The importance of personal freedom is given special emphasis by Maslow. In *Motivation and Personality* he writes of 'freedom to speak, freedom to do what one wishes so long as no harm is done to others, freedom to express oneself, freedom to investigate and seek for information, freedom to defend oneself' (1954). He is of the opinion that 'Secrecy, censorship, dishonesty, blocking of communication threatens all the basic needs'. Having placed a human value on freedom, people at their self-actualizing best will struggle to defend and further this and other higher order needs such as fairness and justice.

Yet people are not always at their best. Maslow observes that in times of insecurity, social, cultural, political or economical, a process of **regression** is likely to take place, of retreating from higher order aspirations to attitudes and behaviour dominated by self-preservation. Propagandists have long understood how insecurity and fear in the population can be manipulated, to the point where fairness and justice are no longer recognizable.

In these circumstances identity can take a beating if we see ourselves as persons with opinions concerning fairness and justice, who take pride in expressing those opinions. Speaking out might suddenly become dangerous, as the Spiral of Silence model suggested by German research professor Elisabeth Noelle-Neumann indicates (see Figure 1.18).

The model can be applied in all sorts of situations. It is about inhibition and self-censorship. In a free society we may feel no inhibition about speaking our opinions, even if those opinions are 'deviant' in the sense that they are not in accord with the majority view. In a less free society, indeed in a society where it is positively dangerous to speak out – for example, in Germany during Nazi rule, in America during the McCarthy witch hunts of the 1950s, in the Soviet Union under the Communists, in Chile in the time of the generals, in China today and many another country across the globe – silence begins to take hold of even the most outspoken.

As the Noelle-Neumann model indicates, faced with the risk of being singled out for notice, isolated, reported (and worse), people withdraw from expressing their opinions. This fear of exposure is reinforced when public

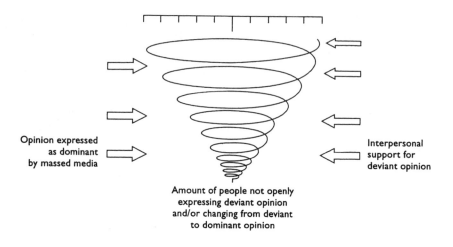

Figure 1.18   Model 18: Noelle-Neumann's spiral of silence model (1974)

discourse manifested chiefly in the mass media is intolerant of divergent or opposing voices.

The most worrying feature of a spiral of silence is that the powers that induce that silence may become persuasive, their ideology irresistible. A person's inner conviction is in danger of undergoing alteration through isolation: 'Maybe I was wrong about this all the time?' Our sense of identity as something unique can be subsumed into that of the group, the community, the 'nation'.

Even in fairly commonplace situations individuals can feel uneasy about expressing their opinions, usually when others in a group or society disagree on issues of importance. The pressure to conform causes dissonance, and in order to shift from under that pressure and work towards congruence, individuals may have to suppress their true opinions. In some situations this silence becomes betrayal, giving rise to dissonance of a type not easily resolved.

The targeting of identity

The pressure to conform to a stereotype of personal communication or behaviour is not only the strategy of those exercising power over individuals, groups and communities. That other myth-maker, the marketing and advertising industry, has for generations taken its cue from Maslow's hierarachy of needs to shape people into stereotypical categories that better serve consumerist goals.

The formula is to match human needs with consumer products and services. By purchasing a certain product, the consumer also buys into a desirable identity. Shampoos, as advertised, not only improve the appearance of your hair, they bring you beauty, style and guarantee the admiration of others, all 'because you're worth it!'

Consumerism has not been slow in creating its own models of communication, usually with the aim of specifying the needs of differing sections, or segments of the population. Drawing up typologies of characteristics responsive to persuasion has made it easier to identify and target consumers. These begin as lists. The public is scrutinized according to its consumer activities, then segmented – labelled and boxed. What places us in one 'box' or another is **lifestyle**, what it is at present and more significantly what we would like it to be.

Eventually lists graduate into models, which brings us to one of the best-known consumer need orientated classifications, the VALS (Values And Lifestyles) Typology and the VALS model (see Figure 1.19). In *New American Lifestyles: Who We Are and Where We're Going* Arnold Mitchell (1983) summarizes the aims and findings of a far-reaching research project carried out in the US in 1980 by SRI International. Further research was conducted in five European countries: Britain, France, Italy, Sweden and West Germany. Both our needs and our lifestyles, Mitchell explains, fluctuate according to circumstance and 'drive', or motivation. The pursuit of a lifestyle is linked with

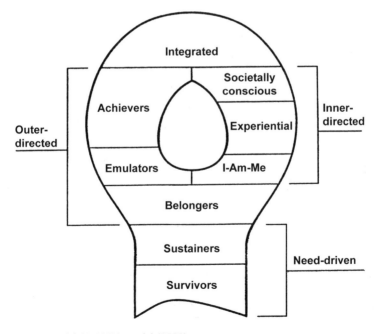

Figure 1.19 Model 19: VALS model (1980)

our desire for personal growth. As this growth takes place, we discover new goals, 'and in support of these new goals come new beliefs, new dreams and new constellations of values'.

The VALS model is complex and ambitious. As Maslow does in his hierarchy, the model seeks to identify the ideal, or a close approximation to it. Where self-actualizers in Maslow are the model to aspire to, in VALS there are those who integrate **outer and inner directedness**. By good fortune or their own efforts these members of the community have long since ceased to experience conditions in which they are need-driven, in terms of survival. Indeed they may never at any time have had to face the challenges of those at the bottom of the VALS hierarchy, those for whom life is a desperate battle for survival (**survivor lifestyle**) or a struggle simply to keep heads about water (the **sustainer lifestyle**).

The outer- and inner-directed groups have moved upwards from the need to belong, emulate or achieve. They will have experienced phases of individualism (I-am-Me), tried out the experiential lifestyle and embraced considerations beyond the self – caring for, working for the good of society. As **Integrateds** they may even be resistant to the siren voices of consumer marketing; that group of individuals, always in a minority in society, who the advertisers find difficult to manipulate.

Do you recognize yourself in the VALS model – your friends, parents; or do you sense the danger of stereotyping becoming a **self-fulfilling prophecy**[6], of people being defined, then the definition repeated until it becomes a norm; something to conform to? When we sit in a Starbuck's coffee bar, what roles are we playing; what narratives are we subscribing to? Are we simply drinking coffee, in the belief that the signifier (coffee) is also the signified (pleasure from the taste of coffee); or is the signified something else? The models we have been looking at may not necessarily give us answers, but they supply us with patterns of analysis – cues (in Barnlund's sense), significant signs (according to the semiologists) or the various indications of 'noise' as developed by model-makers since Shannon and Weaver.

Subject to circumstance

What is of vital interest in the study of interpersonal communication is the relationship between **identity** and **circumstance**, the one struggling for definition and constancy, the other subject to change, to its many twists, turns and uncertainties. Our wealth, our health, our upbringing, even our seeming luck or bad luck in life, are major contributors to our self-identity and our confidence in it at any given time. The problematic of identity, indeed its mystery, is the focus of attention of Eric M. Eisenberg in his Model of Communication and Identity (Eisenberg 2001: see Figure 1.20)[7].

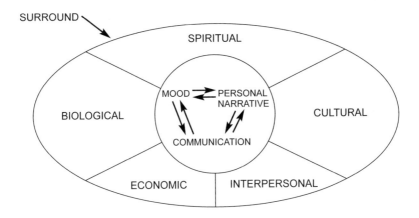

Figure 1.20 Model 20: Eisenberg's model of communication and identity (2001)

For Eisenberg, communication is the means by which we search for, define and establish personal identity; and this quest takes place within a modern day situation of flux and insecurity. What we have so far been calling context or environment, Eisenberg refers to as **surround**. His model demonstrates the interconnectedness of influences upon us as human beings in communities, and the process of communication. Most of the periodical in which this model is discussed, the *Journal of Communication* (September 2001), is given over to the scrutiny of insecurity in contemporary world society and Eisenberg's ambition here is to offer a model that might serve as a mechanism to put the negativity of insecurity into reverse.

He lays the blame for much insecurity on the way identity has been traditionally seen as a **fixed entity**, something that, once formed, is alterable only with great difficulty, even if there was a wish to make this alteration. Eisenberg writes, 'How we respond to the fundamental uncertainty of life shapes everything we do and is driven in part by how we think about our place in the world, our sense of identity' (2001: 534–5). The author sees identity as 'another name for emotional or mental health' governed by our relationship to the future as well as to those around us – family, friends, neighbours, other races, other religions or other nations.

Eisenberg talks of a 'perennial quest for a single, literal, fundamental truth, whether it be found in nationalism, capitalism, or religious fundamentalism' (2001: 536), producing certainties which are essentially divisive and potentially destructive; which result in the establishment of boundaries, of the stress on difference rather than an emphasis on what we have in common, seeing ourselves 'as a living expression of an interconnected universe'.

The surround's mix of influences and pressures, determining how we see ourselves and activate ourselves in relation to others, runs counter to the idea of a fixed self; indeed the key theme that Eisenberg and other commentators urge is of the 'multiplicity of selves'. It can scarcely be otherwise considering how bound up we are with a surround itself subject to constant flux.

Eisenberg's model places a dynamically interactive trio of forces within the surround: **communication**, **mood** and **personal narrative**. In relation to surround, if that is to be taken as regional, international or global, we encounter a problem with rival definitions, or models, of communication, critically subject to cultural differences. In the West, for example, 'the definitions of communications that have dominated both academic and public discourses since WW2 have emphasized instrumentality, intentionality and the autonomous self, fitting well with the challenges of the 20th century' (Eisenberg 2001: 539); but, he argues, 'not so well with those of the 21st'.

Transmission versus ritual

In an increasingly multicultural world,

> social life will be characterized by a much broader view of information exchange ... less concerned with persuasion than connection, less focused on self than system, and less preoccupied with maintaining a fixed identity (of persons, organizations, nation-states) than with developing a robust but dynamic conception of identity that continually adapts to a turbulent environment.
>
> (Eisenberg 2001: 539).

Eisenberg is suggesting we turn away from the traditional, Western transmission model of communication in favour of one much more **culturally orientated**; not the least one more sensitive to the power of language as a weapon of dominance.

Eisenberg points out, 'We run into trouble, both individually and collectively, when we seek clarity at all costs, when we aspire to establish some transcendent truth "once and for all". Harbouring such aspirations leads people to "lock in" to a particular way of thinking and being' (2001: 540) – a way that appears to justify 'our' definitions against 'theirs'.

The use of communication in this manner is essentially defensive; and it has the effect of making others defensive, as individuals or as nation-states; hardening their own definitions. Eisenberg argues, 'The prevailing cultural attitude is something like this: "When our way of life is threatened ... if only we can succeed in classifying the other as irreparably deviant – as another species, really, not at all like ourselves – then we will be safe"' (2001: 541). This way, communication produces demons if not monsters.

An innovatory feature of Eisenberg's model is the inclusion of **mood**, that is whether we as individuals (or groups, communities, nations) 'are hopeful or anxious, happy or depressed' and these factors, affected by surround, are future-orientated: 'By the future, I am referring to everything from the next moment to the rest of one's life' (2001: 544).

Eisenberg acknowledges the generic model of human life as a series of stories. He writes of 'ongoing authorship (and editing) of one's personal narrative or life story, which tells a great deal about our attachments, interpretations, and view of our own possibilities' (p. 544). These narratives can be open to, or closed to, change: what happens in the stories, or does not happen, depends on the nature of mood and communicative style. The processes are 'mutually reinforcing, and repeated patterns get locked in, with varying consequences' (p. 544).

The model suggests that 'Positive change is most likely to occur when each sub-process [communication, mood, personal narrative] is taken into account' (p. 544). What is of special note is the stress on the importance of the body, the **physicality of existence** in the process of the authoring of identity. Models, and to a certain extent, communications theory, may have neglected the role of the physical/psychological but those in the business of addressing people's minds through their bodies ('the body in the world' as Eisenberg puts it) have long seen this as the basis of a range of strategies to influence identity and behaviour.

In this sense, Eisenberg is connecting with, though not affirming, the VALS typology and its own surround, the capitalist-consumerist society whose prime target could be said to cultivate the 'mood to spend'. As Eisenberg points out, 'There are numerous cultural mechanisms that encourage the development of a well-bounded self, so long as that self wants to go shopping' (p. 545).

In a world saturated with consumer persuasion on the one hand and on the other economic and political necessities, to what extent do circumstances permit us **narrative possibilities**? A healthy identity suggests a degree of power over our lives. A sense of powerlessness leads, Eisenberg believes, to 'rigid, defensive, fearful communication'. Again, this might apply as much to groups, communities and nations as to individuals.

Personal power is viewed as central to the process of self-narrative, but discrimination is necessary between two modes of power – 'power over', as in authority over, or control over, and 'power of': 'Whereas "power over" is bounded, instrumental and attached, "power of" is limitless, inclusive, non strategic, and open' (p. 546). Power *of* means the existence of, or potential for, empowerment; and is contributory to our narrative possibilities.

The second of these classifications of power accords with what Eisenberg calls a 'planetary identity', inclusive rather than exclusive, open to uncertainties and differences over ideology, belief and values. He is of the view that

'For our future, we require a global declaration of interdependence, a central tenet of which must be the release of grasping after self and tribal identity' (pp. 546–7) and that means giving up the idea of a fixed truth; refusing to turn 'purposely ambiguous' signifiers into signification that takes on the rigidity of dogma, with all the consequences, social, cultural, economic and political that ensue. The challenge is how to resolve the desirable goal of stability in a world of dynamic change, without settling for certainties.

Only connect

If there is one feature common to all the major models of communication it is **interconnectivity**. We have seen how in the Eisenberg model the connectivity of process, between mood, narrative and communication links with surround, the complex of influences on the central activity. Wilbur Schramm invites us to focus on the nature of interaction when fields of experience overlap, or equally significantly for our understanding of personal and cultural differences, when they do not overlap. In Newcomb, the interconnectivity of A, B and X, and the ways communication is shaped by consonance or dissonance reveals the relationship of inner and outer dynamics.

Just as Eisenberg says that communication is central to managing insecurity, Newcomb makes a similar point, emphasizing our tendency to work from dissonance towards consonance. Both are talking about **convergences**. In an increasingly multicultural world it could be deemed crucial that individuals and communities strive to increase the degree of overlap. Where differences of culture, belief, values and attitudes are marked, there is an especial need for the exercise of **reflexivity,** that is, reflecting upon our own attitudes and responses to Other, empathizing with Other's often contrasting projects of self in context, being not only self-aware but Other-aware.

This means developing the will and having the power to review self and performance, in Eisenberg's terms, to scrutinize the interaction between mood and personal narrative as expressed through communication. In the Johari Window disclosure and attention to feedback draw back the curtain of misunderstanding, prejudgment and often false perception, on the Blind, Hidden and possibly even Unknown Areas. Barnlund gives weight to the significance of internal as well as interpersonal reflection, while Eric Berne warns of the dangers that might ensure from ignoring the 'voices' of our past.

Throughout, we have seen that no model is all-inclusive of the processes of communication; none comprises more than a tentative approach to a fuller understanding of the complexities of human interaction. Yet models are timely reminders of what factors to consider. They are guides to the evolution of our studies of communication, from the early days of mechanistic approaches to communication, the traditional models of information transmission and reception, to ones culture orientated, dealing with signs, codes and signification and advancing towards encapsulating matters of identity, the inner and outer self in relationship with contextual influences in a world of swift and ceaseless change.

The search for the ideal model for any given communicative situation may, in the nature of things, always be just out of reach. That should motivate us to be model-makers, charting and re-charting the salient features of process, examining the dynamics of their interaction, while at the same time taking into account the fruits of ongoing research, study and theorizing.

Exercise

1 Examine the model in Figure 1.21 and give it a 'make-over', perhaps adjusting its shape, repositioning elements and adding features that may have been omitted.

2 Make two lists: a) the factors that contribute, in interpersonal communication, to self-esteem; and b) those that lower or damage self-esteem. Consider how the two lists could be re-shaped into model form.

3 In the capacity of Person A, create a pathway diagram comprising boxes and arrows in which you map your step-by-step strategy of changing your friend B's view on X, avoiding the danger of forcing B into silence or other diversionary communication. Take into account unexpected as well as predictable responses.

4 Study a communicative interaction, either live or on screen, and pick out aspects of that interaction which might reveal themselves according to transactional analysis.

5 Create a model that incorporates what you consider to be the salient features of a multicultural society.

Key points

- Models remind us of the vital constituents of communication.
- They assist us in making connections between those constituents.
- Early models saw communication as information exchange.
- To these were added the role, often complex, often subject to error or misunderstanding, of feedback.
- Where fields of common experience overlap there is the potential for effective communication.
- The shapes of models evolved from the linear to the circular to the

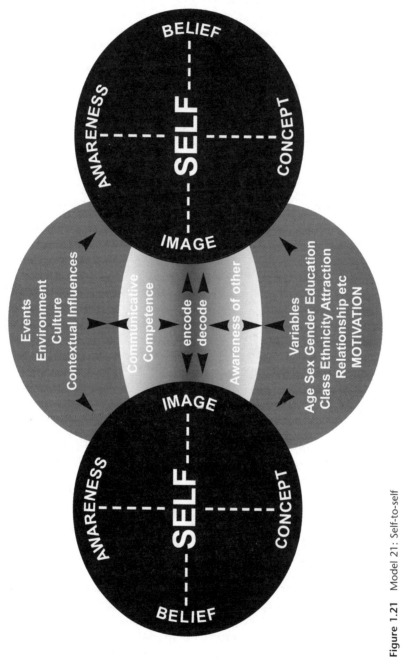

Figure 1.21 Model 21: Self-to-self

With thanks to graphic designer Marion Kember of West Kent College for converting my hand-drawn sketch into something easier on the eye.

spiral; while the image of the mosaic attempts to include intra-personal factors.

- As model-making progressed, vital features such as perception, previous experience or personal history were added.
- Newcomb focused on the orientation of persons A and B towards issues or third parties, represented as X.
- The Johari Window illustrates that the communication process includes that which we are unaware of about ourselves and others as well as what we know.
- Barnlund saw 'cues' embodying the dynamic of interpersonal communication, while semiology placed the sign at the heart of the process.
- Transactional analysis sees individual behaviour as being conditioned by our past experience and manifesting itself in the interacting roles of Parent, Child and Adult. We take up 'life positions' such as 'I'm OK – You're OK'.
- Just as we play roles, we also play games in interpersonal communication, these operating according to scripts.
- For Maslow, what motivates and drives us is a range of needs, formed into a hierarchy, a theory that has inspired propagandists of all types to identify our needs, turn them into wants in our project of and narrative of, self.
- The VALS typology matches notions of identity with lifestyle.
- Noelle-Neumann's spiral of silence model suggests the conditions in which we retreat from communication, resorting to self-defence and often ending up isolated.
- Eisenberg suggests the model of communication for the twenty-first century should seek to break through the frames of self, as shaped by Western-dominated culture, by emphasizing interdependency and greater reflexivity.

Notes

1   Admirable as Berlo's model is – he was the first to include the five senses in the communication process – he does omit feedback from his design.

2   In relation to the Newcomb model and to the experience of dissonance/consonance in interpersonal communication, see Leon Festinger's *A Theory of Cognitive Dissonance* (US: Stanford University Press, 1957). Cognitive dissonance occurs when a person holds two contradictory or inconsistent beliefs which cause psychological uneasiness or discomfort. Festinger argues that people will be motivated, indeed driven, to seek to reduce or eliminate dissonance; and he examines various strategies for doing this.

Newcomb's ABX model was later built on by Bruce H. Wesley and Malcolm S. MacLean Jr in 'A conceptual model for communications research' published in *Journalism Quarterly*, 34 (1957). To the scenario AB and X they introduce C, which they identify as a gatekeeper; largely though not exclusively the role played by the media. A subhead in the article summarizes the orientation of the model: 'From face-to-face to mass'. More recent illustrations of the model itself can be found in Dennis McQuail and Sven Windahl's *Communication Models for the Study of Mass Communication* (London: Longman, 2nd edition, 1996), or *The Dictionary of Media and Communication Studies* (UK: Hodder Arnold, 7th edition, 2006) by James Watson and Anne Hill.

3   See also two books published in the USA by Holt, Rinehart and Winston, both edited by Frank Dance, *Human Communication Theory: Original Essays* (1967) and *Human Communication Theory* (1982). Dance's chapter in Sereno and Mortensen opens with an excellent analysis of the usefulness of models as does Dean Barnlund's chapter 'A transactional model of communication' in the same book.

4   See also, Tom Burns, *Erving Goffman (1922–1982)* published in the US by Routledge (1992); Lemart, C. and Branaman, A. eds. (1997) *The Goffman Reader*. UK: Blackwell.

5   The need-driven framework was taken up by Michael Argyle in his *The Psychology of Interpersonal Behaviour* (UK: Pelican, 1967 and subsequent Penguin editions). Argyle talks of 'drives' orientated towards a range of key human needs, which he lists as biological, dependency, affiliation, dominance, sex, aggression, self-esteem and ego-identity needs and other 'motivations which affect social behaviour'. Argyle stresses that the list he produces is provisional, stating that 'There is as yet no final agreement on how social motivation should be divided up'. See also D.C. McClelland's *Human Motivation* (Cambridge: Cambridge University Press, 1987).

6   Self-fulfilling prophecy: occurs when the act of predicting behaviour helps cause, prompt or fulfil that behaviour. For example, a child typecast as a failure, and frequently classified as such by Other (parents, teachers, peers) may fulfil low expectations. On the other hand, such typecasting can prompt a 'revolt'; a determination to prove Other wrong.

7   Eisenberg's article connects with URT (Uncertainty Reduction Theory) outlined by C.R. Berger and R.J. Calabrese in 'Some explorations in initial interaction and beyond: Toward a development theory of interpersonal communication' in *Human Communication Research*, 1 (1975). Berger followed this up with 'Beyond initial interaction: Uncertainty, understanding, and the development of interpersonal relationships' in *Language and Social Psychology* (Oxford: Blackwell, 1979), edited by H. Giles and R.N. St. Clair, and, in 1986, 'Uncertainty outcome values in predicted relationships: Uncertainty reduction theory then and now', *Human Communication Research*, 13. Theory and research examine how in encounters and interactions communicators use

strategies to reduce uncertainty about each other, a key aim being to increase the ability to predict the behaviour of self and other in communicative situations. Much depends on information-seeking, especially when strangers meet, knowing little or nothing about each other. As our knowledge of Other grows, we know better how to respond, how to manage interaction, how to predict and cope with response. An important factor in the successful progress of interpersonal communication and uncertainty reduction is seen to be similarity – of attitude, values, etc. Berger and Calabrese in 1975 posed 21 theorems of URT. Much work has since been done on many aspects on uncertainty reduction, the relationship between different cultures being particularly apposite, as Eric Eisenberg emphasizes.

2   Exploration of the Nature of Identity

Identity in the 21st century is primarily self-constructed.

Polhemus and Uzi Part B (2004: 12)

'Who am I?' is a question that has resonated across the centuries and this chapter considers how we, as individuals, try to answer that question. As Stella Ting-Toomey (1999: 26) notes: 'individuals acquire their identities via interaction with others' and several perspectives from the disciplines of psychology, sociology and linguistics have been influential in exploring the links between social interaction and the formation and maintenance of self-identity. Central to this exploration is the ongoing debate about the relative importance of structure (societal influences) and agency (an individual's thoughts and actions) in the formation of the self.

Introduction

Self-identity also involves cognitive awareness of the self 'To be a "person" is not just to be a reflexive actor, but to have a concept of a person . . .' (Giddens 1991: 52–3). An individual's self-concept is commonly seen as having three main components: the self-image, self-esteem and the ideal self (Gross 2005). The self-image can be seen as the descriptive part of the self and can be seen to contain perceptions of aspects of the self, such as body image, achievements, personality traits, roles and relationships. The self-esteem is the evaluative part of the self, that is how we feel about ourselves. The ideal self contains our aspirations for the self. The nature of self-identity can also be seen to be bipolar, that is to have a sense of self is also to have a sense of not-self, of those who are different – the other (Bannister and Agnew 1976).

Ting-Toomey (1999: 27) proposes that, 'Two sources of identity typically influence an individual's everyday interaction: group-based identity and person-based identity'. With reference to the work of Tajfel and colleagues, she argues that social identities stem from our membership of 'emotionally significant categories or groups' – examples here could be the cultural, ethnic, gender, sexual and social class identities discussed in later chapters of this book. We usually have overlapping membership of these groups, for example, gender and ethnic groups, and the relative impact of these various identities on interaction may vary with the situation.

In contrast personal identities stem from the aspects of our self-concept that we use to differentiate ourselves from others and provide a sense of uniqueness. Personal experiences and personality traits may, for example, contribute to the notion of a personal identity. Our interaction with others also helps shape our sense of identity. There may be differences betwe we see ourselves and how others see us; differences that are likely to p both the messages exchanged in social encounters as well as our ow reflections on who we are or where we are at in the development of a self.

As Ting-Toomey (1999: 28) points out: 'No individual person develops a sense of self in a vacuum ... Both social identity and personal identity are acquired and developed within the larger webs of culture'. Within these webs are to be found definitions, evaluations and expectations of social identities along with the ideologies that underpin them, though these are subject to change and may be resisted. Further, general definitions of social identities may be limited in what they reveal about the self-identity of any one individual. We are also likely to be members of small groups such as family, work or friendship groups and these too generate role identities and associated expectations of behaviour. Cultural sources of behavioural expectations can overlap and be mutually reinforcing but they can also be in conflict. As individuals we may also decide to challenge or change such expectations. Interpersonal communication is arguably at the heart of the process of identity formation as much of the work of defining, performing, evaluating and changing identities can be seen to be carried out in everyday social interactions. Such interactions provide us with much material for reflection on the nature of our identity.

Cultures may hold different views of the nature of the self. Individualistic cultures typical of Western societies tend to stress the unique and independent nature of the self whereas the collectivistic cultures typical of Asian societies, for example, emphasize commonality and view the individual as 'important only to the extent that they are part of a web of socially meaningful relationships' (Eisenberg 2001: 535). Even within Western cultures the degree to which any one individual sees themselves as independent, free and in control of their own destiny is likely to be dependent on circumstances. However, Giddens (1991: 53) argues that although concepts of what a 'person' is may vary across cultures, 'The capacity to use "I" in shifting contexts, characteristic of every known culture, is the most elemental feature of reflexive conceptions of personhood.'

Development of the self

A number of theorists have pointed to the importance of social interaction in both the development and maintenance of the self. Charles Cooley and, especially, George H. Mead were important in the development of what later became known as **symbolic interactionism** (Blumer 1986). From this perspective identity is constructed through social interaction and thus communication – the creation of meaning through the exchange and negotiation of shared signs and symbols – is seen as central to this process. A process viewed as ongoing and dynamic, somewhat in the spirit of Dance's helical spiral of communication discussed in the previous chapter.

Cooley (1902) developed the idea of the **'looking-glass self'**. For Cooley an important influence on the development of the self is the responses that others make to us and to our behaviour. These responses serve as a looking-glass from which we learn to see ourselves as we imagine others see us. This feedback aids us in understanding who we are. For Mead (1934), the self is made by a reflexive process, involving self-interaction between **the 'I' and the 'Me'**, the 'I' being the act of experiencing and the 'Me' the socialized part of the self, the object which the 'I' experiences and interacts with. The 'Me' is the view of the self that an observer might have. Language is seen as a crucial medium by which the individual represents itself to itself. Self-interaction enables the human being to develop the self, to define and interpret their world and to organize actions based on such interpretations; in short to be an active social agent.

It is through interaction with others, especially role-playing, that the individual learns the ability to see themself as others do, an ability which aids awareness and identification of the self, and allows the 'Me' to expand. In particular, through developing the mechanism of the 'generalized other' the individual acquires the ability to predict how people in general might evaluate them in the light of their behaviour and thus has the potential to use this awareness to influence reactions. For Mead, the 'generalized other' provides us with a sense of self. Mead's ideas highlight the role that the interpersonal process can play in the construction of self-identity. Through this process we can be socialized by others' expectations but as active social agents we also have the potential to shape others' views of us.

For Carl Rogers (1961) a crucial aspect of the development of the self is the drive towards **self-actualization**, to achieve one's potential. A drive that can be, and often is, frustrated by the consequences of our communication with others. Rogers argues that the individual tries to maintain a consistency between their self-image and their actions. However, at times such consistency may be difficult to maintain, partly as a result of social pressures. Such incongruent experiences can threaten the self-image. One way of dealing with such threats is to deny them access to awareness through the employment of defence mechanisms. However, Rogers argues, such strategies inhibit growth and change in the self and increase the gap between self-image and reality; a situation which invites anxiety and emotional problems. It is when an individual's self-image and actions are congruent that they are most able to engage in behaviour that contributes to self-actualization.

Other people are often the source of pressure to deny aspects of the self. Through the process of socialization we learn what of our behaviour is and is not valued by others, especially significant others such as parents, relatives, teachers and friends. We learn, therefore, the **conditions of worth** under which positive regard from others is forthcoming and internalize these. Rogers argues that individuals have a strong need for both positive regard and positive self-regard (the internalization of that of which others approve) and they are thus an important influence on behaviour. If these conditions of worth lead to an individual denying part of themselves, what is received, according to Rogers, is conditional positive regard. Such denial and distortion form a rift between what Rogers terms the 'organism' (the total of an individual's possible experiences) and the 'self' (that which the individual is prepared to admit and accept about their experiences). Rogers believes that the ideal is that these two should be the same but a consequence of socialization is that often they are not.

However, consciously examining what is denied and developing awareness and acceptance for the whole of one's experiences, leads to greater unconditional positive regard and greater congruence between the self-image and reality and the self-image and the ideal self. Consequently the rift between the organism and the self is reduced and self-actualization is boosted. Nevertheless for Rogers social interaction may often create problems for the self that may contribute to its fragility and fragmentation as well as frustrate self-actualization. Everyday interactions may encourage a negative self-regard. Eisenberg (2001: 546) argues, for example, that where an individual (or group) develops feelings of powerlessness this can result in 'rigid, defensive, fearful communication' that then 'elicits fear and defensiveness from others, which over time reinforces negative self-regard'.

Self-presentation

Erving Goffman (1959) highlights the way in which the concept of self can be seen to develop through **self-presentation**, a process by which the individual presents aspects of the self to others on which they then receive feedback. The degree of calculation in acts of self-presentation, though, will usually vary with the situation. Some acts of self-presentation can be classed as acts of self-disclosure. **Self-disclosure** is normally open and reciprocal in nature and integral to the building of relationships with others. We often make careful choices about what we disclose and to whom. Self-disclosure carries risks: risks of rejection, ridicule and damage to relationships. Self-disclosure may threaten the **face** needs of both ourselves and others and, as discussed in Chapter 6, there are cultural differences in the degree to which openness is considered desirable within everyday interaction.

However self-disclosure is a means by which we can progressively share our view of ourselves and explore how others see us (Jourard 1971). The **Johari Window** discussed in the previous chapter is one model that can be used to inform attempts at self-disclosure. Messages from others about ourselves can carry **labels**, labels generated within our groups or the wider society. These run the risk of producing the self-fulfilling prophecy effect. This occurs when the expectations others have of our behaviour is communicated to us and then has the effect of producing that behaviour, so that we fulfil the prophecy.

Goffman's **dramaturgical perspective**, in which performances on stage are employed as a metaphor with which to analyse social interaction in everyday life, provides a range of useful concepts for examining self-presentation. He writes: 'life itself is a dramatically enacted thing. All the world is not, of course a stage, but the crucial ways in which it is not are not easy to specify ... In short, we all act better than we know how' (Goffman 1959: 63, 64). Goffman uses the term 'performance' to describe the act of self-presentation and in many cases these **performances** can be viewed as 'staged'. In staging a performance an individual may use props to aid their act of self-presentation, some of which are likely to be consumer goods. A key concept developed by Goffman is that of the 'persona'. The **persona** is the character an individual takes on to play a part in and to deal with the demands of a particular social situation; once chosen it influences the manner in which the individual communicates in that situation, both verbally and non-verbally.

Different social situations usually require the adoption of different personae. Thus an individual can be seen to command a range of personae and the ability to shift from one persona to another as situations demand may be seen as an important social skill. It is also one which requires careful **self-monitoring**, an activity to which not all seem equally attuned. Snyder (1979) identifies high and low self-monitors: high self-monitors are motivated to and able to assess the demands of different situations and adjust their self-presentation accordingly; low self-monitors on the other hand tend to behave in a similar fashion regardless of the situation and their behaviour tends to be influenced more by their own internal states. Further, it is likely that the **role** an individual is playing (and in particular, the role expectations) may dictate the kind of persona that it would be appropriate to adopt. According to

Goffman we also perform from behind a 'front'; standard parts of the **front** are the 'setting' (e.g. one's local pub) and the 'personal front' (e.g. clothing, for instance a leather jacket).

Goffman argues that the sustaining of everyday performances is important both to the development and maintenance of the concept of self, and thus also to self-identity. Disturbances in such performances constitute, therefore, a threat: 'Life may not be much of a gamble, but interaction is' (1959: 215). Thus 'impression management', the ability to carefully control the impression given off to others, becomes key. Successful impression management also requires sensitive self-monitoring. Competent performances require considerable day-to-day control and the appropriate employment of personae. Personae may then be seen as part of the biography which the individual supplies about the self and the fit between these and the biographical narrative could be expected to influence feelings of security. Giddens (1991: 58) argues, 'All human beings, in all cultures, preserve a division between their self-identities and the "performances" they put on in specific social contexts'. However situations will exist, for a variety of reasons, in which an individual may feel particularly distant from a performance, and perceive it to be false; in such situations they are likely to feel less secure.

Anthony Giddens reinforces Goffman's view that competent and successful control of bodily appearance plays an important role in both self-presentation and sustaining notions of self-identity. When such control breaks down, feelings of anxiety may result. The successful maintenance of bodily appearance may involve the more disciplined control of 'regimes' such as those involved in constructing gender differences in appearance, differences which are crucial to notions of self-identity. Polhemus and Uzi Part B (2004: 12) explore various techniques by which we construct our bodily appearance, and also argues that, 'body style is undoubtedly our most powerful and effective means of signalling "where we are at"'.

Performativity

Judith Butler (1999) in discussing gender identities also highlights the importance of everyday performances in the construction of identity. She argues that the construction and maintenance of identity can be understood 'as a signifying practice', a practice that calls upon cultural tools, such as language, non-verbal signs and commodities in its execution. It is through the repetition of performances that identity is constructed, maintained and also, crucially, modified. Butler sees gender identity as something of a fabrication created out of successive acts of signification, of the process of performativity. Whilst societal expectations may frame the way such performances are enacted, Butler (1999: 185) argues that individuals have the space to challenge and thus modify such expectations: ' "agency" then, is to be located within the possibility of a variation on that repetition', so that 'a subversion of identity becomes possible'. Gender identities thus have a dynamic quality and subversions extend the possibilities as regards gender identities and sexual orientation to include, for example, homosexual or hermaphrodite identities.

The psychoanalytic perspective

Broad societal influences can clearly impact on our sense of self-identity but so too can psychological processes. Woodward (2002: 16) comments that 'Identity involves the interrelationship between the personal and the social; between what I feel inside and what is known about me from the outside.' Psychoanalytic theories, such as those of Freud and Jung, argue that much of our behaviour is influenced by forces within the **unconscious mind**, thus self-knowledge is limited and self-identity partial, provisional and vulnerable to fracture. Central to these theories is an examination of the interplay and conflict between these forces, in particular the conflict between our inner desires and the demands of others, of society. Freud's theories have been influential in the development of Transactional Analysis – a widely used series of techniques for analysing interaction discussed in the previous chapter.

Freud argued there are three components of an individual's personality: the **id**, the **ego** and the **superego**, and these are inevitably in conflict. The id is that part of the personality that reacts to basic biological instincts and drives; it operates on the Pleasure Principle in that it encourages us to seek pleasure and avoid pain. The ego according to Gross (2005: 602) is the ' "executive" of the personality, the planning, decision-making, rational and logical part of us'. The ego operates on the Reality Principle. It is concerned with the social consequences of our behaviour and the resulting evaluations others make. It seeks to control those influences from the id that would, if acted on, result in social criticism or rejection. The superego contains our ideas about what is morally right or wrong – ideas much influenced by the moral values to which we have been exposed during our upbringing. It also seeks to control influences from the id and does this through the ego. It attempts to control those influences that seem likely to result in behaviour of which our own superego would disapprove. The ego may though on occasions counsel against acting on the superego's demands.

Gross (2005: 746) comments, 'the ego is pulled in two opposing directions by the id and the superego'. It also has to consider the dictates of reality. The id lies in the unconscious part of the mind, while parts of the ego and superego are in both the conscious and unconscious mind. The ego mediates between these demands to obtain a compromise and, according to Freud, is aided by three processes: dreams, neurotic symptoms and defence mechanisms. We though are often unaware of the operation of these processes.

The notion that we unconsciously develop defence mechanisms can also be useful to the study of social interaction. Take, for example, the defence mechanisms of denial, displacement and projection. Denial is the refusal to acknowledge the objective facts in a situation as when refusing to engage in a conversation about problems in a relationship. Displacement occurs when we transfer our feelings towards one person/object onto another because it is safer to do so. We may, for instance, feel that we have been unfairly treated by a superior at work but also feel unable to do anything about it so instead we pick an argument with a shop assistant in order to vent our frustration. Projection, for instance, is the transfer to others of our own less than acceptable emotions and characteristics. Thus we may distrust the motives of someone paying us a compliment because when we compliment others it is often with covert motives, such as to help persuade them to do us a favour.

Psychoanalytic theories focus on the internal dynamics that impact on self-identity while acknowledging the role of societal influences on their functioning. It can be seen that in late modern societies, the dynamic between the id, ego and superego may be particularly fractured. Giddens (1991) proposes that in these societies there are few undisputed moral truths, authority is often questioned, and the pace of societal change undermines the comfort or guidance to be gained from traditions. It could be argued, therefore, that the certainties required to facilitate the operation of the ego or superego may be difficult to find in contemporary Western societies.

The self in discourses

The sociological and psychological perspectives discussed so far highlight that within everyday interpersonal communication are to be found a considerable number of messages with the potential to influence the process by which we construct and negotiate a sense of self-identity. These are likely to reflect prevailing expectations regarding social identities found within the differing social contexts in which interaction takes place and within the wider social structure. Mass media messages also contain many messages that may impact on a person's sense of self. Discourses relevant to thinking about identities are to be found within both interpersonal and mass communication and these can, of course, inform each other.

All discourses are framed within narratives of one kind or another and they operate to uphold particular interpretations of social life; as such they can be viewed as being underpinned by certain ideologies and the power differences articulated within them. Identity discourses refer to how we talk to or discuss those belonging to certain social or cultural categories, the verbal and non-verbal language brought into play. Suzanne Romaine, for example, comments that, 'Nothing is more personal or as closely related to our identity as our names' (2000: 116). In discussing the common practice of women taking the surnames of their husbands on marriage she notes that it is not uncommon for a married woman to be addressed as 'Mrs', to differentiate her from an unmarried woman although there is no equivalent term used for a married man. Men are referred to as 'Mr' whether married or not. These linguistic practices arguably help to construct a subordinate identity for women and reflect as well as reinforce patriarchal ideology.

As several theorists have pointed out, we do though have the potential to challenge, negotiate, change and create social and cultural expectations. One linguistic perspective that seeks to explore how we do this is **conversation analysis**. Charles Antaki and Sue Widdicombe explain that the focus here is on the way in which individuals mobilize and co-produce identity in everyday interactions on 'how identity is something that is *used* in talk; something that is part and parcel of the routines of everyday life, brought off in the fine detail of everyday interaction' (1998: 1). It is during our everyday conversations that 'Membership of a category is ascribed (and rejected), avowed (and disavowed), displayed (and ignored) in local places and at certain times' (1998: 2). The relevance of a social identity to the context of interaction is thus seen as a key variable as regards its impact on communicative behaviour.

In addition to social identities we also have discourse identities within a conversation such as listener, speaker and questioner and it is argued that 'These discourse identities are the materials out of which larger and more recognizably "social" or "institutional" identities are built' (1998: 11). Someone occupying a leadership role, for example, may occupy the speaker role more than the listener role at a business meeting in order to display and reinforce their role identity.

This linguistic perspective, while not denying social or psychological influences on our sense of self, does view the individual as a very active creative agent in a dynamic and ongoing process of constructing a sense of self; a process that is seen to be sensitive to context and the expectations of others. It casts light, arguably, on the interplay between the 'personal and the social' (Woodwood 2002: 16) in an individual's identity. The influence of social identities on the sense of self-identity is seen as one that can be substantially modified, or even rejected, during interaction. Several of the case studies throughout the following chapters explore this process.

The challenges of late modernity

Social interaction, it can be argued, generates much raw material from which notions about the self and self-identity can be exchanged, explored and constructed. In doing so it can also presents threats that may lead to feelings of insecurity, fragility and fragmentation; further, social structures within which social interaction takes place may exacerbate such threats. Anthony Giddens (1991: 52–3, original emphasis) defines self-identity in the conditions of late modernity as *'the self as reflexively understood by the person in terms of her or his biography'*. While self-identity is seen as normally having a degree of continuity it is, 'such continuity as interpreted reflexively by the agent' and thus is subject to modification over time.

Giddens (1991: 54), further argues that, crucially, 'A person's identity is not to be found in behaviour, nor – important though this is – in the reactions of others, but in the capacity *to keep a particular narrative going'*, a narrative that enables us to make sense of ourselves. Building such a narrative clearly requires ongoing **intrapersonal communication** as we reflect upon our acts of interpersonal communication as well as upon messages received in mass communication. Everyday life in late modernity is likely to present such a task with significant challenges.

Giddens identifies four features of late modern societies that make the task of maintaining a coherent self-identity, a difficult one. First, identities can only be achieved through choice: 'we have no choice but to choose', given that much of the tradition which allowed them to be ascribed or indicated has lost its hold. The adoption of a lifestyle may be a significant aspect of such choices in that Giddens argues that lifestyle gives 'material form to a particular narrative of self-identity'. Second, individuals are seen to inhabit a 'pluralization of lifeworlds' in which they have to move between a number of different milieux, presenting a number of differing personae, as they move from one social sphere to another, often negotiating differing expectations of their behaviour as they do so (1991: 81–5), encouraging perhaps a 'multiplicity of selves' rather than 'a singular, core identity' (Eisenberg 2001: 537).

Another feature is 'methodological doubt' where certainty is seen as fragile, as truth often depends on context and viewpoint. Spheres of authority and recognition of expertise are often limited and provisional. Radical doubt permeates many aspects of everyday life as we negotiate the claims of often competing and at times conflicting experts. The fourth feature 'mediated experience' is seen to be at the heart of social life. Through the mass media and travel, a vast range of 'lifeworlds' are presented to audiences, thus increasing the range of options available in the construction of identities. The self has to be reflexively made, 'amid a puzzling diversity of options and possibilities' (Giddens 1991: 3). Further such identities have to be adjusted to cope with the range of changes that an individual is likely to encounter in such a society; the change to self-identity that usually accompanies a divorce being but one example. Don Slater (1997: 84) notes that another influence on late modernity – 'commercialization' – has resulted in, 'a greater fluidity in the use of goods to construct identities and lifestyles'. It has also resulted, arguably, in individuals perceiving themselves in part as consumers – a perception that reinforces the notion that we must make choices and one that is explored further in Chapter 5.

The mass media make us even more aware of the potential risks of modernity: the possibility of global warming, for example. Such awareness may promote feelings of insecurity and anxiety, though Giddens does not argue that everyday life in late modernity is any more insecure than that in previous times. Nor, for that matter would it be easy to say that self-identities are necessarily more fragile and fragmented than they were. The awareness of risks has been made more acute, Giddens argues, by the need to make lifestyle choices from a number of options.

The **reflexive project of self** thus requires that individuals work hard at the persistent self-monitoring needed to carry off, successfully, everyday acts of self-presentation, to organize lives and to develop selves in ways which allow for coherent narratives to be sustained in changing circumstances. Rogers (1961), among others, argues that self-actualization is a basic driving force of the individual. This view is certainly reinforced by many of the messages to which the individual is subject in late modernity; not least are those from advertisements, as Featherstone (1991: 86) notes: 'Consumer culture publicity suggests that we all have room for self-improvement ... whatever our age or class origins'. There is a pressure to develop the self and to make the most of opportunities present at various stages of the human life-span. This presents, according to Slater (1997: 84) 'a recipe for identity crisis on a mass scale. Individuals must, by force of circumstances, choose, construct, maintain, interpret, negotiate, display who they are to be or be seen as, using a bewildering variety of material and symbolic resources.'

The dilemmas are compounded for Giddens (1991: 81) in that modernity 'confronts the individual with a complex diversity of choices and, because it is non-foundational, at the same time offers little help as to which options should be selected'. The forces of modernity, though, may promote integration as well as fragmentation and 'feelings of self-identity are both robust and fragile' (1991: 55). The fragility of self-identity is bound up with the potentially fragile nature of the biography that the individual supplies about themself and the difficulty of keeping a coherent narrative going in the conditions of late modernity.

Late modernity can be seen to present the self with a number of dilemmas (Giddens 1991). One is that of **unification versus fragmentation**.

The individual has to master a variety of personae in order to negotiate the diverse contexts of social interaction, without the self-identity fragmenting into a mere collection of personae. Some consumer goods are promoted with the promise that they can help the individual master the art of self-presentation. **Consumer culture** can, Slater notes, offer us, 'resources – both material and symbolic – through which we produce and sustain identities' (1997: 85). Many advertising messages, arguably, encourage and enable us to read off the symbolic properties of consumer goods, to judge what they may or may not being saying about ourselves.

Denis McQuail (2005) provides an overview of the various gratifications and satisfactions the mass media may offer individuals. A number of these, such as 'identity formation and confirmation' and 'social contact' illustrate the use we may make of media artefacts as sources of reference for not only thinking about self-identity but also for dealing with the demands of social interaction. This is particularly likely to be the case when the individual is unfamiliar with the expectations of a particular situation. An individual playing the role of health/sports club member for the first time, for example, could find inspiration for their performance from magazines, books, sports shops, websites and advertisements as well as from personal experience. We are likely though to look for the reactions of others during interaction for confirmation that we have we have carried off a successful performance.

A willingness to believe that commodities have such symbolic properties and that they communicate what is intended (always questionable given the variables influencing the act of decoding) may therefore seem useful to the individual in their task of mastering a range of personae, of controlling the gamble of interaction, and such may be the reason why they are purchased. They are unlikely, however, to promote a sense of coherence for the narrative of the self without reference to some integrating structure. To some extent lifestyle may offer such a structure. Lifestyles establish routines within everyday life that help promote feelings of stability and security for the self. Giddens argues that choice of lifestyle is thus important to the self-identity, both 'its making and re-making' (1991: 81). However, such stability is conditional. Lifestyles are likely to change, and the choice of a particular lifestyle may mean that some of the social settings in which the individual has to operate do not fit comfortably with it.

'Powerlessness versus appropriation' is a dilemma, Giddens argues, identified by many commentators on modernity. Modernity, particularly in the present era of intense globalization, is seen to encourage feelings of powerlessness in the individual. He regards this as an oversimplified view that overlooks the fact that in pre-modern societies most people often had little power. There are clearly areas of modern social life in which most individuals do enjoy some degree of power – the right to vote in democratic elections, and to choose a partner in marriage being but two examples. It can also be argued that consumer culture provides material resources that give the individual a range of opportunities to exercise control over the development of their life. The **decline of traditional authority structures** and their **replacement by a plurality of expertise** faces the self with another dilemma according to Giddens: the uncertainty engendered by a choice of who to turn to for guidance. This dilemma, he explains, 'is ordinarily resolved through a mixture of routine and commitment to a certain form of lifestyle, plus the vesting of trust in a given series of abstract systems' (1991: 196).

The fourth dilemma for the self argues Giddens 'is that between **personalized versus commodified experiences**. The individual has to work on the project of self and on establishing a lifestyle (and indeed changing it) in, 'conditions strongly influenced by standardizing effects of commodity capitalism' (1991: 196, emphasis added). Markets may promote individualism and celebrate freedom of choice but it is within already defined options – options to be shared with many others. Consumer culture may encourage the individual to equate individual freedom with the freedom merely to choose between the various commodities on offer and freedom of expression with the ability to choose from a range of commodities – those which the individual believes, possibly as a result of advertising, send appropriate signals about their self-identity. Other freedoms, such as freedom of speech, and other means of individual expression such as writing and painting may be overlooked as regards their contribution to the project of self.

The emphasis on the individual may also be seen to deny the fact that for the most part people live, love and work within social relationships and networks which give support and a sense of belonging to the individual as well as demanding obligations from them. Personal relationships and membership of such networks are likely to play an important role in the construction of an individual's biography and of their self-identity. A stress on individualism and its expression through the purchase of commodities may weaken the ties that offer some coherence and stability to self-identity. That we are encouraged to purchase consumer goods with which to express aspects of identity raises questions about the impact of consumer culture on 'the project of self' – questions explored further in Chapter 5.

Giddens argues that another feature of modernity that has implications for the biography of self is the **pure relationship** – a relationship that 'is sought only for what the relationship can bring to the partners involved' (1991: 90). It is built on the process of mutual disclosure and the trust and intimacy that stem from this as the relationship develops and deepens. The process of mutual disclosure requires the exploration of the self and the other; it is reciprocal, and thus 'connects very closely to the project of self' (1991: 90), given that, 'self-identity is negotiated through linked processes of self-exploration and the development of intimacy with the other' (1991: 97). Commitment is central to such relationships as it allows the partners to take the risks involved in forming such relationships, for they are sustained primarily by the strength of the emotional rewards that they can bring to those involved. They may be dissolved relatively easily compared to say the marriages of pre-modern, Western societies cemented as they were by economic, religious and community links.

The degree to which individuals will develop pure relationships will vary depending, for example, on such factors as socio-economic and ethnic background. The practice of arranged marriages, for instance, is still to be found in modern societies. Pure relationships tend to be found 'in the domains of sexuality, marriage and friendship' (1991: 98). Pure relationships, once established, can arguably offer the security that enables the individual to negotiate the demands and insecurities of modernity and thus have the potential to be a force against fragmentation and fragility. They may make the individual less vulnerable to the rhetoric of consumer culture. However the very nature of such relationships and the process of mutual disclosure required for their development also create risks for the self-identity. They are, as Giddens notes, 'double-edged'.

In the conditions of late modernity prevalent in Western societies then, it can be argued that cultural consensus has frayed with consequences for the process of developing self-identity, a process that can be seen to now require considerable self-conscious thought and action; it is not 'something that is just given ... but something that has to be routinely created and sustained in the reflexive activities of the individual' (Giddens: 1991). It is thus an ongoing project, for self-identity has to be explored, developed and modified against a background of changing circumstances – circumstances which may contribute to feelings of fragility as regards an individual's self-identity, an individual's biography. Eric Eisenberg (2001) supports Giddens's proposition that awareness of uncertainty, while not confined to modern times, can pose a significant challenge to the development of self-identity and particularly to the development of a flexible self-identity that is capable of successfully negotiating such uncertainties and insecurities.

The challenges noted by Giddens, in part, stem from changes within the socio-economic structure of Western societies. Changes in or modifications to the **class structure** of a society present insecurities for some individuals. While the middle classes have expanded to include new areas of occupation, the traditional working class in Britain has seen the decline of employment opportunities in the manufacturing sector of the economy (Babb et al. 2006) and with it the decline and fracturing of traditional working-class communities. Many of these communities have also experienced periods of high unemployment along with an influx of immigrants and migrant workers. Changes in the occupational structure along with the rise of female participation in the workplace has also, arguably, implications for the class and gender identities found in both communities and in the wider society. Such changes coupled with the pace of globalization and the increased geographical mobility within Britain since the 1950s are, for some, likely to impact on those aspects of self-identity tied to **place,** to a sense of belonging to an area or community. For some the ties maybe weakened, for others geography mobility offers choice and the opportunity to select the locations that 'announce their identities' (Savage et al. 2005: 207).

Cultural identity is also part of an individual's self-identity and threats to our sense of cultural identity can be a threat to our self-esteem (Ting-Toomey 1999). Colonization, civil war, emigration, immigration and **globalization** are examples of forces that can throw such identities into confusion and insecurity. The degree to which cultural identity influences communicative behaviour is seen to depend upon two factors: 'the strength of our identification, and the content of our identity' (Gudykunst and Kim 1997: 92). Being British may be much more meaningful to some British citizens than others. Gudykunst and Kim (1997) argue that we are often made more aware of our cultural identity and may feel it more strongly when surrounded by those from another culture as, for example, on a trip abroad. We also differ in the degree to which we embrace the dominant cultural values, norms and beliefs. Membership of a subculture or co-culture could be expected to be a significant variable in this respect.

The movement of people around the globe through the processes of immigration and emigration may also leave many unsure about the nature of their cultural or national identity. These processes generate hybrid cultural identities reflected in the terms African-Caribbean or Asian British. For immigrants there is the dilemma of negotiating a sense of cultural identity that acknowledges both their roots and their new home. For existing members of the host society there too may be anxiety about the impact of immigration upon their sense of both national and cultural identity (Hall 1996; Sardar 2002).

Cultural identity thus stems from a complex mix of factors and can be problematic. Britain is composed of four different nations: England, Scotland, Northern Ireland and Wales – each with its own distinct cultural heritage and language as well as that which is shared in common with other British citizens. Added to this cultural mix have been elements of the cultural backgrounds of immigrants who have settled in Britain over the centuries. Jeremy Paxman (1998) reminds us that Britain has a long history of immigration resulting from invasions, colonization, peaceful settlements, trade, and flights from persecution elsewhere. Into this fabric of identities has been woven those resulting from more recent immigration.

One feature of Western cultural identity, particularly British and French identity, according to Edward Said (1978) is that it defines itself in relation to the '**Other**' – in this case those from the 'Orient' and in particular India and the Middle East. A perspective he defined as **Orientalism**. Orientalism embraces stereotypical views of the Orient and defines the West as all that the 'Orient' is not: modern, developed, universalistic, rational, powerful and superior.

David Morley and Kevin Robins (1995) argue that awareness of the Other has intensified as a result of the mass media and crucially also because the forces of globalization have resulted in a movement of peoples that means increasingly those once seen as the 'Other' will reside within Western societies bringing challenges, particularly to the ethnocentric assumptions of Orientalism. Such movements also create **diasporas** – communities who strongly identify with those from similar origins and cultural backgrounds spread across the world. These changes bring challenges to cultural identities and not just to those long settled in Western European countries, but also by those recently arrived – some of whom may see incorporation into Western, secular culture as a threat to their identity. It will also bring the challenges and potential gains of a rising number of cross-cultural encounters. Social change brings opportunities as well as challenges and along with technological developments like the Internet and the increased opportunities for travel, offers the possibility to explore and form new identities. Change can be liberating as well as daunting.

Thus there seem to be many forces in the contemporary world that act to make **our sense of identity uncertain** – a feature, perhaps of the postmodern condition. Sardar (2002) believes that, 'We are in the middle of an identity crisis, not just in Britain but throughout the world. Most of us do not know who we really are.' In such circumstances we are, arguably, forced to become increasingly active agents in the shaping of our own identities through the process of interpersonal communication. The following chapters examine key social and cultural influences on the dynamics of this process.

Exercise: Who am I?

In 1960 Kuhn (Gross 2005: 575) conducted a now classic study of the self in which he asked respondents to give 20 different answers to the question: 'Who am I?'

Conduct a similar survey yourself. Ask each of 10 fellow students to address this question to themself and to provide 20 different answers.

a) Analyse the answers for common themes.
b) What do the themes suggest may be the key sources of self-identity?
c) How do they relate to the theories discussed in this chapter?
d) Reflect on circumstances in which you have sought to either highlight or downplay an aspect of your self-identity – why did you do so?

Key points

- The construction of self-identity can be seen as an ongoing project because in contemporary Western societies self-identity has to be explored, developed and modified against a background of changing circumstances. Consequently an individual's sense of self may be rather fragile.

- Psychoanalytic theories, like those of Freud and Jung, argue that much of our behaviour is influenced by forces within the unconscious mind, thus self-knowledge is limited and self-identity partial, provisional and vulnerable to fracture. Freud argued there are three components of an individual's personality: the id, the ego and the superego, and these are inevitably in conflict.

- The ego mediates between these demands to obtain a compromise and, according to Freud, is aided by three processes: dreams, neurotic symptoms and defence mechanisms. Freud's theories have been influential in the development of Transactional Analysis – a widely used series of techniques for analysing interaction.

- A number of other theorists, such as Cooley, Mead, Rogers and Goffman, have pointed to the importance of social interaction in both the development and maintenance of the self.

- The processes of self-presentation and self-disclosure can play a crucial role in forming our sense of self. Goffman's dramaturgical perspective offers a number of useful concepts – such as performance, persona, staging and front – for analysing everyday interaction. The ability to shift from one persona to another, as the situation demands, can be seen as a valuable social skill, one that requires careful self-monitoring, an activity to which not all of us appear equally attuned.

- Goffman argues that the sustaining of everyday performances is important both to the development and maintenance of the concept of self, and thus also to self-identity. Impression management is crucial to the successful staging of performances.

- Butler highlights the importance of everyday performances in the construction of gender identities through a process she terms performativity. She argues that the construction and maintenance of identity can be understood 'as a signifying practice', a practice that calls upon cultural tools, such as language, non-verbal signs and commodities in its execution.

- Linguistic perspectives on identity formation are provided by discourse analysis and conversation analysis. Identity discourses, how we talk to or discuss those belonging to certain social categories, clearly have the potential to shape self-identity. Conversation analysis focuses on the way in which individuals mobilize and co-produce identity in the 'fine detail of everyday interaction' (Antaki and Widdicombe 1998: 1).

- Giddens identifies four features of the post-traditional societies typical of late modernity, that make the maintenance of a coherent self-identity difficult: self-identity can only be achieved through choice; individuals tend to belong to a 'pluralization of lifeworlds'; there is increased awareness of methodological doubt; and a proliferation of mediated experiences. All of these features arguably interact with another crucial feature that of consumer culture.

- Giddens also identified four resulting dilemmas facing the self: 'unification versus fragmentation'; 'powerlessness versus appropriation'; the 'decline of traditional authority structures and their replacement by a plurality of expertise'; and the tension between 'personalized versus commodified experience'.

- Giddens argues that another challenge for the self is the development of the pure relationship. It is built on the process of mutual disclosure and the trust and intimacy that stem from this, as the relationship develops and deepens.

- In recent decades the considerable pace of social change has presented challenges for gender, class, and cultural identities.

3   Groups, Roles and Identities

Many groups are located within the social structure of a society and much of our life is spent as a member of one group or another, thus groups, and the roles that exist within them, can be seen as a key feature of what Eisenberg (2001: 543) terms the 'surround': a collection of influences 'that is pervasive in shaping people's moods, life stories, and communication'. Groups have the power to shape not only the nature of our interaction with others but also our sense of social identity. This is not a simple one way process, as Gahagan (1984: 21) comments, 'Human beings are both prisoners of their social and physical environments and creators of them'. In particular, social-identity theorists, such as Tajfel, view our sense of self-identity and self-esteem as grounded in our group memberships. While we may use groups to explore and forge a sense of self, we do not have to bow mindlessly to expectations about our behaviour and can seek to challenge and change them.

However, we need to be mindful of research that points to the considerable power groups can exercise over their members. Greenberg and Baron (1993) identify a number of our **common needs** that membership of a group(s) may satisfy: the need for security, the need for social identity, the need to achieve certain goals, the need for knowledge and information, the need to belong and the need for affection and attention. That group membership meets important needs helps to explain why individuals may be reluctant to behave in ways that might result in their expulsion from a group. This chapter explores some of the ways in which small groups can influence the process of interpersonal communication and our sense of self.

Self and social identities

Rupert Brown (2000: 28) argues that:

> our social identity – our sense of who we are and what we are worth – is intimately bound up with our group memberships. Thus, one of the first consequences of becoming a member of a group is a change

in the way we see ourselves. Joining a group often requires us to redefine who we are which, in turn, may have implications for our self-esteem.

Cathcart, Samovar and Henman (1996: 233) note, 'The treatment that we receive from other group members plays a role in determining how we will feel about ourselves and our place in the group.' Two key processes can be identified in this respect: reflected appraisal, when attitudes of group members towards us become reflected in our self-concept, and the self-fulfilling prophecy effect when we live up or down to others' expectations of our behaviour.

Michael Argyle (1983) identifies four key influences on the development of an individual's self-concept: the reaction of others; comparison with others; social roles; and identification. The groups that we belong to can provide a basis from which to compare our own behaviour and achievements with those of others – such groups are known as reference groups and clearly have considerable potential to influence our sense of self-esteem.

Given that we may belong to numerous groups, we can acquire several social identities and the roles we play in groups can have a significant impact on our sense of self. Kuhn (1960) conducted a now classic experiment (see Chapter 2) to demonstrate this. His results suggested that not only are the social roles we play an important aspect of how we see ourselves but that their contribution to the sense of self increases with age. The social context also affect the importance we attach to certain roles and social identitie example, Brown (1988) notes studies conducted by Trew (1981a,b) and C (1982) in Northern Ireland (a country that has witnessed much sectarian between Catholic and Protestant communities) that demonstrated the degree to which religious affiliation particularly featured in respondents' self-descriptions.

Social identities that stem from group membership may be viewed as voluntary or involuntary (Deaux 1991). Voluntary identities stem from groups that we choose to belong to, for example student, while Involuntary social identities result from group membership over which we have little control, for example age, gender. Deaux comments that more effort is needed to sustain voluntary as opposed to involuntary identities. Deaux (1991) also notes that we class some of our social identities as desirable and some as undesirable; understandably we tend to downplay those we feel are less desirable – a task that, arguably, calls for some considered impression management.

The nature of groups

Brown (2000: 3–4, original emphasis) offers the following definition of a group: '*a group exists when two or more people define themselves as members of it and when its existence is recognised by at least one other.* The "other" in this context is some person or group of people who do not define themselves so.' A number of **criteria** have been identified as essential for determining the existence of a group. There should be identifiable common goals, interaction between members and a structure for interaction, interdependence of fate or task, a stable relationship among members, a sense of group identity and developing and dynamic social integration. Key characteristics of a group are that it allocates roles to members, generates norms and an ideology, often has status differentiation, develops cohesiveness and has the power to encourage conformity and discourage deviance among its members (Baron and Byrne 1994). Lewin (1948) argued that a recognized 'interdependence of fate' (that is the fate of the individual being tied to that of the group) was a key element of group consciousness. However, Lewin considered 'interdependence of task', more crucial to group processes. Such interdependence can be either negative or positive. Positive interdependence, that is when the group members need to cooperate in order to achieve the task(s), is thought to strengthen group relationships (Brown 2000).

number of **structures** have been identified within groups, the most on being the **role**, **status** and **liking** structure. A role consists of ed and accepted patterns of behaviour associated with a position the group. Some expectations may be generated by the group while others may stem from general societal expectations about how a particular role should be played – the role of student, for example. Not all roles are attributed equal worth and some roles carry more status and power within the group thus creating a status hierarchy and leadership roles (Brown 2000). The 'Liking' structure reflects the degree of individual popularity within a group whether for example an individual is a 'star' or an 'isolate' (Moreno 1953). The network of links through which group members communicate is also a key element of its structure (Brown 2000).

Baron et al. (1992) with reference to the work of Leavitt (1951) identify five **networks** that may be found in groups as illustrated by Figure 3.1. Networks have an impact on the flow of communication within a group and on the participation rates of its members. In small groups there are normally fewer barriers to communication but some members may have a much more active part in the communication network than others, often by virtue of their role and identity within the group. Key individuals play a central role in the networks A, C and E and this provides them with the opportunity to control communication. Leaders usually occupy this central position.

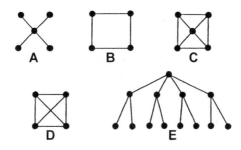

Note: People = ●; Networks A, C, and E are centralized; Network D is fully decentralized.

Figure 3.1   Model 22: Some possible communications networks (Baron et al. 1992, p. 10)

Network E is more typical of a larger group and clearly indicates the difference in access to other group members. The communication network illustrated in B may prove a little frustrating whereas the all-channel network shown in D is that most likely to result in a free flow of communication and more equal participation rates. Baron and Greenberg (1990) explored the relationship between networks and task performance and concluded that centralized networks are better when working on straightforward tasks but decentralized networks are better for complex tasks.

Groups may be **formal or informal**. A formal group, such as an advertising agency, is created to perform assigned tasks and achieve specified goals. It is held accountable for its performance. An informal group, a group of friends say, is created through more spontaneous communicative encounters that result in the formation of mutually beneficial relationships. Typically we are members of a range of groups: friendship, work, family, ethnic, gender, religious, political and socio-economic groups, all of which convey messages that have the potential to shape our sense of self and our behaviour. Cooley (1909) classified groups into two main types: **primary and secondary**. Primary groups are those in which communication is often face to face – the family would be a good example here. It is within primary groups, particularly, that norms and mores are generated, roles allocated and feelings of solidarity enjoyed. Secondary groups, such as ethnic or religious groups, are much larger collections of people and it is likely that an individual will only interact on a face-to-face basis with some members of the group. Interaction with other members may often be at a distance through media such as magazines or the Internet.

Although interaction and relationships may be less stable within secondary groups, membership of these groups may still be a significant aspect of an individual's identity, especially if they feed off membership of primary groups. For example, followers of a religious faith may have a sense of identity with fellow members across the globe, and not just with those in their place of worship. A secular example would be membership of Manchester United football club – a membership that stretches across the globe. The membership of secondary groups can be a significant aspect of an individual's sense of identity and may be displayed in communicative behaviour as when, for example, wearing football club fan regalia.

Group development

Groups develop over time and according to Tuckman and Jensen (1977) there are five major stages in the process of **group formation**. The first of these is the forming stage. This stage is characterized by anxiety as the group seeks to define its goals, clarify the situation, formulate procedures and form ground rules. At this stage individuals often seek to establish identities within the group and may make a play for certain roles. This may require a more conscious attempt at impression management. There is often a felt need for some kind of leadership at this stage. Stage two, the storming stage, is characterized by conflict as members jostle and negotiate about roles, rules and procedures. Personal hidden agendas may be revealed at this stage. The initial allocation of roles, including leadership, may be revised. The group will then move on to the norming stage, during which conflicts are resolved and stability is achieved in the group's structure. Roles, norms, goals, rules and procedures are agreed. Group cohesiveness begins to develop. The group is then ready to move onto the performing stage characterized by the concentration on achievement of group goals. Group cohesion develops further. In the adjourning stage, the group disbands. It is characterized by a sense of disengagement and anxiety along with reflection on and evaluation of the group's activities.

All groups do not necessarily pass through all stages and a group may become stuck at any one of them. Under pressure groups may have to rush to the performing stage without having solved underlying tensions. However, unless conflicts normally evident at the storming stage are resolved it is likely that a group's communication and performance will be hindered. Tuckman and Jensen's framework provides a useful guide to the problems that may beset social interaction as a group develops. It also highlights the proactive stance some individuals take in establishing their identity within a group.

In-groups and out-groups

Groups may also be classed as **in-groups** and **out-groups**. Brown (2000: 312) comments on in-groups: 'Since part of our self-concept (or identity) is defined in term of group affiliation, it follows that there will be a preference to view these groups positively rather than negatively.' In-groups are those to which we belong and whose membership we value. Thus we care for our fellow members and will cooperate with them without any necessary expectation of immediate reward (Triandis 1988). There is also evidence that our own self-esteem is enhanced when our group(s) is positively evaluated against other groups (Tajfel and Turner 1986). Out-groups are those to which we do not belong and some may be viewed negatively. Out-groups help define who we are not. We are not directly concerned about the well-being of members of out-groups. While we may cooperate with them it is usually as part of a reciprocal arrangement of mutual benefit. As will be discussed later the distinction between in-groups and out-groups can often be the source of intergroup conflict.

There are **cultural differences**, particularly between *individualistic* and *collectivistic* cultures, in terms of the influence of the ingroup over its members (Hofstede 2001; Triandis 1988). Individualistic cultures emphasize the centrality of the individual and the individual's goals, achievements, interests and self-development. The expectation is that individuals will be self-reliant, competitive, assertive and take responsibility for themselves and close family. In an individualistic culture it is likely that a person will be a member of a number of ingroups, many of which will have only a limited and specific area of influence over members. A consequence for an individual's communicative behaviour is that arguably this 'pluralization of lifeworlds' (Giddens 1991) generates a 'multiplicity of selves' (Eisenberg 2001) and the demand for considerable adjustment in acts of self-presentation.

Collectivistic cultures, on the other hand, stress the centrality of the group and emphasize the importance of the group's goals, obligations and relationships. The group predominates over the individual and members are expected to accommodate to the demands of the group. Members identify strongly with their ingroups and are expected to behave in a cooperative manner in order to avoid conflict and maintain group harmony. People in these cultures belong to relatively few ingroups and these will have a significant degree of influence over members. Thus the scope for individual negotiation of behavioural expectations or the script for everyday interaction may be quite limited; as Eisenberg (2001: 535) notes there may be, 'little tolerance for individual creativity, difference, or dissent'.

Triandis (1988) argues that while there tend to be significant differences between the way in which people communicate with those in their in- and out-groups in collectivistic cultures, this differentiation is less marked in individualistic cultures. However, it should be acknowledged that people in any culture may have both individualistic and collectivistic tendencies even though one tendency will be stronger. Also, not everyone will identify to the same degree with the predominant tendency of the society in which they live and this may be especially the case in a multicultural society.

Cross-cultural groups

Within a multicultural society it can be expected that some groups will contain members from different cultural and ethnic backgrounds. This may typically be the case in workplaces such as airports and hospitals, for example. Such diversity among the group membership may necessitate a greater and more conscious effort to generate a shared frame of reference, that is a set of working assumptions that guide the group's behaviour. Such assumptions will of course be subject to modification over time through the process of group interaction. In multicultural groups there may also be additional factors at play in the development of the group.

Smith and Berg (1997) identified eight dimensions that could be used to measure the degree to which an individual's contribution to a group might be influenced by assumptions stemming from their cultural background. The dimension of *confrontation v. conciliation* relates to expectations about the manner in which conflict is handled, whether is it openly confronted, ignored or dealt with quietly. The degree to which individuals are expected to stand out from or merge with the group is located on the *individuality v. collectivity* dimension while the *participative v. autocratic* dimension refers to the extent to which members would be expected to give their own views or alternatively to show deference and agree with those in authority. The extent to which group members expect to be genuinely involved in decision making or simply to be rubber stamping decisions made elsewhere is captured by the *spontaneous v. orchestrated* dimension.

The *task v. process* dimension deals with assumptions as to which of these should be the group's main focus; similarly the *quality v. quantity* dimension relates to assumptions about whether it is the quality or quantity of a group's output that matters most. Cultural background can also influence the willingness of group members to openly air criticisms of others in the group and this is traced on the *criticism v. diplomacy* dimension. Finally there may be different assumptions about the way in which creativity is acknowledged, whether it is through its impact on group outcomes or group processes; this is traced through the *productivity v. receptivity* dimension. Smith and Berg argue that multicultural groups would benefit from acknowledgement and discussion of differences in expectations.

Brown (2000) proposes that social behaviour can be seen to lie along an **interpersonal-group continuum** depending on the extent to which a group is important within the social context. Interpersonal interaction outside of the group context, say between a couple enjoying a private romantic dinner, can be seen to be driven more by personal decisions, qualities and characteristics and by the nature of interpersonal relationships. However interaction within and between groups, for example between management and union representatives in a workplace dispute, is driven more by the nature of group memberships, roles, group dynamics and the relationships between the groups in question.

Roles: an introduction

> It is probably no mere historical accident that the word person, in its first meaning, is a mask. It is rather a recognition of the fact that everyone is always and everywhere, more or less consciously, playing a role ... It is in these roles that we know each other; it is in these roles that we know ourselves.
>
> (Park in Goffman 1959: 17)

Typically individuals belong to a number of groups and will therefore occupy a range of roles: for example, daughter, mother, judge, friend, colleague, ballroom dancer, and environmental activist. The concept of role is useful for analysing the way in which we manage the demands made by our membership of the differing groups that comprise the 'pluralization of lifeworlds' we inhabit and which can be seen to contribute to what Eisenberg termed our 'multiplicity of selves'.

Case study

> Shari Kendall (2006) explored the use of 'face-related practices' employed by a female respondent (whom she called Elaine) when performing two of her everyday roles: one as a female manager and the other as a mother. Both roles required the exercise of authority. Examining conversations in both contexts she concluded that 'Elaine creates a demeanor of explicit authority at home by using directive forms that make her authority more visible, whereas she creates a benevolent demeanor of authority at work by using directive forms that interactionally downplay status differences' (p. 620); she is more inclined to protect the face of others in her role as manager than in her role as mother.

All roles also carry with them expectations about the way in which the role occupant should behave. Some may be created through the everyday social interaction between group members but there are many roles that are well established and carry widespread cultural expectations as to how they should be performed: the role of doctor, for example. While some roles are specific to a particular group, others known as social roles are more universal and are linked to positions within a social system; some of these, for example those of mother and father, may be found in most societies although some of the behavioural expectations assigned to them can vary significantly both across and within societies. There may be times when we would prefer not to play a role that others try to assign to us. However we tend to accept to a greater or lesser degree the expectations other group members have of our behaviour in order to remain within the group.

Role expectations can vary over time; arguably gender role expectations have undergone considerable change since the 1960s. Some role expectations may have a moral dimension to them and those who flout these expectations may be subject to moral judgements, significant social sanctions and, in some cases, even criminal proceedings. A GP who, for example, supplies illegal drugs to patients is likely to face critical media coverage, a prison sentence and being struck off the medical register.

Role expectations are often also linked to social **norms** and **stereotypes.** We may, for example, have stereotypical images of doctors, bricklayers, firemen or traffic wardens and of what kind of behaviour is acceptable from them. However, stereotypes are based on oversimplified assumptions about the shared behavioural characteristics of group members so while stereotypes may provide useful mental shortcuts in our attempt to bring order to a complex social world (Lippmann 1922) they are likely to be misleading.

Established roles allow us to assume a certain degree of predictability in others' behaviour as we assume they will behave in line with role expectations and such predictability is socially useful when managing the varied communicative encounters of everyday life. It would, for example, be a source of some frustration if we had to approach every encounter with no expectation of how it might unfold.

Roles are relational in that when we play a role in a particular social context, the other people in that situation are also playing roles. These other people are known as the **role set.** The role set for a doctors' practice will, for example, typically include the roles of doctor, receptionist and practice nurse. Within a role set each member will have expectations of appropriate behaviour for the other role occupants. Effective group interaction, coordination and performance arguably depends upon the level of agreement about such expectations and the degree to which expectations are met. In effect it can be argued that in a group, members 'play up' to each other's roles and identities (Gahagan 1984: 17).

Each person will, however, bring to a role their own personality, motivations, attitudes and experience and no two individuals are likely to play a role in exactly the same way. Within the broad framework of a role there is room for individual interpretation. We have the potential to challenge or modify role expectations through interaction. The degree to which we can do so depends on the role. Some roles, particularly those located within the wider social structure, like that of policeman, carry with them a fairly specific set of expectations to be met and there may be penalties, including legal penalties, for not conforming to these. The opportunity for negotiating role expectations may, therefore, be limited. However there are plenty of roles that do not carry with them a tightly prescribed set of expectations; in such cases an individual may enjoy considerable freedom in negotiating expectations through interaction with others (Gahagan 1984). How we perform a role can also be influenced by the social identities we hold from the wider society such as gender, ethnic and class identities.

Roles, persona and performance

Goffman's dramaturgical perspective, which employs the metaphor of the stage to examine everyday social interactions, offers several ideas useful for exploring how we, as individuals, act out our roles in everyday life. The persona, for example, is like a character that, according to Goffman, an individual adopts to negotiate the behavioural demands of a particular social situation. Once chosen the persona influences the manner in which the individual performs and communicates, both verbally and non-verbally, in that situation. Thus the persona can be seen as the key to acts of performance in everyday life.

Typically the different social situations in which any one individual may participate require the adoption of different personae. Further, it is likely that the role an individual is playing may dictate the kind of persona that it would be appropriate to adopt. The actual persona adopted would also be influenced by factors that we as individuals bring to the role such as our motivations, past experiences and personality. The degree of choice permitted may vary between roles. The role of rock star, arguably, allows for a fair degree of latitude in terms of the choice of personae that could be adopted in order to perform the role effectively. The role of Prime Minister, however, brings with it a considerable number of expectations and consequently less choice about how the role can be played.

Roles can be seen to have well-established **fronts** that role occupants are expected to employ in the performance of them and these facilitate an effective performance. For example, when in court, a high court judge will occupy an established **setting**, the courtroom, and wear the standard dress of robes and a wig. The judge would also be expected to adopt a serious, controlled demeanour. Further expectations, arguably, are that the judge expresses themself in Standard English and refrains from swearing. Goffman (1959) argues that a certain degree of consistency is expected and needed between setting, appearance and manner if a performance is to be convincing to the audience. Thus a careful coordination of verbal and non-verbal behaviour is often required to manage a successful role performance.

From this perspective an individual can be seen to command a range of personae and the ability to shift from one persona to another as situations demand may be viewed as an important social and communication skill. It is a skill that also necessitates careful **self-monitoring**. Snyder (Snyder and Jones 1974; 1979) identified high and low self-monitors as regards awareness of the expectations of behaviour required in different situations. While high self-monitors tend to assess the demands of different situations and adjust their self-presentation accordingly, the behaviour of low self-monitors tends to be influenced more by their inner motives, values and beliefs. It would seem that high self-monitors are more adept at shaping and switching their behaviour to match the expectations within a social context. However it could be argued that a group may benefit from the consistency of the low self-monitor: they may prove a good 'devil's advocate' in group discussions, for example. Fiske (2004) argues that it may be advantageous for a group to have mixture of high and low self-monitors.

The ability to accommodate behaviour to the shifting expectations of various groups may also be aided by what Goffman (1959) refers to as the skills of **impression management**. These skills enable the individual to manage or manipulate their verbal and non-verbal behaviour in order to convey and maintain the appropriate impression to the rest of the group. Impression management, therefore, can be seen as crucial to maintaining, or indeed changing, your identity within the group (Leary and Kowalski 1990). Changing the nature of one's identity or one's role within a group may not, however, be that easy. As Petty and Cacioppo (1996) note there is strong social pressure on individuals to maintain consistency in their behaviour and this would inhibit changes.

Team performances

> In learning to perform our parts in real life we guide our own productions by not too consciously maintaining an incipient familiarity with the routines of those to whom we address ourselves.
>
> (Goffman 1959: 63)

Successful group communication then requires a coordinated effort in role performance and consideration of the identities claimed by fellow group members. Groups, as well as individuals, generate everyday performances, as for example, when in negotiations with another group. In these circumstances a group may be thought of as a **team**. Goffman (1959) pointed to the importance of maintaining a **working consensus** on order for the team to coordinate its behaviour and succeed in fostering the desired impression for its audience. He further argued that analysis of the way in which such a consensus is maintained can provide a valuable insight into cooperative behaviour within groups. Any member of the team might potentially disrupt the performance by an inappropriate act so team discipline is crucial. Such 'reciprocal dependence' is seen to bond the group. Goffman points to the importance of a united front and warns of the threat posed by public disagreement to successful impression management. It strikes, he warns, 'a false note' thus 'dramaturgical loyalty' to the team performance is required. Successful team performances also require tact on behalf of the audience and teams, like individuals, would be wise not to make excessive claims in their acts of performance.

Audiences

All performances, though, require an **audience** and a successful performance, argues Goffman, requires tact on the part of the audience. Any performance can be sabotaged but most are not because of the social expectation that we exercise tact in our everyday encounters: 'few impressions could survive if those who received the impression did not exert tact in their reception of it' Goffman (1959: 12).

However, audiences will only exercise tact if the performer does not stretch credibility in the claims made as part of the act of presentation. The performer must be sensitive to hints that the audience finds such claims implausible and be ready to modify them. Goffman suggests that if an individual or team is intending to misrepresent facts then an escape route should be prepared in case they are challenged. If, for example, a student in a pub conversation claimed wrongly to have gained 80 per cent for an assignment and this was queried by fellow students an adroit response would be: 'I think so ... erm ... maybe I'm confusing it with the mark for that marketing presentation last year'.

Role strain

Role expectations often facilitate communication but they can also present challenges to the individual and these are sometimes termed role strain. Role strain can occur for a number of reasons (Gahagan 1984). Typically an individual occupies a number of roles and so they will have to adjust their communication style accordingly when moving from one group to another. Sometimes switching between communication styles becomes difficult because of wide differences in the role expectations among some of the roles played, for example switching quickly from the role of university lecturer to that of barperson.

This situation is sometimes referred to as **multiple-role conflict** and it can also occur when an individual finds themself in a situation in which the audiences for different role performances unexpectedly come together. Goffman (1959) argues that individuals usually prefer to segregate the audiences for different role performances so as not to be observed behaving in a manner at odds with the usual performance displayed to each audience, particularly if considerable inconsistencies of behaviour would be revealed. For example, few students would wish their parents to attend student parties with them. The unexpected mixing of audiences can tax an individual's communicative competence as it may be difficult to behave in a manner suitable for both.

In some situations there may be uncertainty within the role set as regards the behaviour expected of a role occupant: when a new employee arrives to take up a newly created post, for example, they may find themselves in this position. On occasion members of the role set may disagree about the expectations from a particular role: a work team may expect the team leader to fight for extra resources while the team leader's superior may be pushing for economies.

Role incompatibility can be found when individuals find themselves occupying a role for which they are unsuited. They may feel that they do not have the personal characteristics and qualities necessary: for example someone who is shy might find the role of an MC quite daunting and difficult to play effectively. There are also times when role performance becomes difficult because just too many demands are made of the role occupant. This can also result from an increase in the demands from several of the roles that an individual occupies. As a consequence they may suffer from **role overload**. An example here would be the case of an undergraduate, in their final year of study, being confronted with demands to take on overtime hours in their part-time job and help out with looking after a sick family member at a time when deadline dates for handing in final assignments are imminent.

Whatever the causes of role strain, it has the potential to seriously affect an individual's ability to communicate and thus perform effectively with a given role.

Case study: roles and performance

The student interviewed, while born in Britain, is of Indian heritage. She describes two roles that demand a significant switch in her communicative behaviour: those of great niece and university student.

My great uncles and aunts live in Britain but had no need to learn much English, especially the aunts, because they live their lives largely within a community where Gujarati is widely used. When I visit their houses I will talk to my cousins in English then switch to Gujarati with my great uncles and aunts. It is a matter of respect. Gujarati is seen as more respectful. Respect is a big thing in Indian families. For them showing I know the language, shows I am interested in my family's background ... I also need to maintain a lot more eye contact than normal.

I do not wear traditional outfits unless it is a special occasion. Gujarati is used in serious family discussions – like about wedding and funeral ... arrangements – so I use Gujarati if I am involved in these.

She then talked about her role as a student:

I only speak in English ... sometimes, unknowingly, I slip into Gujarati with Indian student friends. If English students are present too they will always pass comments so I have to explain what I was saying and that I was not slagging them off.

The English students seem to be reminding her that slipping in Gujarati is not meeting with their expectations of the role.

Exercise

   a) Construct a diagram to show all the roles that you play in a typical week. Which of these roles do you consider important to your sense of self-identity and why?
   b) Choose two or more roles that demand quite different kinds of performances from you. How does your use of language and non-verbal cues differ between the performances?
   c) Think of an occasion when you have experienced role strain. How did it affect your performance?

Roles found in groups

A well-known analysis of team roles typically found in work groups was originally developed by the 1970s by Meredith Belbin and his colleagues and was based on their observations of how managers behaved in team simulation exercises. Belbin (1996) identifies nine team roles: plant, resource investigator, coordinator, shaper, monitor-evaluator, teamworker, implementer, completer, and specialist.

Table 3.1 details the particular contribution and allowable weaknesses associated with each role. These roles are adopted on the basis of individual preferences and characteristics, rather than others' expectations, and it is argued that most people consistently play the same one or two roles. Ideally, Belbin argued that all roles were needed for an effective team. Belbin's theory suggests that the individual does have some influence over the roles adopted

Table 3.1 Belbin's nine team roles

roles and descriptions – team-role contribution	allowable weaknesses
Plant Creative, imaginative, unorthodox. Solves difficult problems.	Ignores details. Too preoccupied to communicate effectively.
Resource investigator Extravert, enthusiastic, communicative. Explores opportunities. Develops contacts.	Overoptimistic. Loses interest once initial enthusiasm has passed.
Co-ordinator Mature, confident, a good chairperson. Clarifies goals, promotes decision-making, delegates well.	Can be seen as manipulative. Delegates personal work.
Shaper Challenging, dynamic, thrives on pressure. Has the drive and courage to overcome obstacles.	Can provoke others. Hurts people's feelings.
Monitor evaluator Sober, strategic and discerning. Sees all options. Judges accurately.	Lacks drive and ability to inspire others. Overly critical.
Teamworker Co-operative, mild, perceptive and diplomatic. Listens, builds, averts friction, calms the waters.	Indecisive in crunch situations. Can be easily influenced.
Implementer Disciplined, reliable, conservative and efficient. Turns ideas into practical actions.	Somewhat inflexible. Slow to respond to new possibilities.
Completer Painstaking, conscientious, anxious. Searches out errors and omissions. Delivers on time.	Inclined to worry unduly. Reluctant to delegate. Can be a nit-picker.
Specialist Single-minded, self-starting, dedicated. Provides knowledge and skills in rare supply.	Contributes on only a narrow front. Dwells on technicalities. Overlooks the 'big picture'.

Strength of contribution in any one of the roles is commonly associated with particular weaknesses. These are called allowable weaknesses. Executives are seldom strong in all nine team roles.

Source: From Belbin 1996, p. 122.

within a group. However once a stable allocation of roles has been achieved it might be difficult to negotiate further change; for example, it might be difficult to escape the role of completer and display behaviours more associated with the plant. The classifications make clear that a role carries with it implications for the communicative style of its occupant. Thus the completer may be inclined to 'nit pick' while the plant is dismissive of detail and often fails to communicate fully with fellow team members.

Belbin's ideas have however met with a number of criticisms, for example: that self-reporting is a rather subjective basis on which to identify individual team roles and that it overlooks the influence of social context and related expectations on behaviour and the need for more empirical evidence to support the theory (Huczynski and Buchanan 2004).

Role and status differentiation in groups

A notable characteristic of groups is that of role and status differentiation between members. Some of the key advantages of role differentiation are that it facilitates the allocation of tasks to members, it fosters predictability in the behaviour of group members and it contributes to the individual's sense of identity within the group. Role differentiation is thus often seen to promote effective performance within a group (Brown 1988).

Leadership roles in groups

A key aspect of a group that impacts on individual performance and the pattern of group communication is the leadership structure – that is when some roles, or identities carry more status and power than others. Individuals may enjoy higher status on account of their location within the wider society and this too may affect role performance in a group. For example, as is discussed further in Chapter 4, a number of research studies have indicated that men frequently interrupt women in mixed sex encounters: this may lead male members of a group to behave differently towards a female than a male group leader.

Status hierarchies can be found in informal and formal groups but are common in the latter, particularly in the workplace. Status differences tend to influence, and be influenced by, the process of social comparison within the group and are therefore likely to have an impact on how individual members view their role within the group (Brown 1988). This in turn can affect their communication within the group. Status differentiation can also facilitate effective group performance. 'Social influence is always a reciprocal process, perhaps it would be more precise to say that what really characterises leaders is that they can influence others in the group more than they themselves are influenced' (Brown 2000: 91). It seems that to successfully perform a leadership role within a group requires not only the ability to exercise more influence over other group members than they do over you, but also the capacity to sustain such influence over a period of time: a capacity that clearly has implications for the communication processes within the group. It also raises the question of what determines the allocation of leadership roles within the group.

According to Huczynski and Buchanan (2004: 341): 'The emergence of a leader within any group is a function of its structure. Usually, a group makes a leader of the person who has some special capacity for coping with the groups' particular problems. They may possess physical strength, shrewdness, or some other relevant attribute.' Two significant attributes highlighted by Argyle (1994) are that the individual has a personality appropriate to the group and is motivated to lead. The studies of Hollander and Julian (discussed in Brown 2000) suggest that there are four main sources of legitimacy for a leader: that the leader initially builds up credit points within the group, that the leader has been elected by the group, that the leader is seen by the group as the individual most competent to facilitate the achievement of the group's goals, and that the leader is seen to identify strongly with the group. They also argued that the process of establishing leadership is best done gradually. The need for leadership within a group will depend upon the nature and goals of the group, for example: its goals, its size, the need for division of labour to achieve goals, whether the group is formal or informal, the maturity of the group, the range of knowledge, skills and experiences held by members and the social context. Argyle (1984) points out that leadership can also be shared and rotated among members of a group.

The core functions of group leadership are often placed into two main categories: **task and socio-emotional** or **maintenance functions** (Handy 1993). Task functions are those directly necessary to the achievement of a goal while socio-emotional functions are those directed at maintaining harmonious relationships within the group. Task functions would typically include initiating action; coordinating members' activities; suggesting innovations; researching information, ideas and opinions; evaluating performance; and making decisions. Maintenance functions include encouraging group members, negotiating compromises and maintaining harmonious relationships within the group. The leader can either fulfill these functions themself or ensure that they are performed by others (Handy 1993).

Groups may, of course, have more than one leader. A classic study by Bales and Slater (1956), for example, demonstrated that a group can have split leadership with different individuals performing the role of task and socio-emotional leader. However this is only likely to happen once task leadership has been established. Where leadership is split this may show itself in both the style and content of the communication expected from the leaders; group members may expect a more supportive style from the socio-emotional leader, for instance.

A group may also have both a formal and informal leader. For example, in a work group, the formal leader is likely to be the person appointed to a leadership position such as that of manager; however the group may also have an informal leader – one who has emerged from within the group and who may wield considerable influence (Morgan 1997). In any event groups often move to replace an ineffective leader (Argyle 1983).

Leadership and communication in groups

Occupation of a leadership role has considerable implications for an individual's identity and interpersonal encounters within the group. Those with high status within a group may feel inhibited about asking for help and advice from those of lower status in order to maintain status congruence (Gahagan 1984). Bales (1950), among others, found that those with power in the group contribute more to group discussions; further, it seems that the contributions of high status members can also be accorded more worth than is warranted (Gahagan 1984). Group members are less likely to contradict those with high status and, additionally, may suppress their own contributions and performances in order to enhance those of high status members (Argyle 1983). Baron et al. (1992) argue that a leader is more likely to influence group norms and yet be granted greater freedom than other group members to deviate from them.

McQuail (1984) notes several consequences for communication within informal groups that result from status differentiation: leaders tend to both initiate and receive more communication than others and have a wider range of contacts. However at the individual level there is more interaction with those of similar status. Personality can also be expected to influence the communicative style of those with higher status roles as can the nature of the culture in which the group operates. Lewis (2006), for example, notes that while in Sweden leadership in business organizations tends to be democratic, in Spain it is likely to be autocratic.

Opinion leaders

One important leadership role played within a group, initially identified by Katz and Lazarsfeld (1955), is that of opinion leader – an individual who has an influence, often informal, over opinion formation within a group. While opinion leadership will shift depending on the issue and social context, it would seem there are a number of characteristics that enable an individual to sustain the role of opinion leader: McQuail (2005: 563) argues that opinion leaders tend to be 'better informed, make more use of mass media and other sources, are gregarious and are likely to be respected by those they influence'.

Opinion leaders, therefore, have a potentially significant impact on the reception and interpretation of messages received within the group. Being an opinion leader may also influence not only an individual's expectation of how their contributions to the group will be received but also their sense of self and self-worth.

Leadership styles

There have been numerous studies conducted with the aim of identifying leadership styles in groups and their impact on other group members. An early, classic study carried out by White and Lippitt (1960) examined the effect of authoritarian, democratic and laissez-faire styles on the task performance of groups of boys between the ages of 10 and 11. The authoritarian style did lead to higher productivity but at the price of more hostility, competitive behaviour and aggression than found in other groups. Further it encouraged dependence so group productivity fell when the leader was absent.

Productivity was still relatively high in the democratically led group and the quality of work was higher. Relationships were friendly and cooperative and a good working atmosphere prevailed. The boys worked with greater independence and continued working in the leader's absence; they also expressed satisfaction with being in the group. The laissez-faire style of leadership resulted in poor performance but reasonable relationships – though some aggression was evident. Overall the boys expressed a preference for the democratic style.

The categorization of **leadership styles** has been commonly used over the years in discussion of leadership in workplace groups. For example, Likert and associates (Likert 1961) identified four main leadership styles found in the work environment: exploitative autocratic, benevolent authoritative, participative and democratic. Likert argued that the more supportive styles (participative and democratic) were more effective, however, not all leadership studies suggest this (Handy 1993). Workplace groups do not exist in a social vacuum, and **contingency theories** highlight the importance of matching any leadership style to the cultural expectations that exist in the workplace – these may stem from the culture of the organization as well as that of the wider society. Thus a more democratic style would fit well into what Handy and Harrison's typology of organizational cultures terms a 'task culture'. In this team culture the focus is on utilizing the expertise of its members to achieve goals and status differences tend to be downplayed (Handy 1993).

Cross-cultural differences in preferred leadership styles also need to be considered. Lustig and Cassotta (1996) with reference to Hofstede's dimensions of cultural difference (1980, 1984) point out that attitudes toward leadership styles are likely to be influenced by the degree of power distance, uncertainty avoidance, sex-role differentiation and individualism within a culture. Hofstede's dimensions are discussed in more detail in Chapter 6. In cultures where it is the norm for considerable power distance to exist between the leader and others, and where uncertainty avoidance is valued, it is unlikely that consultative or democratic styles of leadership would be found – indeed they may be viewed negatively. Conversely, in low power distance and low uncertainty avoidance cultures, autocratic and paternalistic styles may be unpopular.

Cultures that emphasize 'masculinity' (gender role segregation, aggressiveness, competitiveness, success) may be more likely to favour autocratic styles while those which are more orientated around 'femininity' – (the importance of interpersonal relationships and work-life balance) may favour the consultative and democratic styles. Finally, it can be argued that consultative and democratic styles are more in tune with the values of individualistic cultures and their emphasis on individual rights, freedoms and self-development than those of collectivistic cultures. In the latter cultures the autocratic or paternalistic leader who projects traditional values and offers protection to the group may be more valued.

Goleman (2000) presents a contemporary view of leadership styles. He identifies six styles that may be employed in the workplace: coercive, authoritative, affiliative, democratic, pacesetting and coaching. Goleman argues that the best leaders are able to switch styles, selecting the most appropriate style for each situation. There are similarities here with Goffman's perspective that individuals manage social interaction by selecting the most appropriate persona for each encounter. While recognizing that the coercive and pacesetting styles are sometimes necessary, in general the other four styles are seen as more likely to set a better emotional tone. Goleman views **emotional intelligence** as a crucial quality for successful leaders, one that enables them to read 'the subtle undercurrents of emotion that pervade a group' (Goleman 2004: 185) and effectively harness a group's emotional energy in pursuit of the organization's goals.

Huczinski and Buchanan (2004: 740) in discussing ideas on contemporary leadership discuss the distinction between the **new leader** and the **superleader**. The new leader inspires, provides vision, coaches, builds a 'shared sense of purpose and mission', and creates a culture in which everyone is tuned in to the organization's goals and is empowered to contribute to their achievement. The superleader on the other hand is concerned with developing leadership in others so that they are empowered to act and make decisions for themselves; this autonomy it is hoped will enhance 'motivation, commitment and creativity'.

The range of theories of leadership styles suggests that there are numerous ways in which an individual might choose to play the role of leader although pressure to adopt a preferred style is likely to arise from socio-cultural expectations and circumstances. The style adopted, however, could be expected to have a considerable influence upon the pattern and nature of that individual's communication with fellow group members.

Analysing interaction in groups

Sociogram

A basic device for recording the pattern of interaction in a group is the sociogram. Sociograms originated within the field of sociometric analysis – that is, the study of interpersonal relationships and communication within groups. An example of a sociogram is given in Figure 3.2. A sociogram can trace the distribution and flow of communication within the group and can provide some initial indication of such factors as the liking and leadership structures, social isolation, and mutual dyads or triads. However it is limited in the amount of information it can yield about the content of communicative acts within a group. To gain additional information participants could be asked to self-report their perception of the group interaction under observation.

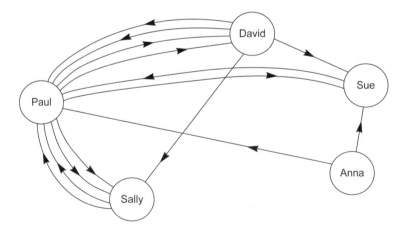

Figure 3.2 Sociogram example

Interaction analysis

One of the most influential schemes for recording and analysing communication within groups is that devised by Bales (1950) and known as **interaction process analysis** (IPA; see Figure 3.3). This is a much more sophisticated device than the sociogram. Bales and his colleagues developed the IPA to track the content of communication within a group discussion. The assumption is that groups are normally involved in some sort of task which forms the focus for communication. Their research suggested that the communicative acts within a group can be usefully classified into 12 types of behaviour which can then be arranged in four main categories: socio-emotional positive acts; task-relevant acts; task-relevant acts – asking questions; and socio-emotional negative acts. For example, in the following dialogue, speaker 1 is exhibiting type 6 behaviour and speaker 2, type 12:

> *Speaker 1*: Right that's agreed, let's set a deadline of Friday 2.30pm by which to complete the project.
>
> *Speaker 2*: That's a really stupid deadline!

Through observation and classification of the communicative behaviour it is possible to track not just the overall pattern of communication within the group but also the relationship between individual roles and communicative behaviour. Bales (1950) argued that task and socio-emotional leaders can be detected by use of the IPA. The task leader would be expected to score highly in the task categories and especially in boxes 4–6 while the socio-emotional leader would score highly in boxes 1–3. An individual who consistently scores highly in boxes 10–12 is likely to be considered difficult. Bales argued that groups encounter a range of frequently occurring problems: typical problems are those of evaluation, orientation, control, decision making, tension management and integration. The IPA can be used to track the way in which a group copes with these.

Conformity and deviance

One aspect of group culture is that it appears to generate pressures towards conformity as several classic studies have demonstrated. Asch (1951)and Crutchfield (1955) found that in a group context, about one-third of individuals conformed to clearly inaccurate majority judgements. These experiments suggest that individuals will withhold their own views and judgments if they believe these to be contrary to those held by the majority. There are clear links here to the work of Noelle–Neumann (1974) who investigated the forces at play in the construction of 'public opinion'. In her Spiral Of Silence model, discussed in Chapter 1, she argues that individual members of the

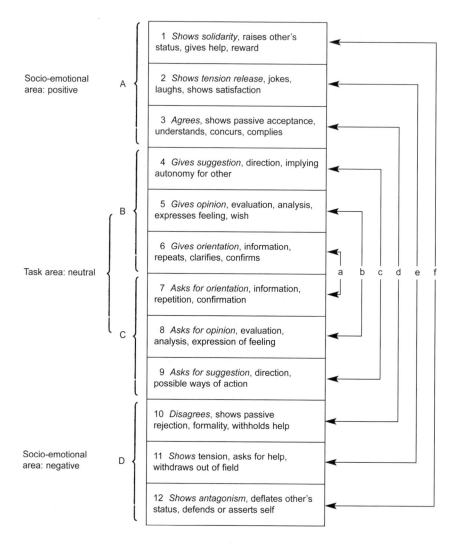

Figure 3.3 Bales's interaction process analysis, 1950 (from Bales 1950. Copyright © University of Chicago Press)

Note: The coding categories in interaction process analysis and their major relations: (a) problems of communication; (b) problems of evaluation; (c) problems of control; (d) problems of decision; (e) problems of tension reduction; (f) problems of reintegration; (A) positive reactions; (B) attempted answers; (C) questions; (D) negative reactions.

public tend to inhibit expression of their views if they believe these to be against the majority view. The consequences of this is that those with the power to represent views as being the 'dominant view', for example the mass media, help to create the spiral of silence. Thus an opinion can be presented as one held by the majority when in fact it is not. Schachter's (1951) exploration of the consequences for those who do speak out against an apparent group consensus helps to explain why individuals may prefer to remain silent. Consistently challenging the majority view led to rejection by the group. However the process of rejection was often subtle rather than open in its nature.

Gross (2005) argues that more recent research has shown that the power of the group to ensure conformity suggested in these experiments may have been overstated and points to later evidence that suggests that, in part, these results may have been due to cultural factors at play in the America of the 1950s. Replications of Asch's experiments have produced varied results with rates of conformity being sometimes higher, sometimes lower than those achieved in the original studies. Gross also points to the cross-cultural comparison of conformity rates achieved using replications of Asch's original experiments, made by Smith and Bond (1998). This indicates that conformity rates are higher in collectivistic cultures than in individualistic cultures.

Group productivity

Being in a group can enhance or inhibit an individual's performance though the degree to which this is the case seems to depend on a variety of factors such as the nature of the task, the effectiveness of group leaders, the cohesiveness of the group and the flexibility of its communication networks. Of interest has been the question of whether individuals exert less effort when working in a group than would have been the case if working on their own. It seems that some people do take the opportunity to coast in a group. Latane, Williams and Harkins (1979) identified the role of social loafing, that is, a tendency to reduce individual effort when working in a group. While it appears that this is not true of all group members, some individuals seem to become social loafers, contributing relatively little to the group's efforts and being carried by the contributions of others (Baron et al. 2006). Once identified as such by other group members certain consequences may follow: for example, the **social loafer** may face rejection by the group. If this identity becomes more widely known, the individual may find it difficult to join other teams or groups.

Baron et al. (2006) note that while research suggests that social loafing is commonplace, cultural factors affect the likelihood of its occurrence. They point to the findings of Karau and Williams (1993) that women are less likely to loaf than men and to research undertaken by Earley (1993) which revealed that social loafing does not seem to take place in collectivistic cultures. It seems that in collectivistic cultures, individuals increase their efforts when working in a group.

While some loaf, others may be motivated to work harder, to undertake *social labouring*. This is thought more likely to occur in real life groups when there are consequences to group underperformance (Holt 1987 in Brown 1988). When individuals are prepared to work harder to cover for their less energetic group members, they are contributing to the process of *social compensation*. Occasions when members do not seem to mind compensating for the loafer(s) include: when there is a strong personal investment in the effective performance of the group's goals, when they wish to avoid negative outcomes for the group and when they believe they will gain credit for the extra effort (Williams and Karau 1991). Baron et al. (2006) note that research studies suggest there are several strategies that may help reduce social loafing: making individual contributions identifiable, increasing commitment to the group and stressing the importance of the outcomes and of each individual contribution to their achievement.

Group decision making

A considerable amount of communication within groups is directed at making decisions – a process that has been the focus of much research. A range of factors may affect such decision making – the quality of leadership, for example. **Cohesiveness** within a group is often viewed as a positive feature. However, research by Irving Janis (1972) led him to argue this may not always be the case.

Case study: groupthink

Janis discovered that cohesiveness might result in a group being more concerned about maintaining the strength of the relationships among its members than with effectively achieving its goals. Janis's study was based on an analysis of a selection of US foreign policy decisions made between 1940 and 1970. The selection was based on those decisions that were seen to have been poor and thus resulting in negative consequences for the US; they included the attempt to invade Cuba at the Bay of Pigs in 1961 and the Vietnam War.

Janis identified eight symptoms by which 'groupthink' could be identified: an illusion of invulnerability; a tendency towards a collective rationalization that discounts any information casting doubt on the group's decisions; a belief in the inherent morality of the group; a stereotypical view of outgroups which makes their views easy to discount; direct pressure being put on dissenters to ensure unanimity; self-censorship being exercised by those group members who have doubts about the group consensus; the existence of an illusion of unanimity among members in part because individuals have remained silent about their doubts; and finally the existence of self-appointed mind guards – group members who act to 'protect' the group from information that may challenge its assumptions.

The dangers of groupthink are obvious. Individual members lose the ability to hold or express independent, detached viewpoints. Concern for group identity is, perhaps, too strong. It is not surprising, therefore, that decisions are not subjected to the level of scrutiny that would reveal their flaws. Janis argued that the role of the group leader was pivotal in the process of groupthink. A strong, dominant leader, rarely checked by other group members, who directed decision making was seen by Janis as likely to encourage groupthink. Other important variables that encourage groupthink are when the group is protected from outside sources, decisions are rarely evaluated against alternatives, and the group is under pressure to make a decision quickly. Later studies have questioned the role of group cohesiveness in this process. Brown (2000) argues that it is more the desire for group cohesiveness than its actuality that may promote groupthink.

Brown (1988) discusses Janis's recommendations for avoiding the trap of groupthink. The role of the leader is seen as crucial here. The leader should adopt a more impartial role, avoid a rush to judgement and encourage alternative and contrary viewpoints. The appointment of an independent evaluator of the group's decisions might also provide a valuable check. Moorhead et al. (1996) examined the decision to go ahead with the ill-fated launch of the *Challenger* space shuttle in January 1986. They found evidence for the symptoms of groupthink but argued that two key conditions contributed to its emergence: time pressures and lack of a clear leadership style which could promote 'open disclosure of information, points of opposition, complaints and dissension' (1996: 167). This later point has echoes of Janis's views.

Another dynamic that appears to come into play when groups make decisions is that of **group polarization** – a tendency to move towards more extreme positions on an issue as a discussion progresses. According to Baron et al. 'Contrary to popular belief, a large body of evidence indicates that groups are actually more likely to adopt extreme positions than are individuals making decisions alone' (2006: 492). During the process of decision making both the group and individual members move towards a more extreme version of their original position. Polarization may sometimes, but not always, result in the group taking increased risks – known as the *risky shift* – but this is only likely to be the case if it was initially inclined to take risks.

Several explanations have been suggested for the occurrence of polarization. The impact of social comparison may be one cause. Group members may compete to be the one whose opinions are the most in tune with those of the group and this process can itself generate more extreme versions of the original position and push the group towards it. Another explanation is that during the discussion the majority of the arguments put forward are those that reinforce the majority viewpoint and the original position taken, the result being that members are increasingly persuaded of the correctness of this position. The strength of the arguments put forward is also an important consideration here. A third explanation points to the power of the group to ensure conformity among its members. It is thought that its ability to do so is enhanced when group members become more keenly aware of their group identity. Several studies have suggested that the polarization of an in-group's initial view may be encouraged by the presence of out-group members, a presence that enhances a sense of shared identity (Brown 2000).

According to Baron et al. (2006) another problem that appears to affect group decision making is the tendency for **biased processing** of information and ideas in a manner that seeks support for initial judgements made. This is at the expense of gaining a wider range of information and exploring all options before coming to a decision. There is also evidence that group members tend to ignore criticism from out-group members – another example of the way in which identities can obstruct effective decision making.

There is a range of evidence to suggest that groups often fail to make the best use of the resources that individual members could contribute, and thus there are often **neglected resources**. Bales (1953) argued that the size of the group could be an important factor: the larger the size of the group, the more likely that some individuals do not contribute much, if at all – the leader's contributions, however, are likely to increase. Groups are also not always able to identify those members that have the most to offer in terms of reaching the best decision.

Intergroup conflict

Identification with a group can also affect the nature of communication with other groups, not always for the better. A classic study of intergroup communication was conducted by Sherif and his associates (1961). A group of boys was taken off to summer camp, unaware that they were part of an experiment. The boys were divided into two teams, given separate cabins and then chose names for themselves – Rattlers and Eagles; the mere act of doing this seemed to foster intergroup rivalry. This was developed when the experimenters further manipulated the situation by introducing competitive activities, tugs of war, for example. These activities provoked aggressive behaviour and negative labelling between the teams that escalated to threats, fights and the stealing and burning of rival banners.

Sherif and his team decided to try to repair the damage by various strategies and were initially unsuccessful. However one did work and this was to introduce the need for intergroup cooperation in order to achieve mutually desired outcomes. For example, the camp's water supply was interrupted and thus it was seemingly threatened with a water shortage. The boys were told that they had to work together to find a solution – which they did. After several such cooperative ventures, the rivalry subsided. This research thus indicated not only the conditions in which intergroup rivalry might be encouraged, group identity clearly playing a role here, but also the conditions under which it could be diminished. Brown (2000: 250), with reference to a range of studies, reminds us that: 'The readiness for people to show partiality for their own group (and its products) over outgroups (and theirs) is not confined to artificially created groups'. The resulting conflicts, it could be argued, are all too evident.

Different group identities, and the stereotypes and prejudice that may accompany these, are not the only source of conflict. Baron et al. (2006), with reference to a range of studies, identify a number of common sources of conflict. One is actual or perceived conflicts of interest or goals. Actual conflicts may exist, for example, over resources or territory – as in the case of the Israeli-Palestinian conflict. Brown (2000) notes here that it seems that strong group identities may intensify perceived conflicts of interest – even where there may not be actual grounds for them. Poor communication is another cause of intergroup conflict and may even lead groups to believe there is a conflict of interest where none exists. A further cause of conflict is the tendency for groups to assume that their own perspectives are objective, and thus reflect reality, but to believe that the perspectives of other groups are biased. The result is that differences are exaggerated. It seems dominant groups are more inclined to make this error and as a result often have a less accurate perspective of a situation as they assume that their perspective is more objective than is the case. Personality clashes and poor group performance can also be sources of conflict both within and between groups.

A number of studies have demonstrated that the need for cooperation to achieve common goals can promote intergroup harmony. However Brown (2000) notes that this is less likely to be successful if the groups concerned actually fail to achieve their common goal. Brown also notes that even in cases where intergroup cooperation can clearly bring benefits it can still be difficult to reduce feelings of favouritism towards an in-group. Dominant groups, in particular, are likely to exhibit in-group favouritism. Further working towards common goals seems to operate best as a mechanism for reducing rivalry when each group's own sense of identity is preserved.

We spend a considerable amount of our life interacting in small groups and the identities we have within these groups can influence our communicative performances and make a significant contribution to our sense of self-identity. However these identities need to be considered in relation to the social identities we hold in the wider society such as gender, ethnic and class identities. These are considered in Chapter 4.

Key points

- Most individuals are members of a variety of groups for a range of reasons. A person's sense of identity may be significantly influenced by such group memberships.
- Essential criteria for determining the existence of a group include common goals, a structure for interaction, the allocation of roles, interdependence of fate or task, a stable relationship among members, a sense of group identity and developing and dynamic social interaction.
- Key characteristics of a group are that it allocates roles to members, generates norms and an ideology, often has status differentiation, develops cohesiveness and has the power to encourage conformity and discourage deviance among its members.
- It is argued that groups develop over time and that there are five major stages in the process of group formation: forming, norming, storming, performing and adjourning (Tuckman and Jensen 1977).
- Groups may be classed as in-groups and out-groups. In-groups are those to which we belong and whose membership we value; out-groups are those to which we do not belong. In-groups help us to define who we are; out-groups help us to define who we are not. There are cultural differences in the degree to which in-groups may influence individual behaviour.
- Cultural differences are likely to impact upon the way in which cross-cultural groups operate and these differences in expectations need to be acknowledged if the group is to run successfully (Smith and Berg 1997).
- Our sense of identity may be significantly affected by the roles we play in the groups to which we belong. A role consists of the expected and accepted way of behaving within a particular social situation. We play a number of roles within everyday life and they have a significant impact on our communicative behaviour. Goffman's dramaturgical perspective, especially the notion of persona, can be useful in analysing the way in which people perform their everyday roles in life.
- Successful role performance can be seen to require a degree of self-monitoring and impression management.
- Role strain occurs when we experience problems in delivering the performance expected by others. Common causes of role strain are

multiple role conflict, role ambiguity, role set conflict, role incompatibility and role overload.

- A number of different leadership styles have been identified ranging from the autocratic to the democratic, suggesting that there may be numerous ways in which an individual might choose to play the role of leader. However pressure to adopt a preferred style may arise from sociocultural expectations and circumstances. The style adopted could be expected to influence the pattern and nature of a leader's communication with fellow group members.
- A number of devices exists for recording interaction in groups such as the sociogram and Bales's IPA.
- Being in a group can enhance or inhibit individual performance. Those who do not contribute much to the group are likely to be seen as social loafers and may face rejection from the group.
- Group identity and the resulting cohesiveness may impede decision making as illustrated in Janis's classic study of 'groupthink'.
- Another feature of group dynamics that can affect decision making is that of group polarization – a tendency to take a more extreme position on an issue as the discussion progresses.
- On some occasions biased processing of information and ideas in a manner that seeks support for initial judgements made by the group, can occur.
- There is evidence to suggest that groups often fail to make the best use of their human resources.
- Strong group identities can encourage intergroup conflict. However the need for cooperation to achieve common goals can promote intergroup harmony.

4   Social Identities

Culture is communication and communication is culture.

Edward Hall ([1977] 1981)

The communication process is an integral part of the culture in which it takes place. The signs, symbols and codes that are the building blocks of the interpersonal communication process are located in cultures. The meanings they convey rely to a considerable extent upon shared cultural understanding. Cultures provide the framework in which social interaction takes place. Culture is transmitted through the process of socialization: a process by which behaviour is shaped in accordance with expectations embedded within the culture and among these expectations are those relating to social identities. However, culture is also dynamic and as discussed in Chapter 2, can be open to considerable forces for change. As a consequence the process of socialization may be fractured rather than seamless.

Within cultures are to be found subcultures, co-cultures, and post-subcultures, discussed in the introduction to this book, and here also are to be found processes of socialization – processes that interact with those of the main societal culture. The postmodernist perspective that contemporary Western is in a state of flux cautions that a dominant culture and thus subcultures may be difficult to define as might the relationships between them.

In this chapter a number of key social identities are explored with a view to examining the way in which language, along with some aspects of non-verbal behaviour, is used to perform and, in part, construct these identities as well as to mark the boundaries between these and other identities. Chapter 5 focuses particularly on culture, non-verbal communication and displays of identity. Social identities such as ethnic, social class and gender identities are rooted in the culture of a society. Individuals can also be seen to have a cultural identity and this is likely to be linked not only to social identities but also to some notion of national identity.

Culture and language

Traces of these movements of people and the resulting cultural exchanges abound within the English language. Bill Bryson (1990) provides some examples of everyday words and their roots: 'shampoo' – India; 'ketchup' – China; 'sofa' – Arabia; 'slogan' – Gaelic; and 'breeze' – Spain. The Vikings, who traded with and invaded Britain, contributed many Scandinavian words to the language such as 'gang', 'bask', 'muck' and 'thrust'. Similarly the French, especially after the Norman Conquest and occupation, have contributed many words – some also rooted in Latin. These include words relating to law and governance such as 'parliament', 'sovereign', 'ennoble', 'annuity', 'annul' and 'divorce'.

The language of scholars and clerics in mediaeval times had been Latin, not just in Britain but also across Europe – a convention that lasted for some centuries. This too has left its trace. Even now it can be argued that more formal ways of speaking English are often marked by the use of words with Latin roots; compare for example: 'accommodation' (Latin) with 'shelter' (Old English), 'holocaust' (Latin) with 'slaughter' (Middle English/Old Norse), and 'alcohol' (Latin) with 'booze' (Middle English/Middle Dutch). Another scholarly language, Greek, has also left its mark with words like 'paediatrics', 'democracy', 'semantics', and 'galactic'.

The many encounters between people of different cultures can also leave its mark on language use. A **pidgin** for example, may be generated between people who do not share a common language but who need to communicate. When conducting trade and business with the English in the Far East, the Chinese and other peoples, such as the Malays, developed in a very basic, utilitarian mode of half English – a pidgin. Pidgin is a Chinese corruption of the word 'business' but the term is now more widely used to refer to a basic form of communication. Traugott and Pratt (1980) argue that a pidgin may be 'roughly defined as a language that is nobody's native language'. Pidgins meet only the basic needs of communication and are very dependent on the accompanying use of non-verbal communication for their effectiveness.

If the social context is relatively stable, the pidgin can be expanded into a **creole**. Creoles are more complex and more flexible languages. Both pidgins and creoles tend to reflect a mix of the original languages of those brought together in a particular context. Typically the vocabulary stems from the superstrate (the prestige language) and the grammar comes from the substrate (the language of the less powerful). The era of colonization conducted by European countries such as Britain, France, the Netherlands, Portugal and Spain saw the development of many pidgins and creoles over the seventeenth to the nineteenth centuries (Romaine 2000). Over a period of time a creole will often change to resemble more closely the prestige language that was its base, if this language is still used in the area, a process known as **decreolization**.

One such creole is **Jamaican Creole**, one of several Caribbean creoles formed when Europeans colonized the area and established plantations. The workers on the plantations were mostly people of African origin who had been forced into slavery and transported to the Caribbean. Jamaica was an area of the Caribbean colonized by the British. Jamaican Creole is thus based on the English of the plantation owners and managers mixed with the West African languages of the people brought to work as slaves. British Black English is largely derived from Jamaican creole and is today widely used in Britain by people with African Caribbean origins as a linguistic marker of ethnic identity.

Ethnic identities

During the 1950s and 1960s people came to settle in Britain from New Commonwealth countries – in particular the Caribbean, India and Pakistan. Later came people from Bangladesh, Hong Kong and Africa. From the 1980s onwards there has been a substantial rise in asylum seekers and more recently the expansion of the European Union has resulted in people migrating from Eastern Europe to Britain. A survey reported in the *Independent* newspaper (6/10/06) found that in Brent, London, if two people are chosen at random in the street there is an 85% chance that they would belong to different ethnic groups. Not all areas of Britain contain such ethnic diversity, however.

According to Social Trends (Babb et al. 2006) by 2001 the 'ethnic minority population' stood at just over 8% of the UK population. The largest ethnic group was that of Indians (23% of the ethnic minority population) followed by Pakistanis (16%), Black Caribbeans (12%), Black Africans (10%), Bangladeshis (6%) and Chinese (5%). Added to these are people from a range of other countries including the USA, Australia, Poland, Germany, France and Spain. Since the 1960s there has also been a considerable increase in those born of mixed ethnic background.

Despite this diversity of backgrounds, when respondents were asked in the 2004 Annual Population Survey to consider what their national identities were, a majority of those from the main ethnic minority groups reported themselves as having a British identity – amongst those from the more established groups, this majority was considerable (Babb et al. 2006). These findings suggest that a sense of being British is a common thread running through many identities within this society.

Although Britain is now a multicultural society, according to Paxman (1998) the dominant culture for the last few centuries has been that of the English. Interestingly the majority of White British respondents in the 2004

Annual Population Survey described themselves as English (58%) rather than British (36%). It should be borne in mind that England's cultural dominance, as Sardar (2002) points out, was founded on its history of colonization and on class and gender oppression, both within and outside Britain. England's cultural dominance may now be subject to challenge but such a past inevitably leaves resentments and tensions within the present cultural mix (Sardar 2002).

Ethnic identity can, but does not necessarily, form part of cultural identity. The objective characteristics that identify an ethnic group may include common customs, faith and beliefs; common cultural traditions; and a common language. Others may try to assign an individual to a particular 'ethnic identity' but such labels can and may be resisted. Stella Ting-Toomey (1999) argues that ethnicity 'derives from more than the country of origin. It involves a subjective sense of belonging to or identification with an ethnic group across time' (1999: 32). The degree of identification may vary significantly between those from the same country of origin, particularly across generations. Roxy Harris and Ben Rampton (2003: 5) point out that ethnicity can be viewed as a resource 'that people can emphasise strategically in a range of different ways, according to their needs and purposes in particular situations'.

There is a diverse mix of people from different ethnic backgrounds in Britain and as Social Trends (2006) records a considerable number have mixed ethnic backgrounds thus there is the potential to generate hybrid or new ethnic identities. Such hybrids may also arise from the desire to incorporate aspects from one's heritage into a sense of 'British' identity. Global communications and travel also make it easier for diaspora identities to be sustained among some ethnic groups. It seems then that the boundaries between ethnic identities are likely to be fluid and blurred and 'ethnic identities' elusive in nature.

Religion can also be an important source of identity; one example here is Islam. Omaar (2006) argues that although Muslims in Britain come from a variety of backgrounds and traditions, their shared faith is an important component in their sense of identity and of their identification with fellow Muslims in other parts of the world. Religious beliefs can also provide much comfort and support when the individual is faced with the task of assimilation into a radically different culture. Britain is home to people from a diverse mix of ethnic backgrounds and at any one time these groups will be as Storry and Childs (2002: 226) note: 'experiencing different levels of assimilation and alienation'.

Ethnic background and identity has the potential to influence the way in which an individual communicates in many different ways. It can present the choice of whether and, if so, when to use English or one of the many other languages spoken in Britain. Asian-British women, for example, may choose to display their identity through wearing the traditional dress of say India, Pakistan or Bangladesh, while members of the Caribbean-British community may display identity through the use of British Black English in everyday conversations. However people usually belong to a range of social groups and ethnic identity may not be seen as a relevant aspect of our sense of identity or performance at certain times and in certain contexts.

A significant number of immigrants to Britain have come from countries within the former British Empire and these people may have identified, to some extent, with British culture before settling in Britain. Others will have arrived with few prior cultural links. Whatever their backgrounds most new arrivals in a country, experience a degree of **culture shock**. Samovar and Porter (2004: 295) argue, 'When you are thrust into another culture and experience psychological and physical discomfort from this contact, you have become a victim of culture shock'. Culture shock normally becomes evident after the initial excitement of encountering a new culture wears off. It can affect not only those who move to settle in a new country; anyone who finds themselves in unfamiliar surroundings for a period of time may experience it. We take for granted the degree to which our habitual patterns of behaviour are adapted to the cultural context in which we normally operate. Once out of that familiar cultural environment we have to rethink many aspects of our behaviour including our use of language and non-verbal communication. This challenge is likely to produce anxiety.

Such culture shock may be short term but in circumstances where individuals move to spend long periods of time in a very different culture, symptoms may be more debilitating. Samovar and Porter (2004: 296) note some of these: 'depression, serious physical reactions (such as headaches or body pains), anger, irritability, aggression towards the new culture, and even total withdrawal'. Such symptoms clearly have implications for interpersonal encounters. However, as discussed in Chapter 7, the process of interpersonal communication strategies can also be harnessed to aid adaptation to a new culture.

Ethnicity and language

The dominant language in Britain is English, an everyday practice that, arguably, mirrors the dominance of English culture. Not all have been happy with the consequent marginalization of the many other languages spoken (Storry and Childs 2002). Examples here range from the traditional languages of the other nations that make up the political entity of Britain, such as Irish and Scottish Gaelic and Welsh, to those of more recent arrivals such as Punjabi, Bengali, Polish, Urdu, Arabic, Hindi, Gujarati, Russian and Chinese.

Ethnic groups, other than the English, also seek to preserve the use and vitality of their language and this may even extend to a resistance to use English. Storry and Childs (2002) note, for example, that older residents of the Chinese community in Liverpool make little use of English. Many residents in North Wales similarly prefer to use Welsh rather than English for everyday conversation. There has been an active campaign to keep the Welsh language alive and it has met with some success. Bowie (1997: 184) reports on the way in which fluency in the Welsh language is still used, by some, as a contested boundary marker of Welsh identity. She found that native Welsh speakers tend to regard fluency in the language as a marker of the 'true Welsh' a claim disputed by many non-Welsh speakers who nevertheless regarded themselves as Welsh.

Jean Mills (2004: 177) found that respondents in her study of Asian mothers in the West Midlands saw language as a 'crucial component of identity'. Language is seen as a crucial tool for both constructing and displaying identities. While strongly recognizing the need for both themselves and their children to be proficient at English, the mothers also saw it as an important responsibility to pass on their 'mother tongue' (Urdu, for example) as a means of maintaining a Pakistani-British identity and links with their cultural heritage. In the words of one mother, Khalida: '*it is important for, I think, for my children to know that there is another language, that maybe their roots are in another language*' (Mills 2004: 180, original emphasis). Without the mother tongue it would also be difficult for their children to communicate with some members of the extended family – particularly grandparents and those who still lived in Pakistan. There is a tread running through comments made by the respondents and that is of a connection between the performance of role identities, ethnic identities and language. The 'mother tongue' is associated with their identity as Pakistanis and is more likely to be used when playing roles within the family and local community whereas English is associated with their identity as also being British and is seen as crucial for successfully performing roles within educational and occupational contexts. The mothers were active agents providing their children with an essential tool – multilingual competence – for building and negotiating multiple identities.

Ethnic boundaries can also be found in the use of English in Scotland. Trudgill (2000) notes the different ethnic backgrounds of the Highland and Lowland Scots: many Highlanders originated from Ireland and traditionally spoke Gaelic – indeed Gaelic is still spoken in parts of the Highlands; Lowlanders, on the other hand tend to be of Germanic Anglo-Saxon origin. This difference is reflected in the variations of English spoken today. Both groups speak Standard Scottish English but the local dialects of Lowlanders is much further away from the standard form than those of Highlanders. Trudgill gives an example: Lowlanders may say *I dinna ken* but Highlanders are more likely to say *I don't know* (2000: 50).

The African Caribbean community is another ethnic community some of whose members make use of language as a marker of identity, in this case British Black English. The roots of this version of English lie in Jamaican Creole – a creole, or patois, that is widely spoken in this former British colony in the West Indies. According to Montgomery (1995) the main differences between this creole and Standard English are in the expression of plurals, time, possession and the negative, in addition to differences in vocabulary. Montgomery (1995: 84) provides some examples:

> the other girls (Standard English) – di addah girl dem (Jamaican Creole)
>
> I went yesterday (Standard English) – mi go yeside (Jamaican Creole)
>
> where are you going? (Standard English) – whey you a go? (Jamaican Creole)
>
> the man's hat (Standard English) – di man hat (Jamaican Creole)

Most British people of African Caribbean origin will switch between the use of British Black English and Standard English depending on the social context and on what aspect of their self-identity they wish to display. Some of course, may not use British Black English at all, nor may they have much knowledge of it. As with other variations of English the degree to which those of African Caribbean origin use British Black English will depend on the speech communities to which they have been exposed and that to some extent depends upon their location within the socio-economic structure.

Elmes (2005) discusses, for example, two groups of young people, of West Indian origin, who live in different areas of Nottingham. One, a group of male musicians, made extensive use of patois in everyday speech while the other group, of females from a different area of Nottingham, did not. Members of both groups, however, were adept at switching from patois to Standard English as the situation demanded. The musicians seemed very aware of the importance of patois to their 'street' image in the music business – evidence perhaps of the usefulness of ethnicity as a resource in this context.

Case study: code switching – some examples

There follows a summary from interviews conducted in 2006 with three undergraduate students of African Caribbean background in which they discussed their use of code switching. Two students have parents originally from St Lucia and Guyana and one student has parents from St Lucia and Jamaica. All the students were born in Britain and have resided for the most part in London.

For all of the students switching between patois and Standard English is a normal feature of their everyday use of language; indeed one student observed that her 3-year-old sister is already quite adept at switching. 'Patois' – described as a mixture of Caribbean patois and English – is used when talking with family members or with close friends who are considered 'family'; it is also used a lot at Caribbean parties. Patois is seen as a 'very direct way of speaking' and is associated with situations in which they feel relaxed and comfortable. It would not be used, though, with friends 'who are not close enough to be considered family'. The reason being is that it is felt that they would not fully understand what was being said and might be offended. Patois is, therefore, used as a boundary marker in relationships: 'You can tell how close people are by whether they are using patois or English'.

Within the home environment the use of patois also indicates a person's position in the family hierarchy. Their parents and older relatives use patois more than younger members of the family. Younger members of the family have to be careful when talking to older members of the family: 'you do not to use too much patois and are careful not to use certain words otherwise it will be considered disrespectful'.

The use of patois is also considered to be an important marker of Caribbean identity. The Caribbean is referred to as 'home' even though the students had visited it only once. Two students had recently visited St Lucia and found the patois spoken there quite difficult to understand initially – partly because it also contains French words; however the visit had 'refreshed' their command of it. It seemed to the students that Jamaican Creole has had the biggest impact on the patois spoken in London and that the slang that crossed over into everyday use was mainly of Jamaican origin.

Standard English is used in more formal situations at university, for talking to non-patois speakers and for writing. It can sometimes be difficult to remember to switch in more formal situations. Sometimes cockney is used with friends and they have observed that younger family members are much more likely than they are to use cockney as opposed to Patois.

Another interviewee whose 3-year-old grand-daughter is Jamaican-English offered the following as an example of the impact of a recent visit to Jamaica on her code switching:

'Where are the stuffed olives, Grandma? Me lookin' fo' dem'.

Exercise: language and identity

Conduct interviews with 3–5 people who acknowledge that they regularly switch between the use of Standard English and another language *or* variation of English. Try to find answers to the following questions:

a) In what situations do they use the other language/variation of English?

b) Does the switch relate to their sense of identity in that situation?

c) Are there any similarities with the findings discussed in the case study?

Elmes (2005) also documents evidence of speakers who use words from their country of origin alongside those from the local dialect. Elmes (2005) records some examples. Words of African Caribbean origin found in use in Liverpool include: 'duffy' – unattractive, 'liquored' – drunk, and the word 'bredren' – a friend, was found in Liverpool, Midlands, London and the South-East. Within London and the South-East, words of African Caribbean origin also to be found include: 'bling' – showy jewellery and 'butters' – unattractive. Words of Punjabi origin include 'bibi' – paternal grandmother and 'nani' – maternal grandmother (Midlands). Some of these words, 'bling' for example, have become widely used.

There are a number of other variations that have emerged in the use of British Black English. Followers of the Rastafarian movement, for example, replace the use of 'me' with 'I' and we with 'I an I' (Montgomery 1995). This makes their everyday speech quite difficult for those outside this subculture to follow, a feature that perhaps serves well a subculture that has traditionally taken an oppositional stance to the dominant culture and has viewed its members as exiles within and alienated from the dominant white society (Hebdige 1979).

British Black English along with the closely associated African American Vernacular English spoken in the USA, is evident in many of the lyrics within popular music genres such as reggae and rap as well as among numerous movie characters. The popular British poet Benjamin Zephaniah also makes use of Jamaican Creole. Consequently British Black English has become known outside of the African Caribbean community and some of the lexicon has been adopted more widely, especially among young people.

An ongoing study by researchers from Lancaster University and Queen Mary College, University of London on linguistic innovation in inner city areas of London has identified the emergence of a new dialect of English, Multicultural London English (MLE), spoken by young people from a range of ethnic backgrounds – including white Anglo-Saxon. MLE, however, seems to be used more by young people from ethnic minorities, particularly those who are more mobile and have more social contacts. The dialect reflects a strong linguistic influence from British Black English mixed with influences from West Africa and Asia – a mixture reflecting perhaps the dynamic nature of culture, language and identity (see >*www.lancs.ac.uk/fss/projects/lingustics/innovators/*).

Social class identities, dialect and accent

Several researchers have argued that there are a number of ways in which an individual's social class background may influence their use of verbal and non-verbal communication. The variations of language use reflected in dialect, of which accent is a part, can serve as linguistic markers of an individual's socio-economic background to the extent that social-class dialects or sociolects and social-class accents have been identified. In addition accent can also serve as an indicator of regional identity (Trudgill 2000). The relationship between socio-economic background and language use is complex because the socio-economic structure of society changes over time as may an individual's location within it and further, the dynamic nature of language means that patterns of language use are also subject to change. There are also other influences – periods of time living abroad, for example – on any one individual's way of speaking, that is on their idiolect (Trudgill 2000).

While differences in Britain between the different **dialects** of English may be diminishing, there remain noticeable variations between what some might term the standard and non-standard dialects. Typical differences are in the use of vocabulary, tenses, pronouns, double negatives and tags such as 'is it?' (Montgomery 1995). Below are some illustrations:

> The team did well to score in the last minute. (Standard)
> The team done well to score in the last minute. (Non-standard)
>
> Where is my make-up bag? (Standard)
> Where's me make-up bag? (Non-standard)
>
> I had nothing to do with that break-in. (Standard)
> I hadn't got nothing to do with that break-in. (Non-standard)
>
> Ladies first, is it not? (Standard)
> Ladies first, init? (Non-standard)

Martin Montgomery notes that there are regional variations in the degree to which such variations operate. However in general there is greater use of non-standard dialects among those in the lower socio-economic groups.

There are numerous variations in pronunciation aligned with social-class accents. Trudgill (2000) studied those found in Norwich, for example. He discovered three main variations: the pronunciation of 'n' as opposed to 'ng' in words like running, walking – the working-class speakers tending to say workin' as opposed to working; the pronunciation of 't' in words like butter – working-class speakers being less inclined to do so; and use of the infamous dropped 'h' as in 'ouse – again working-class speakers were more inclined to drop the 'h'. However as Trudgill (2000: 37) notes while class-based differences in the degree to which non-standard variations were used exist, 'The vast majority of Norwich speakers use both pronunciations'. The differences rather than reflecting a divide, rest more on 'a continuum, with most speakers using sometimes one pronunciation, sometimes another' (2000: 36). The influence of social context on idiolect has to be acknowledged.

The findings of the BBC's Voices survey documented by Elmes (2005) revealed the considerable variation in dialect and accent still to be found across Britain. The survey revealed many regional variations in vocabulary. Thus to be 'cold' is to be 'starved' (Lancashire), 'fruz' (East Anglia), or 'shrammed' (The West of England), while to be tired is to be 'jiggered' (Lancashire, Yorkshire), 'wabbit' (Scotland), or 'lampered' (Cornwall). To be drunk is to be 'rubbered' (Northern Ireland), 'kaylied' (Lancashire), 'meddwyn' (Wales), or 'skimmished' (London and the South-East, and the West of England), while to be 'moody' is to be 'thrawn' (Northern Ireland) or 'mardy' (The Midlands, Lancashire, Yorkshire and Northumbria).

Accent can also be considered an aspect of non-verbal communication (Argyle 1988). Regional accents are still evident in everyday speech and as Montgomery (1995: 70) notes, 'the standard dialect is spoken with many differing regional accents'. Such accents maybe an important component of geographical identity. Elmes (2005: 61) notes that even now 'A striking feature of many of the Voices interviews has been the way in which specific accents and words are identified as belonging very narrowly to a particular village or town.'

Regional accents spoken within Britain also appear to trigger wider social evaluations and these may well influence both perceptions of the speaker and reception of the message. The prestige accent is Received Pronunciation (RP). It has its origins in the area of England that runs south-east from the Midlands to London but also encompasses Oxford and Cambridge. This region has long contained the centres of power and influence in Britain and it is perhaps unsurprising that the accent spoken by those wielding power also acquired status. Once a regional accent, RP is now used within Britain among upper and middle-class speakers (Montgomery 1995).

Trudgill (2000) identifies a continuum as regards the use of dialects and accents. Essentially the higher an individual's social class the more likely it is that they will use the standard dialect and an accent closer to RP, the lower the social class the more likely it is that a person will use a non-standard dialect and a localized, regional accent. To some extent, then, the stratification that exists among dialects mirrors the social stratification found within society. However, as is evident in testimony found in Elmes (2005), for example, people do adjust their accents to fit in with the social context. Individuals can modify not just their accents but also their use of standard or non-standard English in order to highlight aspects of their self-identity. This flexibility needs to be considered when analysing everyday communicative encounters. Individuals may view regional accents and the use of non-standard class dialect as an important marker of regional, group and class identity and may be reluctant to use more prestige forms of speech even though they could (Montgomery 1995). Indeed as both Edwards (1979) and Trudgill (2000) note a 'covert prestige' seems to be attached by males generally to non-standard dialect due to its associations with toughness and masculinity so it can also be utilized in displays of gender identity.

It seems that different accents trigger different kinds of evaluation and a number of studies have tracked such evaluations. Accents associated with large urban centres like London, Birmingham, and Newcastle are often viewed negatively while those of more rural areas such as Welsh, Scots and West Country accents are warmly received (Trudgill 2000). Montgomery (1995) notes that RP is rated as the most correct way of speaking and connotates a range of favourable attributes – intelligence, for example. Regional accents, though, are more likely to trigger judgements of social attractiveness – that the speaker is good-natured or has a sense of humour.

Giles and Trudgill (1983) argue that perceptions of regional accents are influenced by associations made with the accents – for example in the case of the Birmingham accent: smoke, grime and heavy industry – rather than by any objective criteria. When they asked native English speakers in Canada and the United States to evaluate regional accents used in Britain, they found that the Cockney accent, which had been rated as the least popular by the English respondents, was rated second favourite by the North American respondents. Giles and Trudgill argue that this may reflect the fact that for North Americans, London is associated with holidays and leisure.

Trudgill argues that evaluations that lie behind the use of the terms standard and non-standard or reactions to accents are social rather than linguistic as 'There is nothing at all inherent in non-standard varieties which makes them inferior' (2000: 9). Reactions to regional accents are subject to change though. Coggle (1997) argues that regional accents are becoming more acceptable in professional occupational roles, lawyers for example, for which RP had traditionally been the norm. He is also of the view that Estuary English – an accent found among those who live in and around London and the Thames Estuary area – is gaining ground from RP, reflecting a less class-conscious society, perhaps. Awareness of the evaluations that may be made does explain our attempts, as part of our performance, to switch our use of dialect and accent to blend into a social setting or to create the desired impression. Coggle argues that many of us can do this and that it is a valuable communication skill.

Gender Identities

> Actually, the first thing you notice about somebody when you first meet them is what sex they are.
>
> (Trudgill 2000: 60)

Gender is a key component of an individual's identity and a significant sociocultural variable impacting upon communicative behaviour. Richard Gross notes (2005) that sex is the term often used when referring to the biological or physical attributes that classify us as either male or female, while gender is used to refer to the sociocultural expectations attached to the behaviour of those classed as males or females. Crawford and Unger (2004), taking a social constructionist approach, argue that the construction of gender as a significant sociocultural category is heavily dependent on inter-personal processes. In everyday life then, 'Gender is a kind of performance, and the actors must learn their lines and cues. Like good acting, gender is best performed when it appears most natural' (Crawford and Ungar 2004: 68).

There are differing sociocultural expectations as regards the behaviour of males and females, and there are pressures to conform to such expectations. Failure to do so is likely to result in the application of social penalties (Crawford and Ungar 2004). Such sociocultural expectations do, of course, vary over time and across cultures; they are also the focus of conflicting ideas. As Gross (2005) notes, the link between gender identity and sexual identity is complex and can be problematic; there is not a simple correspondence between sex and gender: transsexuals, for example, identify with a gender different to that normally associated with their biological sex. A number of theorists have explored the use of verbal and non-verbal communication in the development and display of gender identity and some of these are considered in this section.

Gender and language

Martin Montgomery (1995: 148–9) comments: 'If obvious gender differences are signalled in part by surface contrasts in dress and demeanour, it is likely that even more profound differences of gender role and identity are carried by language.' A line of argument taken by some researchers is that the English language itself is biased towards expressing and celebrating the male rather that the female experience of life. An early proponent of this argument was Dale Spender (1985). She argues, with reference to a range of studies, that the English language, far from being neutral, denigrates women and assigns them to an inferior, **negative semantic space**. It is therefore seen as unfit for the purpose of allowing women to fully and positively express and develop their ideas, emotions and experiences. Spender discusses a number of key points to establish her argument.

Spender argues that one rule running through the use of English is that the male is the norm and the female is deviant. This rule is evident, for example, in the way that words are typically added to nouns describing occupations, particularly prestige occupations when referring to women in these roles: hence 'lady doctor', 'female surgeon', 'female judge', 'female presenter', 'women soldiers', 'career girl'. Romaine (2000: 117) recounts that she looked in the British National Corpus (1995) and found the following examples of use: '*lady doctor* (125 times), *woman doctor* (20 times), *female doctor* (10 times), compared to *male doctor* (14 times)'. She found no use of 'gentleman doctor' and only one use of 'man doctor'. Another way of marking gender to the same effect is with the addition of endings, as in 'waitress', 'stewardess', 'actress', 'hostess' (Spender 1985: 20). What is also being argued here is that traditional societal expectations about occupational roles and identities are reflected in and, more worryingly, may be reinforced by, the English language.

Suzanne Romaine (2000: 117) argues that a similar message can be found with reference to family roles. In the British National Corpus she found 'family man' occurred 94 times compared to a mere four references to 'family woman'. Further, while 81 references to 'working mother' were noted, none were found for 'working father'; 153 references to 'single mother' were found but only 2 for 'single father'; and 59 references were made to 'teenage mother' while only 2 to 'teenage father' (2000: 111). These findings are, arguably, a reflection of differential role expectations for males and females within the family. In the same vein the different standards of sexual behaviour tradi-tionally expected from men and women may well account for the fact that that while there are thought to be 220 words in the language relating to sexually promiscuous behaviour among women, there are only about 20 to describe the same behaviour by men – a case of the language attempting to guard female sexuality, perhaps (Spender 1985: 15).

Swear words, arguably, reveal something of the ideologies of the society in which they are found. A number of feminist linguists have argued, in relation to the English language, that many swear words reflect a patri-archal ideology and the attitudes and expectations regarding gender identities that stem from it. Deborah Cameron (1992) argues that the greater number of taboo words that relate to women's bodies, as opposed to those of men, reflects the way in which swear words and sexual insults are used by men to exercise social control over women, especially over their sexual behaviour. She also points out that these words are also more strongly tabooed. It is likely that 'this network of misogyny' as Cochrane (2006) describes it, helps to set the boundaries, for sexual behaviour seen as appropriate to gender identities.

Spender argues that another way in which the subordinate status of women is reinforced is by the process of **perjoration**. That is the negative connotations attached to words that are used to describe women and their experiences. She argues that the words bachelor and spinster, for example, both denote that a person is unmarried. Yet the term bachelor has positive connotations in contrast to the negative connotations attached to the word spinster. Romaine (2000) also provides examples of the collocations of the word spinster to illustrate this point: 'gossipy', 'jealous', 'eccentric', 'frustrated', 'repressed' and 'lonely'. These are in contrast, she notes, to the mostly neutral or positive collocations found for the word bachelor.

Romaine (2000) argues that the same bias can be found in the collocations of the words woman, man, girl and boy as further evidence of perjoration. In a survey based on the British National Corpus (1995) she found that the word 'intelligent' is much more likely to be associated with man than woman, though interestingly slightly less likely to be associated with boy than girl. 'Honest' was more likely to be used with man than woman but had similar levels of usage with girl and boy. 'Blonde' was overwhelmingly used more in relation to woman and girl and hardly used at all in relation to man and boy – reflecting, perhaps, a greater tendency to comment on female appearance. 'Hysterical' and 'silly' were also associated much more with woman and girl – indeed there was no evidence in the survey of the collocation of these words with man (2000: 110).

Romaine notes that it is still more common for women than men to be addressed by their first name. The use of first names is normally a sign of informality and friendship; however when such use is one-sided, it suggests an unequal power relationship and it seems women are still more likely than men to find themselves reminded of this situation. In a similar vein, Romaine notes, adult women are also often referred to as 'girls'. Of course, such practices are open to challenge within everyday conversations.

However, there is some evidence that women may also use the term 'girl' to downgrade the status of the person being referred to. Edwards (1998) studied conversations that took place within relationship counselling sessions, and analysed the use of 'girl' or 'woman' when referring to the identities of those involved. In one section of conversation Connie, the wife, talks about the woman with whom her husband has been having an affair:

Counsellor: To explore what happened.=
Connie: =*To* explore: what happened ex*a*ctly y'know, because I c*a*n't
               ac*ce*pt (1.0) I c*a*n't ac*ce*pt (1.0) y'know: (.) wh*a*t he's *te*lling
               me, (0.5) y'know? = = I just belie:ve that this girl was here all
               alo:ng (0.2) and that's why. (0.5)

                                                        (Edwards 1998: 25)

Edwards notes that 'girl' may be used here as a tactic to downgrade the other woman's status – Connie's purpose, arguably, in this extract. However it should be noted that in other extracts the terms 'girl' and 'woman' do not seem to carry this connotation – indeed Connie uses both terms to describe herself and her friends depending on their relevance to her purposes in the conversation. Such purposes are seen by Edwards as a key variable affecting 'what people do with the words they use' (1998: 31) and the identities they choose to highlight – a reminder of the influence of agency.

Commenting that 'Nothing is more personal or as closely related to our identity as our names' (2000: 116) Romaine points out that it is still quite common for women to take on her husband's surname after marriage. That a woman's name may have temporary features may have deeper significance for her sense of identity. The practice has also made it difficult to trace the female line within a family and thus the history of female family members. Spender (1985) argues that such conventions, along with the actual restrictions that traditionally existed on the publishing of women writing and on their speaking in public, contributed to **female invisibility**. An invisibility that, she argues, resulted in a wall of near silence in the public domain as regards women's experiences and perspectives on life. A silence that has contributed to 'the male-defined hierarchical world-view' (1985: 227) a world view that helped locate women in identities associated with subordinate roles in life. While this silence may have been broken, to some extent, in recent decades, its legacy is, arguably, still evident. Another feature signalled out by Spender (1985) is what she refers to as '*He/man* language.' This is the principle that 'he' and 'man' are generic terms that include she and woman, as in for example the use of the term 'mankind' to refer to both men and women. The principle she argues contributes to the male as norm rule with its associations of male superiority but arguably also renders women invisible as in effect it denies them a separate identity. Spender recounts the considerable effort that male grammarians have made over the centuries in their quest to establish that 'he stood for she' (1985: 150). Spender also recounts that another principle that they sought to establish is that of placing the term for males before the females in lists as in, for example, husband and wife, brother and sister, son and daughter' (1985: 147).

As Romaine (2000) points out in everyday speech people often use, as they have done for centuries, 'they' or 'their' when referring to that which includes or applies to both sexes. She also notes experiments that have demonstrated that women do not feel included when they read texts using 'he'. Harding considers that the tendency of management textbooks to use the term 'he' as the generic form when referring to managers, might help in a social construction of an image of management that has 'a masculine gendered identity' (2003: 139).

The thrust of argument here is that the English language, linguistic conventions and subsequent gender-related **discourses** are active players in helping to construct a subordinate, incomplete and negative gender identity for women. However, that the language may reflect certain biases does not necessarily mean that Spender is right to argue that it cannot be used by women to express themselves, their experiences and perspectives and to challenge expectations, to explore possibilities and construct more positive identities. Cameron (1985), for example, puts forward three propositions to argue that women do not necessarily need to be alienated from the English language. First the assumption that language determines thought can be called into question. There is scant evidence that language has the degree of power accorded to it by supporters of the linguistic determinism hypothesis. Language is only one factor that may influence an individual's perceptions and its influence interacts with others.

Second, it is impossible for a group to exercise such a degree of control over meaning, not least because the generation and exchange of meaning is a dynamic process open to numerous influences and 'Meanings have to be constructed by the individual language user' (1985: 79). This is why communicative signs, symbols and messages are prone to differing interpretations. Third, language is a dynamic, renewable resource used creatively by individuals to express their thoughts, experiences and perspectives. It is possible, therefore, to find the words with which to explore and express women's experiences and to challenge patriarchal assumptions. Cameron is not denying that language has been and can be used to 'oppress, silence and marginalize women' (1985: 79) she is, however, pointing out that it can also be used to fight back.

Gender and interaction

Deborah Tannen (1992) argues that men and women have sufficiently different conversational style as to justify the application of the term **genderlects**. When in conversation, men 'speak and hear the language of status and independence' whereas for women it is the language of 'connection and intimacy' and she observes that 'communication between men and women can be like cross-cultural communication, prey to a clash in conversational styles' (1992: 42). It seems that men tend to engage in what she terms 'report-talk' displaying knowledge in order to establish status and dominance.

Women on the other hand are more inclined to engage in 'rapport-talk' and use conversation to establish cooperation and intimacy; hence their greater inclination to talk about relationships. Both Tannen and Romaine (2000) note that some studies have found similar differences in the language use of girls and boys. Tannen's notion of genderlects is also consistent with findings that women are more inclined to self-disclose than men (Jourard 1971). Self-disclosure tends to be a reciprocal process and can be seen to play an important role in identity formation as it is a means by which we intentionally reveal information about ourselves to others and in return receive feedback on our revelations, feedback that may then influence how we perceive ourselves.

Tannen further argues that these styles partly explain why men seem to dominate in mixed-sex company. However, this may not be the case in conversations between men and women in more intimate contexts, as here 'rapport-talk' maybe more appropriate. Tannen observes that one of the results of the differing motivations for conversations is the common complaint of women that men seem reluctant to engage in everyday conversations as much as women would like, and offers the following scenario as an example: 'Women's dissatisfaction with men's silence at home is captured in the stock cartoon setting of a breakfast table at which the husband and wife are sitting: He's reading a newspaper; she's glaring at the back of the paper' (1992: 81). The television, computer screen or ipod might also serve as alternative sources of focus. However, she also notes that some research suggests that the class and educational background of the couple is a variable here: it is less likely to be the case among educated, middle-class couples as they are more likely to view each other as close friends, with whom experiences should be shared.

Everyday **interaction within the family** is seen by a number of researchers as a rich source of information about the interplay between family roles and gender identities. It is, arguably, within family conversations that many of the expectations surrounding gender roles and identities are negotiated. Tannen, for example, argues that 'the conversations that take place in families reflect the divergent expectations of family members of different genders' (2006: 187). Based on an analysis of a number of transcripts of everyday interaction in American families, she concludes that the different gender-related patterns of rapport-talk; report-talk are evident. Among the transcripts reviewed, is one of a sister and brother (both adults) that records some reluctance on the part of the brother to engage in conversation about his everyday life:

Sister: So how's things with Kerry?
Brother: Cool.
Sister: Cool. Does that mean very good?

> *Brother:* Yeah.
> *Sister:* True love?
> *Brother:* Pretty much.
> *Sister:* PRETTY much? When you say pretty much, what do you mean?
> *Brother:* I mean it's all good.

(Tannen 2006: 187)

A similar reluctance was also evident, however, in transcripts of conversations between a mother and her teenage daughter, revealing that age and the closeness of relationships are also variables that impact on the pattern of interaction in families.

Tannen (2006) also looks at the 'telling your day' ritual common in many families. Mothers are more inclined here to use interaction to involve family members, maintain relationships and share problems whereas fathers are more inclined to use interaction to make judgements on the actions recounted by others and to offer solutions to problems raised. Fathers are though less inclined to share their problems. This creates the 'father-knows-best dynamic'. This dynamic results in mothers feeling that they have been placed in a less powerful position but 'without knowing how they got there' (2006: 187). Such snapshots of family interaction, Tannen argues, reveal the way in which the dynamics of intimacy and power can be embedded in family interaction.

These dynamics, arguably, send out messages about role expectations, i.e. that women are expected to play a more active role in maintaining relationships. They also send out messages about power differences. If mothers appear less powerful as a consequence of their different priorities, the message may be that men are more powerful than women. The family is a prime agent of socialization and family interaction clearly has the potential for shaping expectations relating to gender identities and roles. The dynamics in the one-parent family unit and in families in other cultures, however, are likely to be different.

Another area of verbal interaction in which gender differences have been noted is in the differing degrees of use of non-standard English, prestige accents and swearing in everyday encounters. Trudgill (2000) argues that a range of studies have demonstrated that women are more likely to use pronunciation that is closer to that prestige accents such as PR. They are also less likely than men to use non-standard forms of English. Romaine (2000) notes that in a study she undertook amongst children in Edinburgh, a similar pattern was evident; the boys using both more non-standard English and swear words than the girls.

Trudgill (2000) considers some suggestions as to why this might be the case. As noted in Chapter 4, males do seem to accord a 'covert prestige' to the use of non-standard English because its associations with working-class dialect lend it allied connotations of masculinity. Another possibility is that women feel under greater pressure to conform to social norms, and this shows itself in linguistic behaviour as in other forms of behaviour. Romaine (2000) also found evidence that females are under pressure to be more 'correct' in their use of language, particularly in more formal contexts, and that they felt that they would create a negative impression if they used too much non-standard English. Montgomery (1995) with reference to the studies such as that of Milroy (1980) argues that not all women will demonstrate the tendency to move towards prestige registers; the degree to which they do this will depend upon their social context. Those who are located in tightly bound local communities often keep to the vernacular.

Traditional folklinguistic belief was that women used taboo and swear words less frequently than men and, further, that men ought not use such words in front of women. How truly this belief reflects the realities of everyday life is questionable given the limited data available (Coates 2004). Elizabeth 1, it is rumoured, was well known for the frequency with which she swore. Jennifer Coates comments that these beliefs may well reflect ideas of what ought to have been the case rather than what actually was – a patriarchal hope rather than a reality, perhaps. The evidence from more contemporary studies of gender differences in swearing paints a more complex picture.

A study for the Broadcasting Standards Council (Millwood Hargrave 1991) contained a detailed exploration of views on swearing in everyday life as well as on television. The study did find evidence that there was social acceptance of men swearing when together socially but not of women; but both older men and older women were more sensitive to swearing and older men tended to use milder swear words. The study did find one notable gender difference still evident among the under 35s and this was in the response to sexual swear words – younger women were less comfortable with these.

However, Rundell (1995) in discussing trends evident from the British National Corpus comments that as regards the act of swearing, gender differences seem much less evident in the under 30s. There are also regional and social-class variables that cut across the findings on gender differences. Rundell (1995) notes that those who live in the south of England generally swear more and Hughes (1992) found that working-class women in deprived areas made frequent use of taboo swear words and found them unexceptional.

Coates (2004) reviews a range of research, including her own, and draws a number of general conclusions about **differences in male and female communicative behaviour** during encounters. Many of these differences can be viewed as both reflecting and reinforcing a subordinate female identity. It seems that 'men and women do pursue different interactive styles' (p. 110). In mixed sex encounters men are more likely to interrupt women than vice-versa; they also tend to control the topics of conversation and dominate the encounters. Indeed the thrust of research suggests, Coates argues, 'that women and men do not have equal rights to the conversational floor' in mixed-sex encounters (p. 124). Men more than women use silence or delayed minimal responses such as 'mhm' or 'yeah' to close down and withdraw from a mixed-sex encounter. Women are more likely to use minimal responses to support and encourage another person's contribution to a conversation.

Women also appear to use more **hedges** than men in conversation. Hedges are verbal utterances such as 'sort of', 'perhaps' and 'if you know what I mean'. Hedges have a number of functions that include expressing confidence, suggesting uncertainty, and facilitating face-saving when sensitive topics are being discussed. When giving directives or instructions it seems, men are more inclined to use aggravated directives, using the imperative, as in for example: 'This is the schedule we will adopt' whereas women seem more inclined to make use of more inclusive, mitigated directives as in, for example: 'Let's adopt this schedule then'. As previously discussed it seems that men do tend to swear more than women and that women are more polite.

Tannen (1992) also comments on another feature of mixed-sex encounters, one that echoes Spender's comments on female invisibility, and that is the apparent reluctance of others to listen carefully to what women have to say – indeed both males and females have a tendency to divert the conversation back to male speakers. It has also been observed that female suggestions are often overlooked until later repeated by male speakers. Such acts of disconfirmation have the potential, perhaps, to undermine a sense of self-identity.

Cameron (2006) examines such gender differences in interactive styles in the light of what she describes as the emergence of a new 'linguistic ideal' – that of the 'skilled interpersonal communicator who excels in such verbal activities as cooperative problem-solving, rapport-building, emotional self-reflexivity and self-disclosure, "active" listening, and the expression of empathy' (2006: 458–9). She argues that two key social changes that have led to the emergence of this ideal: the growth of service industries within the economy, and thus of occupational roles for which such skills are seen to be crucial; and the need, identified by Giddens (1991), for individuals to engage in the reflexive project of developing self-identity – an engagement that requires individuals to put considerable conscious effort into creating and maintaining relationships. Cameron argues that this contemporary definition of the **skilled communicator** preferences those skills traditionally associated with female interactive styles and thus can be viewed as *'feminizing the values and the language of public discourse'* (2006: 461, original emphasis). It may lead, of course, to a change in male interactive styles.

The assumption that women may be better at such skills may both contribute to and reflect the gendered nature of occupational roles within the British economy and in particular the tendency for women to work in the service sector. Cameron (2006) cites research conducted in call centres, for example, that evidenced a preference for male managers to employ women rather than men on the everyday assumption that women were likely to be better at such communication skills. Liz Yeomans (2006) argues that this assumption may also explain why the majority of employees within the public relations sector are women. She also points out that such jobs often require considerable emotional labour and this may be a significant cause of stress to the employee. Cameron points out that within the service sector women are often required to employ these skills in a performance that simulates empathetic and friendly relationships. Given the emotional labour required to maintain such performances throughout the working day and week, it is perhaps not surprising that they create stress. A further point made by Cameron is that skilled communicators or not, women are still more likely than men to have poorly paid, low status jobs.

Gender and non-verbal communication

As Crawford and Unger (2004: 79) note, 'Many non-verbal behaviours vary by gender' along with other social variables and there are thus numerous examples for consideration. Morris (2002) also argues that an important aspect of our non-verbal behaviour is that it can send out 'gender signals'. These signals he argues, are 'clues that enable us to identify an individual as either male or female' (2002: 347) and they also help to confirm known gender identities. Morris describes many of these signals as 'invented' in that they are cultural rather than natural markers of gender and thus vary across cultures and throughout history; examples of such invented signals include differences in hairstyle and dress and in the use of cosmetics. Morris (2002) further comments that as regards the use of these 'invented' signals the, 'most interesting feature is that they are so common' (2002: 359), their frequent occurrence reflecting, perhaps, a particular need, on the part of individuals and societies to emphasize gender differences.

Looking at Western societies, Polhemus and (2004: 160) argues that despite the loosening up of conventions as regards male and female appearance in recent decades 'make-up, nail art and various hairstyles continue to be taboo for real men'. It can be observed that women are more likely than men to wear colours such as lemon, lilac and lime green. Though both men and women wear trousers in contemporary Western societies, it is much less common for men to wear skirts – when they do it is likely to be a sarong for the beach rather than a skirt to the office. Morris (2002) also notes that there remain gender differences in the way men and women wear trousers. Despite the fact that trousers give women the freedom to adopt the leg-spread posture when seated, they still seem much less inclined to do so than men.

Women, it seems, are more likely to touch their hair and clasp their hands; men are more inclined to fold their arms across the chest (Morris 2002). According to Argyle (1988: 286) 'Women smile more, use less space' and 'look more' than men. Women also seem more sensitive to non-verbal signs, particularly facial expressions, though men seem to pay more attention than women to vocal cues.

Montgomery (1995) argues that people typically experience little difficulty in distinguishing between the voices of men and women. Men generally use a lower pitch and their voices have more resonance. However, as Romaine (2000) points out this may be partly due to socialization. She discusses the disadvantages this can bring for women: people normally raise the pitch of their voice in public speaking in order to make themselves better heard; when women do so in this situation their voices can sound shrill. However, people can be taught to change the pitch of their voice. Romaine mentions the case of former British Prime Minister, Margaret Thatcher, who was famously coached to make her voice sound more authoritative.

Performativity

There seems, therefore, to be a considerable amount of evidence that the way we communicate is, to some extent, influenced by our socialization into gender roles and associated gendered patterns of behaviour; further, however, our sense of identity can be seen to be both constructed and reinforced by our everyday performances. One influential perspective that focuses on the role of such everyday performances in the construction of gender identity is that of **performativity** proposed by Judith Butler (1990,1999). Butler argues that gender categories and the ideas of identity and sexual orientation associated with them are not natural but are rather social constructs that depend heavily upon everyday performances and interaction with others. For Butler (1999: 178) performativity, not nature, is at the heart of gender. Butler argues that there is not an 'essence that gender expresses' but rather 'the various acts of gender create the idea of gender, and without those acts, there would be no gender at all' (p. 178).

These performances are framed by, but not determined by, social expectations of appropriate behaviour and it is in the regular and frequent repetition, though not identical repetition, of these performances that gender identity is both constructed and reinforced. Butler comments that those whose performances stray too far from expectations are likely to receive negative feedback and maybe even suffer social sanctions. Many tools of verbal and non-verbal communication are employed in such everyday performances to create displays of gender identity such as hairstyle, dress and use of cosmetics and these performances seem to be enacted through gendered interactive styles. While our everyday performances may often reinforce expectations and from Butler's perspective may 'constitute the illusion of an abiding gendered self' (1999: 179), up to a point they can also be employed to challenge them: a young female may decide to continually interrupt male speakers just as a young male may decide to wear blue nail polish. If gender is constructed through performances it is also a less stable category than traditionally supposed. As Butler comments, 'the "doer" is variably constructed in and through the deed' (1999: 181).

Butler's concept of performativity can be used to explore recent changes that have been noted in the display of masculine identities, in particular the emergence of the so-called **metrosexual male**. This term is commonly used to refer to heterosexual males who take care with their appearance and seems to have been first used, if somewhat disparagingly, by the journalist Mark Simpson in 1994. A key aspect of this identity lies in the displays of non-verbal behaviour by males and can be seen as a good example of Butler's claim that expectations surrounding gender identities can be modified through everyday performances. Salzman et al. (2005: 36) argue that changes in male occupational roles and in gender roles have resulted in some men rethinking their behaviour; this re-think, they argue, 'has affected not only how men think and behave, but also how they look. Very slowly, men who were previously averse to spending time and money on their appearance began to think again.' This trend is not, apparently, just confined to Western countries. Salzman et al. (2005) name Pakistan, Brazil, Korea and Indonesia as countries in which this 'global phenomenon' has been sighted. The notion of the meterosexual male has been commercially exploited, evidenced by the rise in beauty and fashion products and services now targetted at men, not to mention style guides for metrosexual men (see Flocker 2003). David Beckham is often cited as a classic example of the metrosexual male. However, Salzman et al. (2005) argue that metrosexuality is about more than just a concern for appearance; it reflects a shift towards a concern for relationships and a willingness to be more open about emotions – a shift towards displaying what have traditionally been viewed as feminine qualities. The appearance of the metrosexual male has not been welcomed in all quarters.

Case study

The man of the moment is metrosexual
Matt Keating
Guardian, Wednesday 16 July, 2003

'Ten years ago, I would have looked at certain aspects of my lifestyle and said: "Ponce",' confessed James Brown, the launch editor of lad bible *Loaded*, who was a little surprised to find that he might be 'turning into . . . a metrosexual'.

'I thought a metrosexual was a pervert who frequented the underground in Paris or Newcastle,' said Brown in the *Sunday Times*. Apparently not. 'A metrosexual, according to New York's finest marketing men, is "a guy who is definitely straight, but has embraced the worlds of grooming facials, shopping with women and ... their feminine side".'

The metro bit refers to 'metropolis and, in this instance, means men with money' (*Sunday Mirror*). Such a man, added the *Chicago Tribune*, is to be found with 'sports section in hand ... soccer ball at the ready; he can cook up a blow-your-socks-off pasta feast while discussing the merits of wine and wrenches with equal intensity'.

Celebrity metrosexuals include Hugh Jackman, Justin Timberlake and Ben Affleck, reckoned the *Dublin Evening Standard*. 'But the ultimate metrosexual male is David Beckham.' *The New York Times* agreed. 'The European media have found a metrosexual icon,' it reported, 'in the soccer star who paints his fingernails, braids his hair, and poses for gay magazines, all while maintaining a manly profile on the pitch.'

Unsurprisingly a leading advertising agency, Euro RSCG Worldwide, was behind the study that sparked all the press coverage. 'Paradoxically,' noted the NY Times, 'the term metrosexual ... was coined in the mid-90s to mock everything marketing stands for.'

Australia has also come in on the debate. Peter FitzSimons thought this 'new masculinity' was an excercise in narcissism. 'What gets my goat,' he railed in the *Sydney Morning Herald*, 'is that the whole damn marketing schtick ... is so all-embracing, so pervasive ... that even as we speak there are young blokes out there feeling completely lost and isolated ... All of this stuff leaves them stone motherless cold.'

Guardian Unlimited © Guardian News and Media Limited 2006

Exercise

1   Which current celebrities could be considered to represent metrosexuality? Justify your choices.

2   Select four current advertisements that you feel feature a metrosexual male or products that a metrosexual male might use. Justify your choices.

3   What might be the limits to the performance of a metrosexual identity as regards displaying attributes normally associated with females and 'gay' men? Where do the identity boundaries lay?

Sexual identities

The concept of performativity highlights the possibilities for challenging and changing assumptions about gender identity through everyday performances and opens up a range of possibilities as regards gender, identity and sexual orientation. The formation of sexual identities are, arguably, influenced by role models and social expectations but they are also honed in everyday interaction, through self-presentation, self-disclosure and the feedback gained from such communicative acts. Larry Gross (1998) recounts the difficulty of dealing with an emerging homosexual identity in a 'mid-century America' that provided little interpersonal support for such an identity. He recounts the resultant feelings of isolation and anxiety when faced with the silent void regarding discussion of such possibilities – a denial of the existence of homosexual identities also mirrored by their near absence, then, in the mass media.

Gross's discussion highlights the interplay between mass and interpersonal communication in the development of self-identity. He notes that homosexual identities, gay or lesbian, are now more widely acknowledged within the media, as in everyday life, but there remain the problems of stereotypical, limited and often negative media portrayals of homosexuality and prejudice from some sections of society. While the Internet, cable television and radio networks do facilitate greater opportunity for communication with other homosexuals, Gross argues that unlike other minority groups, homosexuals often find themselves with limited access to everyday social interaction with similar others, yet such encounters could help mediate the impact of mainstream media representations of homosexuality on an individual's sense of identity.

Yip (2004) considers similar problems surrounding the formation of homosexual identity for British Muslims in contemporary Britain. Yip notes that a number of studies have concluded that religious values are particularly integral to Muslim communities and these traditionally convey a negative view of homosexuality. The stress within these communities on the importance of family life and the maintenance of family honour along with a view of marriage as a social and religious duty combine to create a difficult social context in which to explore, disclose and display homosexual identity. Yip examines the interpersonal strategies used by a sample of Muslim males and females to do just this.

Yip found that it was more common for individuals to 'come out' to their mothers and younger siblings. Most acts of disclosure were met with 'cautious tolerance' but some were met with actual or threatened violence and in some cases individuals felt they had to run away from the family and community. Some were encouraged by parents to use marriage to conceal or 'cure' their homosexual identity – a strategy reminiscent of that traditionally employed within the wider British society. Few of the participants in Yip's study had revealed their homosexual identity to the wider kinship group thus it was an identity that was partially enveloped in secrecy and silence and thus partially denied. Yip's study highlights not just the role that interpersonal communication plays in the construction and display of personal identity but also the social constraints within which this process occurs. As Yip concludes it is a reminder of the interplay between structure and agency, a reminder that the project of self is subject to influences and expectations stemming from elements of the social structure.

A review of the cases of prejudice and discrimination against homosexual identity publicized by the pressure group Outrage, for example, further reminds us of the dangers of revealing certain sexual identities, even when such identities are legally recognized. Such dangers can range from pressure to resign a post, as in the case of the homosexual Church of England canon pressured to resign his appointment as Bishop of Reading in 2003, to the current homophobic attacks and murders in Jamaica (*www.petertatchell. net.2006*). As Butler (1999) points out, performances that pose a significant challenge to expectations have to be considered with care.

Queer theory

Butler's (1990) argument that gender is a problematic concept and not necessarily rooted in an individual's biological sex has been influential in the development of queer theory. As Butler argues the central tenet of performativity is that sexual identity is essentially fluid, ambiguous and thus unstable. Queer theory explores the 'mismatches between sex, gender and desire' (Jagose 1996: 3) and challenges the assumption that heterosexual desire is 'natural', unproblematic and to be regarded as the social norm. It challenges the assumptions that there can be any 'natural' and stable sexual identity or orientation and explores not only lesbian and gay sexual orientations but also 'cross-dressing, hermaphroditism, gender ambiguity and gender-corrective surgery' (Jagose 1996: 3).

In the analysis of communicative texts queer theory also 'seeks to locate Queerness in places that had previously been thought of as strictly for straights' (Burston and Richardson 1995: 1). As is the case with everyday performances, a significant number of the clues used to locate queerness reside in the verbal and non-verbal behaviour of the characters. Gross (1998) notes that a number of popular television programmes such as *Dynasty*, *Ellen* and *Cagney and Lacey* have been read in this way and formed a focus for everyday conversations among gays and lesbians, providing a means by which to explore further their sexual identities. Sullivan (2003) also examines a range of texts from *Batman Forever* to *Austin Powers, International Man of Mystery* to demonstrate how queer readings can be constructed. Queer theory shows again the interplay between interpersonal and mass communication in the formation of identity.

Queer linguistics examines the particular role that language can play in the performance of 'queer' identities. Kira Hall (2006: 375) explains that 'queer linguistics is necessarily concerned with how heterosexual normativity is produced, perpetuated and resisted, but seeks to localize these productions within specific communities of practice'. A well-known example of the way in which language can be used to express homosexual identity is Polari – a form of 'British gay slang' (Lucas 1997: 85) popular among the homosexual communities of the 1950s and 1960s. In the 1960s Polari crossed over into mainstream use, an example being its use to portray camp, comic characters. Its crossover into the mainstream, the legalization of homosexuality in the late 1960s, the reduced need for caution in displaying homosexual identities and changing trends within the homosexual scene since the 1960s have resulted in limited contemporary use of Polari (Lucas 1997).

Sexual identity is only one aspect of self-identity and may be more significant for some than others. A number of studies have explored how language can be used when individuals do wish to express a 'gay' identity. Barrett (1997: 192) argues that 'the form of language often reflects a stereotype of gay men's speech'. Barrett notes that key features of this speech include the use of 'empty adjectives', specific terms for colour, 'hedges'; broader scope of pitch in intonation; 'hypercorrect pronunciation'; and specific words widely used in the gay community. Social exchanges may also include the ritual exchange of insults and positive politeness strategies. 'These features', argues Barrett, 'may (in a given context) index a gay identity' (1997: 193). Individuals may not display these features in everyday speech but code switch when expression of a 'gay identity' is appropriate or required. Barrett comments that some of these features are shared with other speech communities: hypercorrect pronunciation, politeness and hedges, for example, have been noted as features of 'women's language' by some linguists. Barrett (1997: 195), in a study of 'bar queen speech' in Texas, noted that a key feature was the use of 'positive politeness' strategies.

Ethnic, social class, gender and sexual identities, can exert a significant influence on an individual's communicative behaviour but it is partly through the use of verbal and non-verbal signs within the process of interpersonal communication that such identities are constructed. Chapter 5 focuses more on the non-verbal aspects of communication and their contribution to our exploration of the relationship between culture, communication and identity.

Key points

- Social identities are likely to influence an individual's communicative behaviour; they are also, in part, constructed and displayed through the process of interpersonal communication.
- There are many variations in the use of English, for example: the use of British Black English or local dialects and accents, and these may be a key aspect of displays of identity. Many languages, other than English, are spoken in Britain and their use too can be integral to displays of identity.
- Individuals may alter their use of language in order to blend in with differing social situations. In part, this switching reflects the differing identities an individual may seek to establish and display in differing social contexts.
- Some theorists argue that the English Language and linguistic conventions governing its use privilege males while denigrating female identities and experiences.
- A number of differences between male and female communicative behaviour have been identified. These include differences in the following: conversational styles and goals; the use of non-standard English, prestige accents and swearing; dominance of mixed-sex encounters; the use of hedges, minimal responses and silence; and in the manner in which instructions are given. Gender identity, however, is only one influence on communicative behaviour, thus other influences are likely to affect the degree to which these general differences in male and female communicative behaviour impact on any one individual.
- Some argue that the current ideal of a skilled communicator celebrates the skills traditionally associated with female interactive styles.
- The concept of performativity proposes that gender identity can be seen to be both constructed and reinforced by our everyday performances and interaction with others. Performances that stray too far from expectations are likely to suffer social sanctions; however, they can also be employed to challenge them. Gender is thus seen as a dynamic and unstable social category.
- A much talked about category is that of the metrosexual male. A key aspect of this identity lies in displays of non-verbal behaviour and its emergence can be seen as a good example of the claim that expectations surrounding gender identities can be modified through everyday performances.
- The formation of sexual identities are, arguably, influenced by role models and social expectations but they are also honed in everyday

interaction, through self-presentation, self-disclosure and the feed-back gained from such communicative acts. Queer theory and queer linguists are examples of areas of study that focus on the role of communicative behaviour in the display of such identities in social encounters.

5 Non-verbal Communication, Culture and Consumption

Nonverbal messages signify who we are via our artefacts (e.g. the clothes we wear), our vocal cues, our nonverbal self-presentation modes, and the interpersonal spaces we claim for ourselves.

(Ting-Toomey 1999: 115)

Like language, non-verbal communication is rooted in culture and depends heavily upon cultural knowledge for its effective use and interpretation. We learn the use of non-verbal communication as part of the process of socialization and may thus be less consciously aware of the non-verbal element of our everyday communication. Yet Mehrabian (1971) argues that 93% of messages we receive in face-to-face social interaction are classed as non-verbal while only 7% as verbal. The basic building blocks of non-verbal communication are identified by Argyle (1988) as appearance, facial expression, eye contact, touch and bodily contact, spatial behaviour (proxemics and orientation), gesture, head nods, posture, and non-verbal vocalizations.

The differing elements of non-verbal communication are often used to convey different kinds of message. These basic elements are thought to be universal but the rules for display of non-verbal communication and the meanings attributed to the various non-verbal signs often vary across cultures. There are significant cultural differences in non-verbal communication and these can pose a considerable barrier to effective interpersonal communication. Thus caution is prudent when communicating across cultural boundaries.

This chapter first explores the use of non-verbal signs within the process of interpersonal communications and the implications for both cross-cultural communication and displays of identity. Appearance is arguably a key component of the act of self-presentation and so the chapter moves on to consider the role of consumer goods in the construction of identity.

Introduction

The main functions of non-verbal communication include the display of emotional states and attitudes towards others, self-presentation, the regulation and synchronization of interaction, reinforcement of verbal messages, showing interest in and helping to maintain conversations, giving advance warning of the nature of verbal communication to follow and, crucially, giving feedback to others (Argyle 1988). It is thus an indispensable feature of everyday communicative encounters and of displays of identity. We often consciously try to manipulate the non-verbal signs we give off in order to cultivate a given impression (Goffman 1959).

There is evidence that some non-verbal signs can act as 'personality displays' and we may try to employ our layperson's understanding of such behaviour in our everyday performances – not always with success (Morris 2002). Argyle (1988) provides examples of actual links found between non-verbal behaviour and personality. For instance, those who sit or stand slightly closer to others and who look more, smile more and talk more are often more sociable, more extrovert, and are also perceived as such by others. On the other hand those who talk quickly, loudly, at a higher pitch, and energetically, with few pauses and who tend to interrupt others may be displaying dominance, or making a claim for dominance, in a social situation. However factors within the social situation also affect non-verbal behaviour and individuals vary in their sensitivity to and ability to read non-verbal signs. Thus, successful impression management is not always achievable.

Non-verbal communication lends to a conversation what Gahagan (1984) calls a 'diplomatic flexibility', that is it can be used to drop hints. This flexibility is grounded in the ambiguous nature of much non-verbal communication, ambiguity that stems from the fact that much bodily movement is not communicative in intent, so it can be difficult for a receiver to be clear about what is intended by any one particular sign. Touching one's face, for example, may result from the need to scratch an irritating spot or be a sign of anxiety (Argyle 1988). Such ambiguity means that non-verbal signs can be used to suggest a response, a suggestion that can be retracted later. It also means they can be prone are to aberrant decoding.

Touch

Touch is typically used to communicate friendship and intimacy within a relationship. It can also be used when offering congratulations, as when footballers hug one another after scoring a goal, to provide reassurance when a friend is upset, or when trying to persuade someone. More negatively, it can be employed to express aggression and dominance – those of higher status in a social situation often initiate touch. Touching is used in many cultures as one of the rituals of social interaction, for example shaking hands in greetings or farewells. Touching may also be part of the ritual interaction found within ceremonies (Argyle 1988).

However, the rules for the use and degree of touch do vary across cultures. A number of anthropologists have recorded cross-cultural differences in the degree of bodily contact expected during everyday social interactions. Those who live in high contact cultures include the French, Italians, Africans, Arabs and Russians while those in low contact cultures include the Japanese and Chinese. Those in moderate contact cultures include the Northern Europeans, Australians, New Zealanders and the US Americans (Ting-Toomey 1999). There are also crucial cross-cultural differences in the rules for the use of touch. In Arabic cultures, for examples, a high degree of same sex touching among males is common in public. Males may even loosely hold hands in the initial stages of a greeting. Opposite sex touching in public, even handshakes, however is not acceptable. Men are much more likely to fully embrace each other in public in Latin American cultures than would be the case in Britain (Ting-Toomey 1999).

Facial expression

The meaning of **facial expression** is thought to vary less across cultures than is the case with some other non-verbal signs. The key role played by displays of facial expression is the conveying of emotion within social encounters. According to Ekman (1982) the main facial expressions are those for happiness, surprise, fear, sadness, anger, disgust and contempt. Facial expressions are an important source of feedback within the interpersonal communication process indicating how others are responding to our messages; they can also provide useful advance warning of the sender's emotional state and its likely impact on their communication. Facial expressions are not always linked to emotions; some are linked to speech. The eyebrow flash, for example is used mainly as a form of social acknowledgement and the eyebrows are often employed to express degrees of surprise, disbelief or misunderstanding (Argyle 1988).

Aware of what they may reveal, we may seek to control our facial expressions in order to conceal our true emotional state or responses. Ekman and Friesen (1982), for example, noted that the 'false' smile, one that does not extend to the eyes and cheek muscles, is often employed in everyday encounters to create a positive impression. Argyle (1988) argues that people are usually better able to control the information given off in facial expressions than in some other areas of non-verbal behaviour. Indeed some

o(
e)
b(
b(
a1
th
(1
ti
o

a(
(1
Ja
w
(/
o
o.

\ews presenter demand careful control of facial
may control our facial expressions, there may
onal state in other areas of our non-verbal
.on. Thus at a formal meeting our annoyance
evealed in the face but in the silent tapping of
: also points to the work of Haggard and Isaacs
ace, despite attempts to control it, can some-
'micromomentary' expressions the true nature
tate.

e main facial expressions appear to be similar
)erhaps their biological links to our emotions
; for display seem to vary across cultures. The
l negative emotions and mask these, in public,
lso be used to mask shyness or embarrassment
xample, cross-cultural differences in the degree
)le. Too much smiling is seen as an indication
ire (Samovar and Porter 2004). Public displays
of grief have ..   l much more muted in British culture than in
some Mediterranean .. . ..bic cultures.

Eye contact and gaze

These serve important functions in regulating social interaction. Establishing
eye contact is normally a means of initiating a social encounter just as a
decrease in eye contact is a sign that an encounter is coming to an end
although there is often increased looking as the encounter is concluded.
During a conversation the listener will signal their attention with frequent
eye contact while the speaker will, less frequently, use eye contact to check for
feedback. Lack of eye contact by the listener will usually be interpreted as lack
of interest. Turn-taking in conversations is also signalled by eye contact,
along with other signs (Gahagan 1984). Individuals will use more eye contact
in a conversation when they are further apart than when closer together.
People seem to reduce the amount of eye contact when discussing difficult
topics and to look less when sad or embarrassed. Increased eye contact may
also lead to more successful efforts at persuasion (Argyle 1988).

Higher than normal levels of mutual gazing is often a sign of intimacy
and mutual attraction; people also tend to look more at those they like.
However, prolonged eye contact can also be used to threaten or intimidate
others. For this reason awareness of the gaze of others can make us feel
uneasy. Gaze aversion can be used as a sign of submission (Argyle 1988).
Argyle (1988) mentions a number of studies which found that status hierarchies within groups can also be tracked by observing eye contact: there

existed an 'attention structure' in which gaze was used by subordinates to follow the behaviour of the leader(s). Higher status individuals tend to look less than normal when listening and more when speaking.

There are, however, cross-cultural differences in the level of gaze considered normal during encounters. In North America, Britain, Eastern Europe and in Jewish cultures direct eye contact is expected during conversations but less direct eye contact is the norm in the West Indies and among many Asians and African Americans (Axel 1998). Samovar and Porter (2004: 182) discuss a number of other studies that show that in some cultures, for example Latin America, the Caribbean, India and some African cultures, looking those who are of higher status in the eye can be viewed as a sign of disrespect.

Gesture

Morris (2002) identifies a number of gestures used to communicate non-verbally. Gestures can be made with a number of parts of the body such as the hands, arms, feet and head – head nods are normally considered as a gesture. 'Primary' gestures are those that have communication as their intention such as the hand wave. 'Incidental' gestures are those that arise not from the intention to communicate, for example scratching the nose when it itches, but may nevertheless be read as communicative by an observer – for example: the scratching of the nose might be interpreted as a sign of anxiety or deceit. Argyle identifies three main types of gestures used during social interaction: 'emblems', 'illustrators' and 'self-touching' movements.

Emblems have direct and well understood verbal equivalents within a group or subculture such as the peace sign. Illustrators accompany speech and illustrate what is being said as when, for example, indicating the size of a pizza eaten; they also include the baton gestures that trace the rhythm of speech. Self-touching is often an indicator of a person's emotional state but can also be used in courtship displays and grooming. Self-touching can be a displacement activity. Morris (2002) discusses the ways in which passengers waiting to board a plane often display subtle signs of nervousness such as earlobe-tugging and head-scratching. Gestures can be useful in the regulation of social interaction and provision of feedback. Rapid head nods, for example, can indicate agreement with a speaker while beckoning a friend over with a hand can signal the wish to start a conversation.

Some gestures are closely linked to certain roles or situations; these Morris describes as 'technical' gestures. These are needed, for example, when it is necessary to communicate over short distances in situations in which it is important to be quiet or secretive, or in which you could not be heard; examples here would include TV studios, auction rooms and casinos. Some gestures, 'coded' gestures, operate as part of a code and are more like a language; Morris provides examples here of sign language, semaphore and the tic-tac code used on a racecourse by those involved in betting on horses.

The meaning of gestures often varies across cultures thus caution needs to be exercised in their use. Gestures termed by Morris as 'symbolic' provide many such examples. Symbolic gestures are abstract signs for an object or action and can thus be ambiguous to those not familiar with the context of their normal use. So while in Saudi Arabia stupidity is indicated by touching the lower eyelid with the tip of the forefinger, this same gesture can have an entirely different range of meanings in other cultures: 'disbelief, approval, agreement, mistrust, scepticism, alertness, secrecy, craftiness, danger, or criminality' (2002: 34). Morris uses the term '*multi-message* gestures' for those that have considerable differences in meaning across cultures; another example is the gesture made by forming a circle with the thumb and forefinger. In Britain and the US this means 'OK' but in southern France it means 'worthless', in Malta it indicates a male homosexual while in Sardinia, Greece, Russia, Germany, Brazil and Bangladesh, for example, it is seen as an offensive gesture. The 'thumbs-up' gesture, while used to indicate all is well in Britain, means 'up yours' in Australia (Axel 1998).

Posture

Morris (2002: 412) comments that, 'General body posture, or "bearing", is one of the most widespread and common of all human Meta-signals' and argues that the ability to maintain a confident and energetic **posture** throughout interaction provides the speaker with a considerable advantage. We can also communicate a range of other messages through posture: those of emotional state, status, threat, fear and discomfort, for example (Argyle 1988). A slumped frame, with hands in pockets can be a sign of depression while leaning comfortably against a wall when talking to a friend suggests a relaxed attitude. An erect posture with the head held high can help convey status just as submission can be signalled by making the body appear smaller by hunching and lowering the body and head. In some cultures, the Japanese and German for example, body lowering, as in bowing, is still used as part of the greeting ritual. Body lowering is also widely used within religious rituals of worship in many cultures, to signify submission to the power of a deity. During a conversation a speaker who makes frequent body shifts may be revealing a sense of discomfort or unease or even the intention to deceive (Morris 2002).

Posture also plays a role in the regulation of interaction. Leaning towards the speaker shows interest in the conversation and provides encouragement just as an overly relaxed posture might suggest that the listener is bored. The sudden folding of arms may be signalling disagreement with the speaker. In many cultures sitting so that you show, or point, the soles of your feet to others is considered offensive. This is the case in Arab countries and also in countries such as Nigeria, Malaysia, Pakistan, India and Turkey (Axel 1998). Both **gestural** and **postural echo** have been observed to take place between speakers who are friends and enjoy a good rapport; each mirrors the other's postures and gestures throughout the conversation. Such mirroring facilitates a productive atmosphere and conversation. While it occurs naturally among good friends it can be consciously manipulated to both create and destroy rapport – the latter by deliberately providing a mismatch of gestures and postures rather than an echo. Spatial behaviour according to Argyle (1988: 168) 'consists of proximity, orientation, territorial behaviour, and movement in a physical setting'. Individuals appear to prefer to keep a certain distance between themselves and others; this distance depends upon the relationship, social setting and culture. In general we stand or sit closer to those we like and those we perceive to be similar to us. However violating these norms, that is getting too close, can be used as a means to dominate or threaten others. We also use space to indicate the desire to both initiate, by moving closer, and terminate, by moving away, a communicative encounter. We do seem able to deal with less space in certain situations where crowding is expected, when on the tube or at the first day of the sales, for example.

Hall (1966) argued that there were four main zones. The intimate zone is reserved for people with whom we have close relationships; the personal zone is for everyday encounters; the social zone occurs in the more formal settings such as business meetings and the public zone refers to the distance maintained between key public figures and the general public or an audience. Hall found that for middle-class European Americans the appropriate distances for each zone were as follows: intimate, 6 to 18 inches; personal, 18 inches to 4 feet; social, 4 to 12 feet; and public, over 12 feet and up to 25 feet. However these distances vary across cultures. Morris (2002) gives the comfortable distance for conversation among Western Europeans as that of the stretched out arm up to the fingertips, for Eastern Europeans it is the stretched out arm up to the wrists, while for those from the Mediterranean area it is the stretched upper arm, as far as the elbow.

Spatial behaviour

Morris (2002) argues that when our **personal space** is invaded in crowds we tend to respond by reducing our social signals: for example we avoid eye contact (think of passengers on crowded tube trains scrutinizing the advertisements) and we reduce the number of facial expressions and body movements we make. Individuals do not react well to those who violate these norms, to those who appear not to respect their space. Reaction to perceived violations seems to vary across cultures. Gudykunst and Ting-Toomey (1988) argue that there are differences between the way those from individualistic and collectivistic cultures deal with such invasions. While those from individualistic cultures tend to respond in an assertive, if not aggressive, manner those from collectivistic cultures tend to respond more in a passive, withdrawn manner.

Reviewing a number of studies, Ting-Toomey (1999) notes that several cultures maintain a closer distance for the typical conversation: some Latin American and Caribbean cultures (for example, Jamaican and Bahamian) maintain a distance of 32–35 centimetres, approximately. For some Arab cultures even that distance is too great: in Saudi Arabia 23–25 centimetres is more typical (Ferraro 1990). In general people in high contact cultures stand closer to one another (Argyle 1988). Clearly cross-cultural differences can be a source of misunderstanding in communicative encounters. Those who prefer to keep their distance may feel uncomfortable and intimidated when those from other cultures appear to stand 'too close for comfort'. Equally individuals used to close contact may judge those who 'keep their distance' as unsociable.

The **orientation** between people can also send messages about the nature of the relationship. Cook's studies (1970) showed that people tend to sit next to or adjacent to those with whom they have a cooperative relationship but are more inclined to sit opposite those with whom they are in competition or negotiation or those whom they do not like. We do, though, sit opposite friends when eating. However Ting-Toomey (1999) comments that in high contact cultures people often prefer a more direct orientation. Argyle (1988) notes that dominance and submission can also be communicated through orientation. Those with higher status in a social setting may be placed so as to be physically elevated above others, for example on a rostrum or stage or even in a higher chair. Orientation can also be used to regulate interaction as when, for example, someone stands up to signal the start of a speech or presentation. When we wish to change conversational partners or groups, say at a party, this can also be signalled by reorienting the body towards to those with whom we wish to converse (Argyle 1988).

Spatial behaviour extends to our use of **territory** and territorial markers. Morris (2002) identifies three kinds of territory: personal, family and tribal. An individual's territory is often associated with a sense of privacy, belonging, **identity** and security. Such personal territories typically include a person's bedroom, study, car, office, flat, house, or garden but can extend to a chair or seat – a student might have a preferred seat in the university library just as a commuter might have a favourite seat on the train. We tend to mark what we consider our territory (Morris 2002). Hence a university student might, in their absence, leave a sock, CD or book on their chair in the living room of a student house to remind the others of its rightful occupier.

The way in which we arrange furniture within our territories can also impact on communicative encounters (Samovar and Porter 2004). Furniture can be used to encourage or discourage interaction. For example, a large desk can be positioned in an office so that it always comes between the occupier and the person entering; desks in a seminar room can be placed in a horse-shoe design to facilitate interaction or in rows to inhibit it. Samovar and Porter point to some cross-cultural differences here. In a typical living room in the United States, chairs are positioned around the television set whereas in France, Italy and Mexico chairs are seated to encourage interpersonal interaction.

Our personal territory is also an important aspect of what Goffman (1959) termed the 'setting' for our everyday performances. Thus we might pay considerable attention to our choice of accommodation and its location, and to matters of interior and garden design, as we may perceive these 'props' to signal something about our social identities. A perspective encouraged, arguably, by numerous television programmes and the way in which certain **commodities** are promoted.

Territory can also be a marker of **group identity**. For a family the home is a key territorial space and many people spend considerable time and effort to stamp, through decoration, garden design and possessions, a particular mark on their home territory. Non-family members normally only enter this space on invitation. This territorial behaviour can extend beyond the home. Morris (2002) provides the example of a family trip to the beach. Once at the beach a family may use many markers of their temporary occupation of a favoured spot: windbreaks, towels, deckchairs and a frisbee, for example.

Ting-Toomey (1999) discusses general cultural differences in the arrangements and significance of the home environment. Within indivi-dualistic cultures the home might be seen as a private personal space but this is not the case in collectivistic cultures in which communal patterns of accommodation are common. Further, while personal privacy is valued in individualistic cultures this is not so much the case in collectivistic cultures and indeed the desire for such levels of privacy may be viewed negatively.

Tribal identity is a longstanding characteristic of human behaviour (Morris 2002). The tribe was once just local in nature, but now feelings of tribal identity attach not just to gangs, groups and neighbourhoods but also to national identity. Morris (2002: 189) notes that much of our tribal identity still rests in the groups to which we belong and that group identities are often marked by 'territorial signals' such as 'badges, costumes, headquarters, ban-ners, slogans and all other displays of group identity'. National flags are also tribal symbols and can be territorial markers. While the English flag may typically be displayed on property to display support for the English national football team, Bodi (2006) notes evidence that some residents of Preston use it as a territorial marker within a multicultural community. Sadly territorial markers can be employed to display deep divisions between people; contemporary examples here would include the murals painted on the end wall of rows of terraces in Northern Ireland that signal either Unionist or Republican areas and the 'separation barrier' that divides Israeli and Palestinian territories.

Non-verbal vocalizations

These can be divided into those that are linked to speech and those that are independent of it. Those that are linked to speech, include prosodic and synchronizing signals and speech disturbances (Argyle 1988). Prosodic signals involve the use of rhythm, intonation and pauses in speech; these features affect the meaning of the verbal content of the message. Take for example, the utterance 'Is that the price?' This can be interpreted as a question or an exclamation depending on the use of pitch and stress. Synchronizing signals are those used to regulate or control interaction; for instance, when falling pitch indicates that a person has finished speaking and someone else can start. Speech disturbances include repetitions, 'ums' and 'errs' and incomplete utterances. These can indicate, for example, nervousness or uncertainty on the part of the speaker.

Vocalizations that are independent of speech are emotional noises, paralinguistic features and those relating to personal voice quality and accent (Argyle 1988). Emotional noises and paralinguistic features convey messages about our emotional state and about our attitudes towards others. The voice also seems to give away quite accurately our true feelings towards someone: it is not what we say but the way that we say it. Pitch, speed and loudness are typically employed to carry these messages. Argyle, with reference to a number of studies, suggests that we can, for example, project friendliness, anger, anxiety, fear, dominance or submission. We also seem to make judgements about others on the basis of the individual quality of their voice: a number of studies have, for example, revealed the tendency to judge those with nasal voices as less credible. The role of regional **accents** in projecting identity and triggering social evaluations has already been discussed.

There are a number of cross-cultural differences in non-verbal aspects of speech and these could be a source of misunderstandings. Samovar and Porter (2004: 188) note, with reference to a number of studies, a range of differences: for example, Arabs speak with considerable volume and emphasis as this is taken as a sign of 'strength and sincerity' while in Thailand loudness is seen as impolite and similarly for the Japanese, 'a gentle and soft voice reflects good manners and helps maintain social harmony'. Thus while an Arab speaker may seem pushy and angry to a Japanese and Thai speaker, they in turn may seen uninterested and thus impolite to the Arab.

Exercise

Review cultural differences that you have experienced in non-verbal communication. Have they caused difficulties when communicating with others? If so, how were these difficulties overcome?

Appearance, dress and bodily adornment

Ellis and Beattie (1986) refer to appearance, dress and bodily adornment as the 'standing' features of interaction. In contrast to most other aspects of non-verbal communication these vary little during an encounter although dress and some bodily adornment can vary considerably between encounters. Aspects of appearance such as body size and stature, skin colour, age and sex are more stable. Dress and bodily adornment can signal the nature of the social setting as well as many messages about the self: cultural or group identity, gender, status, personality, ethnicity, faith, wealth, age, social roles and personal tastes, for example. Dress varies, though, in the clarity of messages sent; everyday dress may be open to a number of interpretations, uniforms less so. Appearance, dress and bodily adornment can be an important factor in the formation of first impressions and can form the basis for a number of assumptions made about us: competence and friendliness, for example. They can also trigger **stereotyping** (Baron et al. 2006). We may construct our appearance with considerable care when trying to cultivate a particular impression (Goffman 1959).

In *Hot Bodies Cool Styles* (2004) Polhemus charts the array of body adornment on display among the young in Western cultures. He argues that in these cultures we have access to a 'global 24/7 supermarket of style' (2004: 8) from which to choose artefacts and adornments to express **personal identity** – our sense of uniqueness as an individual. Evident in contemporary adornments is the influence of tribal styles, for example in ethnic clothing, tattoos, body piercings, scarification and body painting, all of which are to be found on display at numerous music festivals. Polhemus notes that few young people, however, actually belong to those subcultures that try to live a tribal lifestyle. He also reminds us that tattoos and body painting were likely to have been found among the tribes of ancient Britain. Today we can observe the painted faces among the crowds of football, rugby and tennis fans, each individual proclaiming their tribal allegiance.

These contemporary styles reflect the range of intercultural exchanges that have taken place over the centuries; styles of body adornment that borrow from many other cultures to the extent that Polhemus (2004: 115) argues, 'Western culture is affected today by the broadest geographic range of styles in its history'. One example here would be Mehndi art: the use of henna to paint temporary designs on the body – typically the hands and feet. This form of art stems from India, North Africa, the Middle East and South East Asia, where it has been traditionally used to mark significant occasions. While such traditional uses are found among ethnic communities in the West, for example in Indian communities to celebrate weddings, it is also more widely used as a personal body decoration.

There are many cultural differences as regards appearance. Baron et al. (2006) note a number of studies that suggest that while being significantly overweight may be viewed negatively in the USA, to the extent that those thought obese can be stigmatized, in some other cultures, say Mexico, this is less likely to be the case. Wearing traditional dress can be an important signifier of ethnic identity and faith within a multicultural society. According to Pittock (1999) tartan clothing is still a significant symbol of Scottish identity. Similarly wearing a sari can celebrate an Indian heritage. The Islamic faith encourages modesty in dress, particularly for women, and traditional female dress in some middle-eastern countries – Saudi Arabia for example – covers almost the whole body, a style also adopted by some female followers of Islam in Britain. For Sikh males long hair, often worn under a turban, is a sign of spirituality while for Buddhist males this is signified by the shaved head (Mercer 1987).

Style: subculture, tribes and D I Y

Dick Hebdige (1979) highlighted the ways in which dress could be an important signifier of subcultural identity. His original study focused on youth subcultures and the way in which these can use style to signify their identity, values and resistance to the dominant culture. The punk style that emerged in 1970s Britain, for example, made use of everyday commodities such as razor blades, safety pins, tampons and zips, in a way that subverted their normal use – the use of razor blades as earrings, for example – to produce what Vivienne Westwood described as 'confrontation dressing'. The style mirrored punk music in its celebration of shock, alienation, chaos and disjunction and its aggressive rejection of mainstream society – a society that seemed to have rejected working-class youth at a time of high youth employment.

Hebdige argued that, as is the case with a number of styles adopted by youth subcultures in Britain, punk drew on influences from the culture of the West Indian community. For example, the punk aesthetic designed to connotate a sense of alienation and exile echoed themes central also to the Rastafarian subculture of the same era. While for the Rastafarians the exile was from their spiritual homeland, for the punks it was a desolate 'internal exile' in their own land.

As Hebdige points out not all who dressed in the style would have been equally aware of its intended meanings or equally committed to the sub-culture. This is borne out by a later study conducted by Sue Widdicombe and Robin Wooffitt. They used a combination of discourse and conversational analysis to explore what subcultures mean to their members. The study illustrates considerable variation in the way in which members read the meanings of a subculture and its contribution to their sense of identity. The following interview extract illustrates ambiguities as regards the punk subculture:

> R: hhh e::r well I dun*no* i- (.) tch
> it's *har:*d to descri:be 'cos er:,
> there's so *di*fferent *me*anings about punks
>   (Widdicombe and Wooffitt 1995: 194)

Looking at more recent styles, the 'modern primitives' are described by Muggleton and Weinzierl (2004: 17) as 'a peculiarly post-modern phenom-enon'. A cultural hybrid, they draw their style from tribal practices of body adornment and modification but followers are found within 'modern, urban White' locations. Winge (2004) argues that the style reflects a longing for the simplicities and freedoms romantically imagined to be typical of the everyday life of primitive tribes and communicates a rejection of the anxieties and complexities of modern life. Thus control of the body substitutes for a felt inability to control the forces driving and shaping modern societies – echoes here, perhaps, of the sense of alienation evident in the punk and Rastafarian subcultures. However as Widdicombe and Wooffitt's earlier work suggests, there is likely to be individual variation in how the style is used and what it is intended to convey.

Winge (2004: 122) provides some examples of their practices of body modification: 'septum piercings (similar to those worn in Papua New Guinea), elongated earlobes (similar to those of some North American Indians), scar-ification designs (similar to those of the Tiv in Africa) and blackwork tattoos (similar to those of Borneo)'. Winge reminds us, however, that modern pri-mitives may borrow from tribal cultures they have labelled as primitive, but in such cultures modification practices typically marked fixed identities, rites of passage and lifelong membership of the tribe.

It is argued by a number of researchers that subculture and style have become disconnected since the 1980s. While some subcultures may express group membership through style (the tattoos and leathers sported by bikers, for example) many young people raid what Polhemus has termed the 'supermarket of style' primarily to express personal identity and will borrow from and move between past styles with a 'stylistic promiscuity which is breathtaking in its casualness' (1994: 131). Contemporary groupings resemble small tribes more than the larger youth subcultures of the past. What has been lost though, arguably, is the sense of group solidarity lent by such subcultures as the Teddy boys, rockers or mods. Youth subcultural styles also fall prey to the process of incorporation: a process by which they are modified, shorn of their radical potential and repackaged within mainstream fashion. The media, fashion and cultural industries now play a significant role in constructing and marketing youth culture and associated identities.

If the solidarity of class-based youth subcultures has diminished, the emergence of a multicultural society and the development of global communications technology has, arguably, facilitated the emergence of global youth cultures and the resultant hybridization found in styles of music and fashion. Huq (2004), for example, traces the influences of urban Black American music, fashion and language on New Asian Dance Music and its followers in Britain.

Polhemus (2004: 12) argues that in a culturally diverse social environment, 'style has become a crucial, indispensable tool – a language system' for the expression of personal identity and that for many, the contemporary 'DIY' approach to appearance is a potent means of saying 'I am here' (2004: 147). Individual personal style can be constructed using a range of artefacts drawn from other subcultures and cultures, past and present. As regards the Western world Polhemus (2004: 10) comments: 'What you look like is no longer strictly determined by social situation and culture or even fashion. Free from rules, appearance is now a matter of personal creativity'.

Exercise

Consider the above statement by Polhemus. To what extent do you agree that your personal appearance is 'now a matter of personal creativity'? Are there sociocultural expectations that constrain your choices regarding appearance and if so, where do they come from and in what situations do they apply?

Non-verbal communication, identity and consumption

> One of the most important ways in which people relate to each other socially is through the mediation of things.
>
> (Lury 1996: 1)

Western societies are generally regarded as 'consumer' societies in which 'the personal consumption of goods and services becomes an all-powerful force' (Berger 2005: 1). Social interaction within these societies is therefore framed by the emphasis placed on the consumption of goods. Arguably one of the most important aspects of non-verbal communication relates to the things that we consume – things deliberately chosen to send messages about ourselves to others. Featherstone, for example, claims that 'One's body, clothes, speech, leisure pastimes, eating and drinking preferences, home, car, choice of holidays etc. are to be regarded as indicators of the individuality of taste and sense of style of the owner/consumer (1991: 83). We are all sophisticated 'readers' of these non-verbal signs and can swiftly make a range of assumptions about a person from their patterns of consumption. It is possible to argue, therefore, that: 'It is by and large through commodities that everyday life, and the social relations and identities that we live within it, are sustained and reproduced' (Slater 1997: 27).

Objects of consumption clearly act as a mediating factor in social interaction but, perhaps more significantly, they play a key role in the formation of self-identity in modern societies, in which traditional roles and identities are no longer fixed, but need to be constructed. Individuals therefore can use goods, not to shore up an existing sense of self-identity, but to 'become the being they desire to be by consuming the items that they imagine will help to create and sustain their idea of themselves, their image, their identity' (Bocock 1993: 68). Or in other words to 'shop' for an identity.

For commentators such as Giddens, identities formed primarily by consumption are 'non-authentic' identities, constructed by advertisers keen to promote goods as accoutrements to certain 'lifestyle' choices. Such identities, formed by consumption, are also ephemeral, subject to the whims of the rapidly changing marketplace. Within postmodernism an extreme version of this is proposed in which 'society appears as a kind of fancy-dress party in which identities are designed, tried on, worn for the evening and then traded in for the next' (Slater 1997: 30). Giddens argues, however, that although 'identity shopping' can impede the development of the 'true' self, individuals are not merely the 'dupes' of advertisers. He claims that people are able to negotiate individual meanings from the range of goods available, stating that 'mass produced clothing still allows individuals to decide selectively on styles of dress, however much the standardizing influence of fashion and other forces affect those individual decisions' (1991: 200). Although ultimately, Giddens believes that 'The reflexive project of the self is in some part necessarily a struggle against commodified influences' (p. 200).

Berger also points to the pitfalls of 'shopping for an identity' arguing that individuals living within a consumer society have a tendency to adopt a 'marketing personality' by which he means 'they learn to "sell" or market themselves to others by creating a personality geared towards finding acceptance among whatever individuals or groups with which they are involved' (2005: 79). Berger claims that such people become 'alienated from themselves, estranged from what we might call their "true selves"' (p. 79).

The start of the novel *Fight Club* provides a good illustration of this, when Tyler Durden attempts to escape from his 'false' IKEA-fuelled identity and discover his 'true' self by blowing up his condominium and all its IKEA contents:

> Something which was a bomb, a big bomb, had blasted my clever Njurunda coffee tables in the shape of a lime green yin and an orange yan that fit together to make a circle. Well they were splinters, now.
>
> My Haparanda sofa group with the orange slip covers, design by Erika Pekkari, it was trash now.
>
> And I wasn't the only slave to my nesting instinct. The people I know who used to sit in the bathroom with pornography, now they sit in the bathroom with their IKEA furniture catalogue.
>
> We all have the same Johanneshov armchair in the Strinne green stripe pattern. Mine fell fifteen stories, burning, into a fountain.
>
> (Palahniuk 2006: 43)

Ultimately, in *Fight Club*, Palahniuk seeks to expose the ruthless ideology at the heart of American consumer driven society in which everything has a price and citizens are seemingly unaware of their subjugation to the capitalist system.

Unlike Tyler Durden, most individuals in Western societies do not reject the fundamental principles of consumerism, even though they might be concerned about some aspects of consumption, such as environmental issues. In fact most people actively use consumption to indicate their wealth and status. Leiss et al. claim that 'The construction of social relations through goods is one of the strongest threads binding together human development from the earliest times to our own' and that 'material objects, having a certain permanence and being easily distinguishable from each other, serve ideally to mark social distinctions according to who possesses or controls any particular thing and who does not' (1997: 311–12). The American economist Thorstein Veblen in *The Theory of the Leisure Class* (written in 1899) examined the consumption habits of the nouveau riche 'leisure class' in America whom he argued used the consumption of expensive (and tasteful) goods and conspicuous leisure time to indicate their elite **status** to others. He also noted that this conspicuous consumption resulted in social emulation, as those of lower status sought to gain respectability by buying goods associated with the more prosperous group. Veblen (1998: 31) points out that the key problem with social emulation is that there is no end to the 'catch-up' game:

> But as fast as a person makes new acquisitions, and becomes accustomed to the resulting new standard of wealth, the new standard

forthwith ceases to afford appreciably greater satisfaction than the earlier standard did. The tendency in any case is constantly to make the present pecuniary standard the point of departure for a fresh increase in wealth; and this in turn gives rise to a new standard of sufficiency and a new pecuniary classification of one's self as compared with one's neighbours.

Veblen also claimed that wealth acquired from ancestors was 'more honorific than wealth acquired by the possessor's own effort' (1998: 29). This remains true of British society today in which the newly wealthy are not afforded the same status as the aristocracy. In addition Veblen noted that within middle-class families 'there is no pretence of leisure on the part of the head of the household' but 'the middle-class wife still carries on the business of vicarious leisure' (p. 81). Again parallels can be drawn with contemporary British society in which women are still more often associated with both conspicuous consumption and conspicuous leisure activities. Finally, Veblen pointed out that the promotion of social status via consumption was partly a result of increased urbanization and the relative anonymity of city life. In the countryside with smaller centres of population and less movement of people such displays would be unnecessary. Arguably, twenty-first century British society is becoming more fluid and increasingly anonymous hence the continued need to assert one's identity and signal status via consumption.

The communication of social status is clearly inextricably linked with the consumption of certain types of goods, usually resulting in a 'trickle down' effect, in which lower status groups seek to gain status by acquiring 'high status' goods. This is an idea developed by the French sociologist Pierre Bourdieu in *Distinction: A Social Critique of the Judgement of Taste* (1986, first published in 1979) in which he also argues that social groups use consumption habits to help maintain their identities. Bourdieu claims, however, that the key factor that distinguishes the social classes is not their relative wealth, but their relative educational standing and most importantly their sense of cultural **'taste'**. He states that the possession of cultural, rather than economic capital enables the educated group to retain social dominance over the less educated group because of their ability to make 'distinctions' based on 'taste'. Bourdieu

> describes how individuals struggle to improve their social position by manipulating the cultural representation of their situation in the social field. They accomplish this, in part, by affirming the superiority of their taste and lifestyle with a view to legitimizing their own identity as best representing what it means to be 'what it is right to be'.

(Lury 1996: 83)

Bourdieu also introduces the concept of 'habitus' arguing that 'lifestyles are systematic products of habitus, that is, habitus is a system through which we surround ourselves with, and desire, certain objects according to our perceptions of the social world' (Paterson 2006: 44). It could be argued therefore, that habitus determines the clothes that we buy, the places we go and the people with whom we socialize. For Bourdieu the consumption possibilities that have been rejected are as important as the commodities finally selected. For example an individual could define themselves as someone who does *not*: shop at Tesco, wear M&S clothes, drink beer or watch Sky Sports, etc.

This leads to the possibility of consumer choices being conceived as a loose sign system with its own 'langue' and 'parole' (following Ferdinand de Saussure's model). The 'langue' represented by the individual items consumed and the 'parole' by the combination of these items presented at any one time. If an individual is, for example, wearing a certain set of clothes and is found in a milieu that compliments the clothing, then it might be argued that this results in a 'coherent' act of communication. If the various items selected do not 'match' (i.e. don't appear to form part of a coherent system) then their 'meaning' will be more difficult to decode. Finally it is important to point out that the 'meaning' of the individual signs is not fixed, but arbitrary, governed by social convention (and that in any case all signs are polysemic, open to a wide range of possible interpretations).

Goods, therefore, can potentially symbolically transmit complex meanings about the self and are considered an 'important means whereby consumers can communicate to others their relationships to complex sets of otherwise abstract social attributes (such as status), thus identifying themselves within social structures' (Leiss et al. 1997: 292). The key question that arises from this is: how do meanings become attached to commodities? Using Veblen's analysis, it might be claimed that the commodities consumed by elite groups have no more intrinsic value than those consumed by lower status groups. It is merely their association with the high status group that makes them symbolically prized. Many commentators, however, would point to the role played by advertisers who attempt to 'assign' meanings to goods by associating them with desirable 'lifestyles' that individuals can 'buy into' by the purchasing of compatible commodities. The fact that those wishing to sell goods have artificially created these 'lifestyles' returns us to Giddens' (1991) concerns about the formation of 'false' rather than 'true' identities. In addition it has been claimed that advertising

> creates demand, which would not exist in its absence, by manipulating people's normal motivational impulses. Advertisers, it is held, manipulate people by subtly mixing reality and fantasy, by creating a 'magic show' that makes it hard to tell what one's 'real

needs' are or where to draw a line between sensible behaviour and careless overindulgence.

(Leiss et al. 1997: 32)

Although these negative statements can be counterbalanced by Fowles' (1996: 225–6) claim that

> Advertising and popular culture are overestimated as agents in the development of self-identity ... Although visible, the content of the media is only symbolic; it is never alive, never palpable. As such, it has little coercive power and can be accepted or rejected, in whole or in part, according to the needs or whims of the spectator.

Case study: Burberry

The recent crisis at aspirational clothing company Burberry illustrates the extent to which the 'meaning' of consumer goods can be subject to rapid change. The 2000 Burberry clothing and accessory range, which prominently featured Burberry's trademark check, had initially been phenomenally successful. The wearing of Burberry clothing quickly became established as a mark of 'distinction'.

For positional companies such as Burberry, the 'elite' connotations of the brand are vital to its success because 'Consumer culture is crucially about the negotiation of status and identity – the practice and communication of social position' (Slater 1997: 30). Unfortunately for Burberry, the 'elite' connotations associated with the brand were undermined when Burberry check was widely adopted as the badge of an 'undesirable' group, the 'chavs', and within a few months the Burberry brand became synonymous with 'lower' class taste.

The Burberry case study illustrates a number of key points:

- Clearly 'Commodities are not just objects of economic exchange; they are goods to think with, goods to speak with' (Fiske 1989: 31).
- Commodities such as Burberry clothing can, given the right context, serve as a mark of social distinction.
- The 'meanings' attached to such commodities are not fixed, but subject to continual change.
- Advertising can help to establish a certain brand image, but clearly other factors exert a powerful influence over the status of a brand (no amount of advertising, for example, would have altered the public's negative perception of Burberry check after 2002).
- Successful positional consumption in the twenty-first century is a complex affair. Simply being wealthy enough to afford designer

clothes and other aspirational lifestyle accessories is not necessarily a mark of 'distinction', indeed it can be an indicator of 'poor' taste. Consider, for example, the treatment of David and Victoria Beckham in the British press – despite their wealth and success they are often mocked for their lack of 'cultural capital'.

Exercise

a) Examine the argument that the way in which the 'Chav' sub-culture 'adopted' Burberry check was tantamount to a 'tactical raid' on the symbolic meaning of the brand, that is an example of what Eco termed 'semiotic guerrilla warfare'.

b) To what extent do you believe that people consciously 'appropriate' non-verbal signs to construct statements about their identity?

This chapter has explored, among other topics, cultural differences in non-verbal communication. Chapter 6 looks at other factors to be considered in cross-cultural communication.

Key points

- Non-verbal communication is a key feature of our everyday performances. Like language it is rooted in culture. There are, therefore, significant cultural differences in its use. While the elements of non-verbal communication are thought to be universal, the rules for their display and the meaning of some non-verbal signs, vary across cultures.
- Non-verbal signs can be used to display group identity – the use of territorial markers being an example here.
- Elements of non-verbal communication such as appearance and dress may be significant features in the display not only of sub-cultural and co-cultural identity but also of self-identity.
- The commodities that we choose communicate important messages about ourselves to others and 'it is by and large through commodities that everyday life, and the social relations and identities that we live within it, are sustained and reproduced' (Slater 1997: 27).
- Commodities play a key role in the development of self-identity, although commentators such as Giddens argue that 'identity shopping' can impede the development of the 'true self' and that 'The reflexive project of the self is in some part necessarily a struggle against commodified influences' (1991: 200).

- The novel *Fight Club* offers a very good case study of an individual who begins to questions his self-identity in a consumption driven society.
- Veblen's *The Theory of the Leisure* (1998) proposes that high status groups feel the need to demonstrate their status through conspicuous consumption and conspicuous leisure activities. He also noted that this resulted in social emulation, as those of lower status sought to gain respectability by buying goods associated with the more prosperous group.
- Bourdieu emphasizes the importance of 'cultural capital', which allows certain social groups to make 'distinctions' based on taste. He also introduces the concept of 'habitus', 'a system through which we surround ourselves with, and desire, certain objects according to our perceptions of the social world' (Paterson 2006: 44).
- It is possible to conceive of consumer choices as a 'sign system' that loosely follows Ferdinand de Saussure's model. Individuals are as likely to be defined by the commodities (signs) they reject as the ones finally selected.
- The power of advertising has been hotly debated. Can it 'manipulate people by subtly mixing reality and fantasy' (Leiss et al. 1997: 32)? Or has it 'little coercive power and can be accepted or rejected … according to the needs or whims of the spectator' (Fowles 1996: 226)?
- The Burberry case study illustrates that the 'meaning' of commodities is not fixed, but highly fluid. It also introduces the notion of 'tactical raids' on the symbolic meaning of positional brands.

6   Cross-cultural Communication

The multicultural nature of British society ensures that a consider-able number of communicative encounters will occur between individuals from different cultural backgrounds – though some areas of Britain are more culturally diverse than others. Within any single year many people will travel abroad for either business or pleasure and encounter other cultures. Many organizations, including uni-versities, operate on a global basis and thus have a culturally diverse workforce and customer base. Britain hosts many international conferences and festivals. It is also a member of the European Union, a cross-cultural political and economic entity.

The Womad festival of world music held at Reading, in 2006, to take one example, not only celebrated cultural diversity in music, but also hosted stalls promoting an array of artefacts – such as clothes, food and body art – originating from a range of different cultures. Also to be found at the 2006 festival were the stalls and tents of those advocating action on global issues ranging from the plight of the Palestinians and prisoners in Guantanamo Bay to water shortages in Africa and other environmental concerns. One stall with a more local focus was that promoting inter-faith relations within Reading. Both performers and festival-goers were drawn from a mix of countries, cultures and faiths, as are the residents of Reading itself. This one event, alone, provided considerable opportunity for cross-cultural encounters.

There are therefore many contexts in which such encounters take place and where in Schramm's terms 'fields of experience' may not overlap. This chapter considers some of the factors that a range of theorists have argued impact on the process of interpersonal communication in a cross-cultural context and it also considers advice on how to avoid problems in cross-cultural communication. Chapter 5 looks at cultural differences in non-verbal communication.

Introduction

Larry Samovar and Richard Porter (2004: 2) offer a useful definition of intercultural communication: 'Intercultural communication is the circumstance in which people from diverse cultural backgrounds interact with one another', adding: 'The crucial element of this form of communication is culture and the impact it has on your communicative behaviour. Culture strongly influences your beliefs, values and worldviews: it is reflected in your use of language, your non-verbal behaviour, and how you relate to others' (2004: 3).

Samovar and Porter argue that 'intercultural communication will have two major points of contact: international and domestic. International contacts are those between people from different countries and cultures' (2004: 5). It also needs to be acknowledged 'that within each culture there are numerous co-cultures and specialized cultures. These provide the opportunity for domestic points of intercultural contact' (2004: 5). A home student studying at a British university, for example, may interact with international students from a wide range of countries but also with students from different co-cultures within Britain. Trompenaars and Woolliams (2004: 211) make the point that ethnic groups 'often share the same meaning as their forefathers in the inner layer of culture' and the family may remain a particularly important reference point. Thus cultural variables relating to the area from which an ethnic group originated, several generations ago, may still have an impact on the communicative behaviour of its members in contemporary British society. Obviously this is much more likely to be the case for those who have recently arrived.

William B. Gudykunst and Young Yun Kim (1997: 22) remind us that 'the underlying process of communication between people from different cultures or subcultures is the same as the underlying process of communication between people from the same culture or subculture'; thus we should not underestimate the similarities while acknowledging the differences. In addition to the cultural differences found in language and non-verbal communication, cultural identities, assumptions and expectations can significantly influence perceptions and judgements of behaviour and thus affect the way in which messages are encoded and decoded; they can be, therefore, a considerable source of 'noise' within the interpersonal communication process.

Cross-cultural variables

Trompenaars and Woolliams (2004) liken culture to an onion. The outer layer contains that which we can perceive most easily: for example, buildings, clothes and people. Beneath this skin lies a deeper layer of culture, one that significantly influences the way in which its people behave. Here are to be found the beliefs, values, norms and expectations that frame the way in which people perceive and engage with the world. These differences stem from the 'innermost layer' (2004: 15), the basic assumptions that a culture has developed over time in dealing with challenges and crises across the centuries. A society's culture is also dynamic; elements are modified and change over time as these challenges and crises arise and are dealt with.

As Trompenaars and Woolliams point out, while a culture can be viewed as 'a collective sharing the same frame of reference' (2004: 48), both co-cultural and individual differences mediate the way in which cultural variables affect any one individual's behaviour in any one communicative encounter. Ultimately interpersonal communication, though framed by cultural assumptions, is a transaction between individuals. Several studies have identified key cross-cultural variables that may impact on intercultural encounters. The first two, those of Hofstede and Trompenaars and Hampden-Turner, are based largely on data collected from a business context but offer a useful starting point.

Hofstede's five dimensions

Geert Hofstede (2001) identifies five dimensions along which national cultures could be compared. His studies include his original research carried out in subsidiaries of IBM, the research carried out by Michael Bond in formulating the Chinese Value Survey (1985) and a review of other relevant studies on cross-cultural variables. In all 50 countries are covered in his research.

Power distance

> The extent to which the less powerful members of institutions and organizations within a country expect and accept that power is distributed unequally.
>
> (Hofstede, 2001: 98)

Thus **power distance** refers to the power relationships that exist between individuals and the way in which inequalities in such relationships are perceived and acknowledged within a national culture. At one end of the power distance dimension, according to Hofstede, lie high-power-distance cultures, such as Malaysia, India and Arab countries, that regard hierarchies and the power differences that underpin them as the norm, while at the other end lie low-power-distance cultures, such as Britain, Ireland, Austria, Sweden and the

United States, that seek to reduce and downplay power differences among its members.

Hofstede (2001) provides some examples of how power distance may impact on everyday behaviour.

In high-power-distance cultures

- children are taught to obey their parents and respect their teachers;
- people are not seen as equal but have an allotted place within society;
- people expect to be told what to do by those in power at work or in government;
- there is a tendency for 'military, autocratic or oligarchic' systems of government and the dominant religions often also 'stress stratification and hierarchy'.

In low-power-distance cultures

- children are treated as equals by both parents and teachers;
- people are viewed as deserving equal rights and treatment;
- power differences are accepted when such differences are seen as legitimate and convenient;
- governments are pluralistic and democratically elected, and the dominant religions also tend to emphasize equality.

Uncertainty avoidance

> Uncertainty about the future is a basic fact of human life with which we try to cope through the domains of technology, law and religion. In organizations these take the form of technology, rules, and rituals.
>
> Hofstede (2001: 161)

The dimension of **uncertainty avoidance** refers to how different cultures cope with the uncertainties of life and seeks to measure, as Hofstede notes, 'The extent to which the members of a culture feel threatened by uncertain or unknown situations' (2001: 161). High-uncertainty-avoidance cultures, according to Hofstede, such as Greece, Portugal, Spain and Japan seek to minimize the threats posed by uncertainty by actively promoting stability. Examples of such attempts, provided by Hofstede, include:

- the obligatory carrying of identity cards;
- the generation of numerous 'precise laws and regulations';
- intolerance of civil protest and an emphasis on the importance of consensus;
- a tendency to be less tolerant of immigrants.

People living in such cultures also experience more stress and concern about the future. Low-uncertainty-avoidance cultures, such as Jamaica, Great Britain, Ireland and Singapore, are more accepting of and less worried by life's uncertainties. Such cultures are more tolerant of difference and eccentricity and have relatively fewer rules and regulations. Hofstede argues here are to be found, for example:

- greater tolerance towards immigrants;
- no obligation to carry identity cards;
- acceptance of political protest;
- respect for diversity of beliefs;
- a willingness 'to live from day to day'.

Individualism-collectivism

One key cultural variable identified by a number of researchers is the degree to which a culture may be predominately, though not exclusively, collectivistic or individualistic. Hofstede (2001: 209) states that the dimension of individualism-collectivism 'describes the relationship between the individual and the collectivity that prevails in a given society. It is reflected in the way people live together – for example, in nuclear families, extended families, or tribes – and it has many implications for values and behaviour.' Cultures, he argues, in which **collectivistic tendencies** predominate, are those found in Singapore, Pakistan, West Africa and Guatemala, for example. These cultures emphasize the crucial importance of the ties and obligations resulting from membership of in-groups. Hofstede (2001: 225) notes that in such cultures 'people from birth onwards are integrated into strong, cohesive in-groups, which throughout people's lifetime continue to protect them in exchange for unquestioning loyalty'.

Although people tend to belong to a few in-groups, for example: family, friendship and workplace groups, these will exercise a strong, general influence over the behaviour of their members and it is common to find arranged marriages within such cultures. Economic and financial activity also often revolves around family ties. In collectivistic cultures the interests of the in-group are viewed as more important than those of individual members so individuals are obliged to defer to in-group priorities and put the interests of the group first – as Hofstede notes a ' "We" consciousness' prevails (2001: 227).

Hofstede (2001) discusses further characteristics:

- As in-group identification is strong, cooperation, the maintenance in-group harmony, and avoiding conflict is valued.
- Respect for the 'face' of others in the group is also seen as important.

- Those religions found within collectivistic cultures often stress the importance of shared religious practices.

Triandis (1988) notes that in collectivistic cultures there are often marked differences between the manner in which in-group members treat and communicate with each other in comparison to those in out-groups, as they typically apply different standards of behaviour when dealing with out-group members.

In contrast are those cultures in which Hofstede argues **individualistic tendencies** predominate, such as the United States, Australia, Great Britain and Sweden. Here the emphasis is on the importance of the individual as the basic unit of society. Hofstede explains that 'Individualism stands for a society in which the ties between individuals are loose: Everyone is expected to look after him/herself and his/her immediate family only' (2001: 225). Thus emphasis is given to the individual's aims, interests, achievements and self-development. In these cultures individuals are expected to

- speak out
- be competitive
- stand out from the crowd rather than merge into a group identity.

Individuals are often members of a number of in-groups but most of these will have a relatively limited and specific influence over their behaviour. Personal privacy and space is valued. Thus in individualistic cultures, Hofstede argues, an '"I" consciousness' prevails and 'Identity is based on the individual' (2001: 227).

Such cultures place value on individual rights and freedoms, and they may also be seen as hedonistic. Economic activity tends also to emphasize individual rather than group interests. Conflict and confrontation are not unusual and can be seen as potentially beneficial. As regards religious behaviour, the individual nature of a person's relationship with a deity is stressed. Individualistic cultures adopt the same standards of behaviour towards both in-groups and out-groups and fewer noticeable differences are to be found between the ways in which people communicate with in-group and out-group members (Triandis 1988).

Individualism-collectivism is a dimension however, and most societies will have features of both collectivism and individualism within them. Also not all people will necessarily identify strongly with the predominant tendency of the culture in which they live. This is particularly likely to be the case in multicultural societies like Britain in which there are a number of ethnic communities whose members originate, some of course quite recently, from collectivistic cultures. Further, the collectivistic nature of traditional British working-class communities needs to be acknowledged even though these communities have been subject to much change since the 1960s, but especially since the 1980s, as a consequence of social and economic pressures.

Gudykunst and Kim (1997) identify three factors that influence the degree to which individualism and collectivism may impact on any one person's behaviour. These are: **personality orientations, individual values and self construals**. They refer to the work of Triandis et al. (1985) regarding the personality orientations of **idiocentrism** – concern for one's own needs and achievement – and **allocentrism** – concern for others. These orientations can exaggerate or modify cultural influences. Thus within an collectivistic culture, someone with an idiocentric orientation may have considerable regard for self-interest and resent the ties of in-group members in comparison to an individual with a strong allocentric orientation (Triandis et al. 1988). The **values** that an individual holds can also moderate the impact of culture. These values may stem from religious or political beliefs – the importance of charity and compassion for others, for example. Such values are likely to affect the degree to which an individual is influenced, say, by the prevailing values of individualistic societies.

Gudykunst and Kim (1997) argue, with reference to a range of studies, that **self-perception** can also mediate the cultural influences of individualism or collectivism. Markus and Kitayama (1991), for example, identify independent and interdependent self construals as an important influence on people's behaviour. Each person will have both an independent and interdependent self construal but one will tend to predominate. Independent self construals emphasize the individual nature of each person whereas interdependent self construals emphasize the collective nature of human activity and experience. The focus of the independent self construal is on the expression and achievement of individual aims while that of the interdependent self construal will be on maintaining good relationships with in-group members and the achievement of in-group aims.

Gudykunst and Kim (1997: 63) propose that 'The independent construal of self predominates in individualistic cultures, and the interdependent construal of self predominates in collectivistic cultures'. However,

> people with predominately interdependent construals of the self exist in individualistic cultures like that of the United States and Australia, and people with predominately independent construals of the self exist in collectivistic cultures like that of Japan or Korea.
>
> (1997: 64)

These factors remind us that while human behaviour may be subject to broad cultural forces, it is unlikely to be totally determined by these given that they interact with individual and sociocultural variables. It is not that easy, therefore, to predict how any one individual may behave in a given situation simply with reference to the nature of the general cultural influences to which they have been exposed.

There are many contexts in which communication crosses cultures, the business context being one. Ting-Toomey (1999) discusses the impact of individualism and collectivism on the process of **conflict management**. She argues that those from individualistic cultures tend to adopt an 'outcome-orientated model' that judges the process for its 'effectiveness' in achieving the desired ends; those from collectivistic cultures, on the other hand, tend to adopt a more 'process-orientated' model that judges the process for its 'appropriateness' in terms of the behaviour of those involved.

These different assumptions lead to a range of other differences in approaching conflict management. Those from individualistic cultures have a tendency to: focus on the end result; expect frank and open discussions; prefer set deadlines by which decisions should be made; give emphasis to facts and figures; be competitive; perform as individuals; and judge the success of negotiations in terms of obtaining concrete goals. Collectivists, however, have a tendency to: focus on the process and maintaining relationships; pay attention to facework; avoid direct confrontation; seek cooperation; be less concerned by deadlines; give due consideration to intuition and experience as well as facts; perform as a group; consider the wider context of the negotiations; and judge negotiations to be successful if mutually beneficial goals have been achieved while preserving reputations and good relationships. For collectivists there cannot be a successful outcome unless relationships are maintained and there is greater emphasis on long-term perspectives thus it may be considered wise to concede today in order to gain later. Of course there will be differences in the degree to which individuals from either kind of culture are influenced by these general patterns of behaviour.

Cultural variables can also impact upon the reception of **advertising messages**. Advertisements seek to appeal to both the mass audience and the individual; they are decoded in the minds of individual receivers. In attempting to persuade the consumer advertisers can try to appeal to the consumer's self-identity, to make the claim that the product will promote self-development or aid self-presentation. As McCracken (1986) notes products can be promoted for their 'signalling properties', for what they say about us to others. However, how we read these messages about ourselves seems to be subject to cultural influences. In discussing the impact of individualism and collectivism upon the encoding and decoding of advertisements de Mooij (1998: 189) notes that in collectivistic cultures being alone tends to be regarded in a negative light and thus advertisements featuring just one individual run the risk of suggesting that the person has 'no friends, no identity' not the kind of message advertisers usually want to have associated with their product. Thus people are often featured in groups and the benefits the product can bring to the group are emphasized. In individualistic cultures, on the other hand, it is relatively common to feature one person and individualistic appeals.

Masculinity – femininity

This dimension refers to the relative value placed upon what are considered masculine or feminine qualities in different cultures. Hofstede (2001: 297) defines masculinity and femininity as follows:

> Masculinity stands for a society in which social gender roles are clearly distinct: Men are supposed to be assertive, tough and focused on material success; women are supposed to be more modest, tender, and concerned with the quality of life. Femininity stands for a society in which social gender roles overlap: Both men and women are supposed to be modest, tender, and concerned with the quality of life.

He argues that cultures that favour masculine qualities include Japan, Austria, Mexico and Great Britain, whereas those that prefer feminine qualities include Portugal, Denmark, the Netherlands and Sweden. Examples are provided of the impact these differences can have on everyday life. High masculinity cultures are characterized by:

- less emphasis on equality of opportunities in education and the workplace;
- more job-related stress;
- prevalence of traditional family roles;
- relatively few women in high political office;
- dominant religions tending to privilege men.

High femininity cultures are characterized by:

- greater equality of opportunity found in both education and the workplace in affluent countries;
- relatively less job-related stress;
- couples sharing family roles;
- relatively more women in high political office;
- dominant religions tending to emphasize the 'complementarity of the sexes'.

Hofstede also noted that low masculinity cultures tended to place more emphasis on social welfare provision, had fewer people who were poor or illiterate, believed in the integration of immigrants and displayed more public concern about the problems associated with the impact of biotechnological advances.

Long- versus short-term orientation

This dimension was formulated from research involving respondents from 23 countries in the mid-1980s, using the Chinese Value Survey devised by Michael Harris Bond. The values explored stem from Chinese scholars. Hofstede (2001: 359) defines these dimensions as follows:

> Long Term Orientation stands for the fostering of virtues orientated towards future rewards, in particular, perseverance and thrift. Its opposite pole, Short Term Orientation, stands for the fostering of virtues related to the past and present, in particular, respect for tradition, preservation of 'face' and fulfilling social obligations.

Countries with high scores on long-term orientation, according to Hofstede, include China, Hong Kong, Japan and India; whereas those that score low on long-term orientation (and thus have a short-term orientation) include the United States, Great Britain, Canada and Pakistan. Hofstede provides further illustrations of the way in which long- and short-term orientations affect everyday behaviour. Cultures that score highly on long-term orientations are likely to stress respect for status differences, save more and view leisure as not that important; those that score low on long-term orientation save less, value leisure time, look for quick results and have less regard for status differences.

Trompenaars and Hampden-Turner: cross-cultural profiles

An alternative contemporary perspective on the factors to be considered in cross-cultural communication is the database of cross-cultural profiles developed by Fons Trompenaars and Charles Hampden-Turner (THT). It was established from research undertaken with more than 60,000 managers in over 60 countries and has been modified over time. The THT identifies seven dimensions of cultural difference that explore the basic assumptions at the heart of a culture and indicate the differences between cultures that may present dilemmas for resolution within cross-cultural encounters.

Universalism versus particularism

Universalistic cultures expect general rules and principles for behaviour to be applied across most contexts, particularistic cultures do not. In these cultures, for example, it is often considered acceptable to have differing sets of principles for action depending on the circumstances, context and the nature of the relationships involved. Thus friends and family members might be dealt with quite differently to those from out-groups. Examples of cultures that have a particularistic orientation are South Korea, France and China whereas the UK, Ireland, USA and Sweden have a more universalistic orientation.

Individualism versus communitarianism

This dimension is very similar to individualism and collectivism and relates to the degree to which individual or group interests are seen as most important, as having priority. Countries that are viewed as having a communitarian orientation include Japan, France and China; those that have a more individualistic orientation include the UK, Netherlands, Denmark and the USA. Trompenaars and Woolliams (2004) provide an example of the way in which overlooking such differences can thwart the use of interpersonal encounters within a marketing campaign. Yakult, the well-known yoghurt drink, is the product of a Japanese company. In Japan the use of 'Yakult ladies' to distribute the product within their own neighbourhoods, making use of personal contacts and a sense of community loyalty, had been found to be an effective promotional tactic. When this promotional tactic was tried in the Netherlands, however, it met with a cool reception. The more individualistic Dutch regarded such visits to their houses as an intrusion on their privacy. The company also had some difficulty persuading Dutch women to sell the product to those in their own neighbourhoods and to wear the uniforms – both were seen as something of an affront to the norms of individualism.

Specific versus diffuse

There are cultural differences regarding the degree of involvement people expect in their relationships. In some cultures the expectation is to have limited, superficial relationships and interaction with many people while cultivating ongoing, deep relationships with others. Communicative encounters are very much framed by specific role expectations. Thus when ordering a pizza delivery, for example, the conversation is likely to be focused specifically on the details of the order. The characteristic of specificity is typical in countries such as the Netherlands, Germany and the USA. Diffuseness, however, characterizes interaction in countries such as South Korea, Japan, China and Singapore. In these cultures there is more emphasis on acknowledging the general nature of the relationship so ordering a pizza, for example, would also involve some discussion about the well-being of family members. The view in these cultures is that it is necessary to form a relationship before moving on to do business and that such relationships should be carefully maintained. Samovar and Porter (2004) note, for example, that in many Latin American countries personal relationships are viewed as integral to business and thus time must be spent establishing and building up these relationships, usually with the help of mutual personal contacts, before starting business negotiations.

Neutral versus affective

In cultures high in affective orientation, there is often a greater display of emotion in communicative encounters than found in cultures with a more neutral orientation – here the public expression of emotion is often downplayed or concealed. Countries with an affective orientation include Egypt, Spain, Ireland and France; those with a more neutral orientation include the UK and USA. China and Japan score particularly high on the neutral orientation and in these cultures there are strong norms against displaying negative emotions. Such differences in display norms can obviously lead to misunderstandings in cross-cultural encounters.

Achievement versus ascription

In some cultures status is obtained largely through personal achievement and there may be considerable social pressure placed on individuals to achieve their potential particularly in areas like education and employment. The UK, USA and Ireland score highly on achievement orientation. In other cultures, however, status rests on ascription, that is on factors such as gender, age, and one's family and socio-economic background. Japan, China and France are to be found more along the ascribed status end of this dimension. Trompenaars and Woolliams (2004) give the example here of the considerable respect shown in Japan to older members of a company's workforce.

Sequential versus synchronic time

Cultures vary in their attitudes towards time as both Hall (1983) and Hofstede (2001), among others, have noted. Time may be viewed as unfolding in a linear, sequential fashion or synchronically with past, present and future overlapping. Cultures vary in the consideration given to thinking in the short as opposed to the long term, and in the focus given to the past, present or future. Those from cultures with a synchronic orientation, such as France and China, may prefer to undertake several tasks at once, moving between them, while those from cultures such as the UK or USA with sequential orientation often prefer to focus on one task at a time. Tradition is particularly valued in cultures with a past orientation and can be a significant influence on behaviour, whereas in cultures with a future orientation minds tend to be more concentrated on the possibilities that lay ahead.

Internal versus external control

This dimension concerns orientations towards the natural environment, whether there is an attempt to 'control or dominate nature, or submit to it' (Trompenaars and Woolliams 2004: 107). Those cultures orientated towards internal control look to control and exploit the environment for their own benefit and tend to 'take themselves as the point of departure' when planning action. Examples here are the cultures of countries such as the UK, France and the USA. Cultures orientated towards external control, on the other hand, are more focused on environmental factors and tend to take the view that these factors need to be worked with and adapted to rather than controlled when making decisions and undertaking activities. The cultures of Japan, China and Singapore are examples of those more orientated to external control. Trompenaars and Hampden-Turner (2004) provide numerous examples of the way in which such orientations affect management strategies; one example discussed is that in outer-directed cultures there is a greater emphasis on managing by consensus.

The differences and tensions between cultural values, identified by these seven dimensions, give rise to dilemmas that need to be resolved for successful intercultural communication to take place. For reconciliation to occur there needs to be an attitude of mutual respect, flexibility in thinking, a willingness to compromise and a focus on the search for mutually beneficial solutions. It is also important to give due consideration to the local context and to the individuals involved. Reconciliation, of course, is not always possible.

High- and low-context communication

The anthropologist Edward Hall uncovered two other key cultural variables that affect the way in which people communicate, both of which stem from the influences of individualism and collectivism. One significant influence lies in the link between individualism and collectivism and the use of what Hall ([1977]/1981; 1983) termed high- and low-context communication.

High-context communication depends heavily on features found in the social context, for example, the gender and status differences between the communicators, to provide meaning. Further, considerable use is made of non-verbal signs. Hall writes:

> When talking about something that they have on their minds, a high context individual will expect his interlocutor to know what's

bothering him, so he doesn't have to be specific. The result is that he will talk around and around the point, in effect putting all the pieces in place except the crucial one. Placing it properly – this keystone – is the role of the interlocutor. To do this for him is an insult and a violation of his individuality.

([1977]/1981: 113)

Gudykunst and Kim (1997: 68) argue that 'High-Context communication can be characterized as being indirect, ambiguous and understated with speakers being reserved and sensitive to listeners'. High-context communication is common in collectivistic cultures. The crucial importance of in-group membership to everyday life ensures the degree of shared knowledge and understanding of contextual factors – for example, family membership, age, gender, social status – essential for the effective use of high-context communication. Its subtlety is also an advantage when the maintenance of group harmony, the avoidance of open conflict and respect for the 'face' of others are cultural priorities.

Individualistic cultures, however, favour Low-Context communication. In these cultures shared knowledge and understanding of contextual factors cannot be taken for granted so it is necessary to make the meaning carried in communicative encounters more obvious. While non-verbal signs are commonly used to convey meaning, there is greater emphasis upon making messages verbally explicit. Silence in conversations is often seen as an embarrassment and masked (Myers and Myers 1985). Gudykunst and Kim (1997: 68) comment: 'Low-context communication . . . can be characterized as being direct, explicit, open, precise and consistent with one's feelings'. It is, arguably, a manner of communicating suitable for cultures where individualism, competitiveness and assertiveness are valued.

However, although the cultural variable of individualism/collectivism may predispose individuals to favour one pattern over another, they may in some circumstances decide to use the contrasting pattern – for example, when mutual understanding from considerable shared experience can be assumed. Thus people in individualistic cultures may employ high-context communication when talking to a relative or longstanding friend (Gudykunst and Kim 1997: 68).

That in cross-cultural encounters some participants may be employing contrasting communication patterns can obviously be the source of confusion, misunderstanding and conflict. Individuals from collectivistic, high-context communication cultures, for example, may find the direct, open approach of those from individualistic, low-context cultures, disrespectful, impolite and tactless; while those from individualistic, low-context cultures may get impatient and frustrated with the failure of those from collectivistic, high-context communication cultures, to 'get to the point'.

In multicultural societies some individuals may find they have to become highly skilled at switching between low- and high-contact communication styles in order to communicate effectively in the varied social settings encountered. A British-born student, of Hong Kong Chinese parents who emigrated to Britain, may find at a family gathering that chatting with elderly relatives visiting from Hong Kong will require deference to the conventions of high-context communication in contrast to the low-context conventions typical of everyday university life in Britain. Goffman's proposition that negotiating everyday life can be seen to require us to become consummate actors may seem very apposite.

M-time; P-time

In *The Dance of Life: Other Dimensions of Time* (1983) Edward Hall argues that cultures tend to adopt either a monochronic (M-time) or polychronic (P-time) approach to time management. The M-time approach focuses on the clock: time is measured in precise units and is seen as a finite resource; time should be used efficiently; it is expected that people are punctual and meet deadlines; time is represented as having a linear pattern and the focus is on doing one thing at a time. The P-time approach to time, however, focuses on people, relationships and events not the clock: time is seen as fluid and flexible; activities have an inbuilt, unfolding timescale; sticking to rigid deadlines and appointments is not a priority; a number of activities may be undertaken at the same time; and it is not unusual for tasks and conversations to be inter-rupted. Arguably individualistic cultures tend to be driven by M-time while collectivistic cultures tend to embrace the P-time perspective.

Clearly such differences can be the cause of misunderstanding and fric-tion in intercultural encounters. Stella Ting-Toomey (1999: 213), considers problems that can arise in conflict management situations, for example: 'M-time people want to establish a clear timetable to achieve specific conflict goals and objectives; P-time people want to spend more time building up trust and commitment between the conflict parties'.

Facework

Facework strategies, where communication is used to protect the image and reputation of ourselves and others, can be observed in many everyday encounters. However Ting-Toomey (1999) points out that there are cultural differences in how facework is conducted. In Western cultures there is a tendency for people to concentrate on enhancing or protecting their own 'face' whereas in other cultures, Asian cultures for instance, the emphasis is on showing consideration and respect for the face of others. Thus, she argues, that while assertiveness in communication may be admired in Western cultures this is not universally the case and in most Asian cultures tact, caution and diplomacy are the hallmarks of successful communicative behaviour. Lewis (2006: 493) cautions that when engaging in business meetings and negotiations with people from China, Hong Kong and Japan, for example, it is crucial to be polite, avoid confrontation and to maintain the 'face' of all those involved.

Exercise: What do we mean by 'Britishness'?

Several social commentators and politicians have argued that 'Britishness' should be celebrated but what does 'Britishness' mean?

a)   Ask 20 people to list 5 defining characteristics of 'Britishness'.
b)   Analyse the responses and identify the main characteristics mentioned.
c)   Where possible compare and contrast these characteristics with cultural variables mentioned so far in this chapter.
d)   Have you ever encountered or noted any problems in cross-cultural communication? How could they be overcome?

Ethnocentrism, stereotypes, and prejudice

> Intercultural encounters are as old as humanity itself; they occurred as soon as two different tribes of humans met. Such meetings may have been peaceful and used for trade or hostile and a source of warfare, but the same basic processes of comparison, prejudice, and stereotyping that we find today must have taken place also 30,000 years ago.
>
> (Hofstede 2001: 423/4)

The process of interpersonal communication is prey to numerous barriers. Arguably, those that may cause particular problems in cross-cultural communication are ethnocentrism, stereotypes and prejudice.

Ethnocentrism

Ethnocentrism is the use of one's own culture, its practices, beliefs, norms and values, as a benchmark by which to evaluate another culture. The underlying assumption is that one's own culture is superior. Levine and Campbell (1972) argue that there is a tendency for all cultures to be ethnocentric and this will be an obvious potential source of friction when those from different cultural backgrounds encounter one another, particularly as we are often unaware of our own ethnocentric attitudes. Ting-Toomey (1999), with reference to several studies, suggests a dimension of communicative behaviour that ranges from ethnocentrism to ethnorelativism – that is a willingness to take account of the belief, norms, values and practices of other cultures when interpreting and judging the behaviour of those who belong to them.

Ting-Toomey discusses the work of Lukens (1978) who argued that **degrees of ethnocentrism** can be seen to underpin three categories of communicative distance. The *distance of indifference* is the least ethnocentric and is characterized by insensitivity when communicating with those from other cultures as when, for example, talking to them as if they were children by using very simple words and phrases and exaggerated gestures. The *distance of avoidance* is one associated with moderate ethnocentrism and is shown by the marginalization of out-group members during encounters and the general avoidance of communication with those from other cultures. High ethnocentrism is associated with the *distance of disparagement*; here verbal abuse, such as racial slurs, may be combined with physical abuse to deny or even remove the presence of out-groups members. The use of ethnophaulisms, names, nicknames and sayings used to belittle others, fall into this category. Pittock (1999: 29) notes numerous examples of ethnophaulisms traditionally used by the English at the expense of the Irish and Welsh.

With reference to Bennett (1993), Ting-Toomey suggests that there are **stages of ethnorelativism** that to some extent mirror the categories of communicative distance.

- *Interaction understanding* relates to the sensitive use of verbal and non-verbal communication in order to gain a full understanding of both out-groups members' sense of identity and the content of their communication. This involves carefully checking that our interpretations of their communicative behaviour are correct, for example by feeding back interpretations for confirmation.
- *Interaction respect* is characterized by the ability to empathize with those from another culture and thus to step inside their shoes and appreciate their perspective on life.
- *Interaction support* involves the willingness to provide active and appropriate non-verbal and verbal encouragement to those from other cultures so that they may feel fully included in communication encounters. Successful intercultural encounters require considerable conscious effort and goodwill.

Stereotypes

Obviously cultural stereotypes, like all stereotypes, may be the source of much miscommunication and misunderstanding in interpersonal encounters. Gross (2005: 384) argues that the process of stereotyping involves the following:

- 'we assign someone to a particular group (for example, on the basis of their physical appearance);
- we bring into play the belief that all members of the group share certain characteristics (the stereotype); and
- we infer that this particular individual must possess these characteristics.'

Stereotypes thus lead us to assume that all those we have grouped together, based on assumed shared characteristics, are indeed the same; this assumption often leads to inaccurate and ill-defined perceptions of others along with a tendency to overlook individual variations in behaviour. Stereotyping can also lead to the self-fulfilling prophecy effect, that is we see what we expect to see in the behaviour of others and thus the stereotype is reinforced. Our stereotypes of those from other cultures derive from numerous sources, including the mass media, and we may be more prone to be influenced by secondhand sources if we have little or no first hand experience of interaction with those outside our own cultural background. Thus we need to be mindful of the impact of stereotypes on our intercultural encounters, as the following account demonstrates.

Case study: jumping to conclusions

Rageh Omaar in his book *Only Half of Me: Being a Muslim in Britain* (2006: 191–5) recounts an incident that occurred to cousins of one of his aunts while they were visiting a relative in the Royal London Hospital a few weeks after the London bombings of 7 July and shortly after the failed bombings of 21 July. The cousins, called Asha and Habiba, were sisters in their mid-50s and were wearing traditional Islamic dress. They completed the last stage of their journey to the hospital by bus. Once they got to the hospital, however, they were told that they could not see their relative, who had just come out of intensive care, as he needed rest. So they left and stood at a nearby bus stop to return home. Rageh Omaar takes up the story:

> They had been standing there waiting for about ten minutes when they saw the first vehicle speeding towards them, as though it intended to run them down. As it got closer they realized it was a police car. Suddenly

there was another one. Two large police vans skidded in front of them, positioning themselves so as to block the road. They were full of flak-jacketed police officers, some of whom were armed. The officers burst out of the vans and ran towards the two women. In one moment they had grabbed Asha and Habiba and pulled their arms behind their backs. The two women were terrified, trying to calm the police officers down but also desperate to know why they were being restrained. Everything happened very quickly and at least two policemen patted them down beneath their dresses and searched their handbags. As the two women stood shaking on the street an officer took down their names and addresses, and when Asha and Habiba asked why this was happening a policeman replied that they were not able to disclose any information but that a police liaison officer would be in touch. . . . A bus arrived and Asha and Habiba climbed on board, watched nervously by people on the street.

Asha and Habiba have lived in the UK for eleven years. . . . Their husbands' businesses had brought them to Britain and they had settled here . . . as wives of middle-class businessmen. Their appearance as middle-aged, conservative African Muslim women, may have made people think that they were meek and possibly illiterate, at the mercy of a patriarchal culture, but in fact they are educated, self-possessed women.

Once the sisters got home they phoned the police for an explanation. It seems that they had been reported to the police by one of the passengers on the bus who thought they might be terrorists. The sisters asked what had been the grounds for this assumption. Omaar continues:

The officers told them that people on the bus had reported that one of them seemed to be carrying something bulky under her dress. The officer added that many of the people on the bus, including the undercover transport policeman, could not understand why they would be wearing 'such clothes', meaning their Muslim headscarves and long dark gowns, on a summer day in July. Surely even they would wear 'lighter material' on a hot day? The police now accepted that the people on the bus had made a mistake; and that the reason why Asha looked as though she was carrying a suspect backpack and Habiba did not, was because Asha was overweight . . . That's what the problem was: being fat and a Muslim.

Questions for discussion

1   What aspects of the process of stereotyping are illustrated by this story?
2   What sources of information might have contributed to the passengers' stereotype of a 'terrorist'?

3   Consider other examples of how stereotyping might impact on inter-cultural encounters?

Prejudice

Stereotypes are particularly harmful when they lead to **prejudice**. Atkinson, Atkinson Smith, Bem and Nolen-Hoeksema (1996: 701) define prejudice as 'Negative feelings towards a group' adding that the term usually 'implies negative feelings not based on adequate or valid data about the group'. It is often difficult to change attitudes based on prejudice as they are resistant to appeals to reason. Prejudice can be present in many social encounters and clearly such attitudes, when they relate to those from other cultural or ethnic backgrounds, constitute a formidable barrier to successful intercultural communication. Allport (1954) identified five **stages of prejudice** that are valuable in considering the potential impact of prejudice upon interpersonal encounters. The first stage is that of *anti-locution*, the use of insults and 'jokes' – the intention here is to denigrate others. *Avoidance* of communicative encounters with those about whom we hold prejudiced attitudes is a passive display of rejection that tends to result in our negative beliefs and attitudes going unchallenged. Such rejection may be a precursor to the more harmful activities involved in the later stages of *discrimination, physical attack* and *extermination.*

Ting-Toomey (1999: 168) makes the point that feelings of prejudice towards those in other cultural groups are rarely clear-cut for most people. We may, for example, feel positively about some cultural identities but negatively about others. People may be accepting of those from other cultures until their own sense of identity, status or safety seems threatened. We may also be selective about the degree to which we may wish to interact with those from other cultural backgrounds. Of interest here is Brislin's (1993) category of *'Arm's-length prejudice'*. This is characterized by a willingness to be accepting and positive towards those from other cultures in more formal situations, at work, for example, but to be much less so in personal contexts, thus there is not the same willingness to cultivate personal friendships with those from other cultures. Crucially people may try to hide their prejudices because they judge them to be socially unacceptable; however their prejudices are still likely to influence their behaviour and as Merton (1957) argues, if changes in the social environment make displays of prejudice more acceptable, such displays are likely to come to the surface in communicative behaviour. We need therefore to be mindful about the subtle as well as not so subtle impact of prejudice on intercultural encounters.

Transcultural competence

Ting-Toomey (1999: 272) describes the attributes and abilities of transcultural competence, a competence that should enhance the success of intercultural encounters:

- *Tolerance for ambiguity* requires that we approach encounters mindful of the need to be attentive listeners and to consider carefully the perspectives of others; it also requires us to check carefully that we have understood the intended messages.
- *Open-mindedness* requires us to avoid rushing to evaluate others perspectives and actions.
- *Flexibility* enables us to appreciate a range of alternative perspectives on a situation or relationship.
- However, as well as developing an understanding of others' perspectives, it is also important that we display *respectfulness* towards others and their views.
- Successful communication also necessitates *adaptability* so that we can communicate in an appropriate manner.
- The attribute of *sensitivity* facilitates empathy and our capacity to explore others' views and experiences.
- *Creativity* enables us to generate the appropriate and effective communicative strategies necessary in order to successfully manage intercultural encounters.

Adapting to a new culture: culture shock, acculturation and deculturation

Some, if not all, of the interactors within intercultural encounters are likely to be experiencing the problems of adapting to a new culture; the need to adapt may be temporary as in the case of someone backpacking round the world in their 'gap' year before starting a university course or it may be permanent as in the case of a refugee who has fled persecution to start a new life in a safer place and for whom there may be little prospect of a return to the homeland. Gudykunst and Kim (1997) identify four main stages in the process of adaptation: enculturation (that is prior socialization), the interlinked stages of acculturation and deculturation, and finally assimilation into the new culture. Analysing the challenges facing individuals when they negotiate this process, Kim (1997: 405, original emphasis) comments:

They are challenged to learn at least some new ways of thinking, feeling, and acting – an activity commonly called *acculturation* ... At the same time, they go through the process of *deculturation* ... of unlearning some of their previously acquired cultural habits at least to the extent that new responses are adopted in situations that previously would have evoked old ones.

This process generates stress and anxiety and culture shock – symptoms of which include feelings of disorientation, rejection, insecurity, identity loss, social incompetence, loneliness and depression (Ting-Toomey 1999). It necessarily affects the communicative performance of those undergoing it, a factor that may not always be realized by those who are familiar with the culture in question. However communication with members of the host culture is essential to an individual's successful adaptation even though the process of interpersonal communication takes on a whole new dimension of risks, challenges, frustrations and triumphs. Kim also points out that the mass media can be a useful source of information about the new culture for those trying to acclimatize to it.

While the stresses of adaptation may be felt most by those settling in a new country, to some extent similar stresses may be experienced by those faced with the task of temporary adaptation to a new culture. Assimilation is also, arguably, a matter of degree. Essentially, whether newcomers or natives, we are all individuals and are likely to differ in the extent to which we embrace aspects of the culture in which we live and over the course of our lives the strength of that embrace may fluctuate. Some of the case studies presented in Chapter 7 explore the interpersonal strategies used to cope with the challenges of cultural adaptation.

Key points

- Intercultural encounters take place in contexts in which people from differing cultural backgrounds communicate with one another.
- Many aspects of our behaviour, including our communicative behaviour, are influenced by our cultural backgrounds. Cross-cultural differences can be a barrier to effective interpersonal communication.
- A range of cross-cultural variables may impact on the process of intercultural communication and this chapter looked at some examples. Hofstede identified the dimensions of power distance, uncertainty avoidance, individualism and collectivism, masculinity-femininity, and long- versus short-term orientation. Trompenaars and Hampden-Turner's cross-cultural profiles identified the differences of universalism versus particularism, individualism versus

communitarianism, specifc versus diffuse, neutral versus affective, achievement versus ascription, sequential versus synchronic, and internal versus external control. Hall highlights the differences of high- and low-context communication and also of monochronic and polychronic approaches to time management. Ting-Toomey notes cultural differences as regards attention to facework within interaction.

- There are differences in the degree to which the communicative behaviour of any one person may be influenced by these variables.
- Common barriers to successful intercultural communication are ethnocentrism, stereotypes and prejudice – prejudice may be hidden.
- The development of transcultural competence should aid successful intercultural encounters.
- The process of adapting to a new culture involves acculturation and deculturation and often generates culture shock. Problems encountered in adapting to a new culture are likely to hinder the effectiveness of intercultural encounters. However, persistence in communicating with those from the host culture should aid the process of adaptation.

7 Identity, Culture and Outsiders

The starting point for this chapter is that contemporary societies contain many different cultures and that the members of some cultures will see themselves, and be seen by others, as being less integrated into the everyday mainstream of the society – they have the identity of outsiders. In the first part of the chapter, identity and culture are examined in relation to studies of dance musicians, gypsies, body modifiers and the disabled to establish that the grounds for being considered an outsider will vary but, whatever the grounds are, they will affect interpersonal communication with insiders. The studies referred to have tried to get close to interaction, and the sections on musicians and disability have been supplemented with notes and observations from interviews conducted for this chapter.[1] Another type of outsider is considered in the final part of the chapter: outsiders who want to become insiders. This section draws on theoretical approaches to intercultural communication and incorporates interviews with a small sample of migrants who have had to adapt to a new culture.[2]

The dance musician in Chicago

A classic study of the phenomenon of the outsider is Howard S. Becker's study of dance musicians (1966). He conducted the study in Chicago between 1948 and 1949. He interviewed musicians and, as a piano player, was a participant observer of this occupational culture. They were playing music to make a living and, like many other workers, provided a service. At the same time, however, unlike many other service groups their work involved their own highly prized self-expression. The pinnacle of success was to become a jazz professional because this would offer creative freedom and maintain their self-respect and the respect of other musicians. However, the work available made it difficult to fulfil this ambition and they faced the dilemma of whether to play commercial music or to be creative musicians. The costs of choosing the commercial option were that they could not maintain the respect of other musicians or their own self-respect. The cost of the other option was that they could not make a living.

The dilemma had a special intensity because the musicians participated in a culture that made a clear distinction between themselves and others. They saw themselves as having special qualities and saw others who lacked such qualities as outsiders:

> The musician is conceived of as an artist who possesses a mysterious gift setting him apart from all other people. Possessing this gift, he should be free from control by outsiders who lack it. The gift is something which cannot be acquired through education; the outsider, therefore, can never become a member of the group. A trombone player said, 'You can't teach a guy to have a beat. Either he's got one or he hasn't. If he hasn't got it, you cannot teach it to him.'
>
> (Becker 1966: 85–6)

As outsiders, justifiably from the point of view of their special 'gift', the musicians acted, looked, thought and talked differently and supported or tolerated the unconventional and deviant behaviour of others. In return, in recognition of their unusual way of life, others saw them as outsiders. In terms of the occupation and its way of life Becker's study reveals the importance of the group, the subculture of musicians, in maintaining the distinctions between the musicians and others.

Changes have taken place since Becker published his research but, Aaron, an experienced musician based in London, finds it will always be a 'challenge' to be a creative artist and make a good living. He commented that musicians are 'a little bit outside the cultural norms'. A problem for the musician is that 'most people do not have an interest in ability'. And further, the work of musicians is undervalued because, 'It's not seen as beneficial to the social environment; you don't make things or you don't build things. You provide entertainment and people don't take it seriously.' In the work situation their employers can regard them 'almost like a jukebox' and although a booker might want to hear a demo as a check on quality, they 'just want people to buy beer'. As a result, there are often interpersonal tensions between musicians and their audience and musicians and their employers.

Gypsies in Madrid: an anthropological study

There are wide variations to be found in the ways that gypsies live, but they all share the desire to maintain a distinctive culture in relation to the other cultures with whom they come into contact. Paloma Gay Y Blasco conducted a study of the Spanish Gypsies or Gitanos of Jarana on the southern edge of Madrid. Her anthropological fieldwork lasted 15 months in 1992 and 1993. The Gitanos lived in Villaverde Alto, custom-built for them by the state.

Like Becker's jazz musicians, the Gitanos thought they had a special quality that set them apart. In this case it was a belief that they lived according to moral values, unlike the non-gypsies or Payos. Outsiders and insiders often operate according to stereotypes of one another and Gay Y Blasco found that the Gitanos' view of the Payos was that they 'neglect their children, despise their elders and kill each other through terrorism and war; their women are all whores on the lookout for sex, and their men are all weaklings.' Conversely, the Payos' view of the Gitanos was that they were 'people "without culture", who live surrounded by dirt, refuse to work, and earn their living by sponging off the State, stealing, and selling drugs to young non-Gypsies.'

The Gitanos were outsiders and had a sense of collective identity, but did not tend to act collectively. The kinship group was the focus for identification and interaction. Gay Y Blasco says it was striking that in 'Jarana, the Gitanos live with their backs to each other, purposefully restricting daily sociability to their own kin' (Gay Y Blasco 1999: 40–1). Kinship was important too for regulating conflict between kin and non-kin and also had an impact on their relationships with state agencies. For example, difficulties were posed for social workers because the Gitanos insisted that they attended literacy classes with the same sex kin.

Identity

Gitano identity did not rest on birth or kinship. It was not enough to be born a gypsy: it was necessary to act as a gypsy in daily life. Identity was based on a 'way of being' in the 'now' (Gay Y Blasco 1999: 14). Consequently a Gitano could choose to adopt a non-gypsy lifestyle or, less easily, a non-gypsy could choose a gypsy lifestyle. For the Gitanos the body determines identity and a crucial aspect of gypsy life is the biological distinction between male and female. The dichotomy between men and women is absolute and crucial to male and female behaviour and biological developments are intrinsically linked to how males and females have to conduct themselves socially. They need to perform these roles because in doing so the boundaries between themselves and the Payos are maintained.

Dress

Dress was an important aspect of interpersonal communication and was a source of contention, as women, and the girls between childhood and marriage, *mozas*, were expected to show restraint in their dress, in contradistinction to the Payos. Married women were expected to obey their husbands who had the right to enforce the correct modes of dress and hairstyle on their wives. On the other hand, it was admissible to be sensual. As Gay Y Blasco (1999: 80) observed,

Mozas and many young married women make themselves attractive by putting on very tight blouses that emphasise their breasts, and skirts that are long but also very tight and that sometimes have long cuts so that part of the leg is shown. They wear a great deal of makeup and large, shiny jewellery, and they curl and/or dye their hair, pinning it high at the top of their heads so as to display its length and abundance.

Through their dress the young women would be identifiable as gypsies and therefore separate from non-gypsies. Gay Y Blasco noted that young girls could wear mini-skirts or trousers, like the Payos, but as they got older the clear distinctions between men and women and Gitanos and Payos had to be asserted. If young women wore trousers in the cold weather they would wear a skirt over the top to confirm the value of modesty, a style which non-gypsies interpreted, scornfully, as a lack of dress sense.

The young men also had their own style. They paid close attention to their appearance. They wore 'expensive-looking' clothes, colourful scarves and shiny shoes. They often grew their hair long and used gel. Long hair was a sign of beauty and strength as it was for females. The boys adopted an assertive style and were, significantly, allowed to make advances to female non-gypsies. They had the freedom to cross the boundary between the Gitanos and the Payos, and to have sexual liaisons, which fact confirmed the immorality of the Payos and the weakness of non-gypsy males. On the other hand, the life of the *mozas* became more restricted and subject to comment.

Gypsy identity was bound up with the body, and this was demonstrated by the stress on modesty in dress, bearing, and posture and the emphasis on the virginity of a prospective bride. The body, in Gay Y Blasco's terms, worked as a sign that indicated moral worth as well as gender.

Body Modification in the USA

As an indexical sign, the body is an important element in social interaction and, as the Spanish gypsies demonstrate, it is subject to moral judgements. As the body is not a neutral element in interpersonal communication people are willing to modify their bodies. For example, people undergo cosmetic surgery with the aim of boosting their personal confidence and improving their interpersonal communication.

Case study: cosmetic surgery

On a website Wanda and Angela give testimony to the benefits of breast enlargement surgery. Wanda is quoted as saying, 'It's now been 21 days, and

I'm having a lovely time at a party in a dress I wouldn't have worn before my operation. Everything is just fine, and I'm still over the moon with my new bust!' Likewise, Angela, 'Here I am just a few weeks later enjoying myself at a garden party. I feel terrific and full of confidence with my new look. Everyone says how nice I look and I'm really happy with my new figure!' (www.why goabroadforsurgery.com, 23.6.2006). Wanda and Angela's comments illustrate their wish to conform to conventional criteria of beauty.

Other forms of body modification, however, often constitute a challenge to accepted ideas of beauty. For Victoria Pitts 'Body modifiers highlight how the body is a site of significant social contest' (2003: 17). Pitts interviewed twenty body modifiers and professional body modification artists in the USA between 1996 and 2000. Her sample was half men and half women; they were all white and aged between 20 and 53. She wanted to examine the meanings that practices such as tattooing, piercing and scarring had for her respondents.

Her interviewees led her to question the idea that body modification is a symptom of an underlying pathology.[3] Many of the women saw themselves as reclaiming a body that had been subject to male dominance and the dominant ideas of beauty. Some of them had been exposed to sexual violence and/or had been the object of male looking and wanted to assert their own control. Because the process of reclamation involved a painful and stressful ritual that Pitts likens it to a **liminal stage**. (see box)

Liminal stage

A liminal stage is a transitional stage between an old and a new status and identity. Anthropologists have used the concept in their studies of non-industrial societies to refer to rituals that enable individuals to make a transition, for example, from being classified as a child to being classified as an adult. In such rituals, or rites of passage, individuals are disconnected from everyday routines to enter the liminal stage and fulfil the requirements of the culture in question. Finally, they are brought back into their society with their new status.

In industrial societies there are not the same social prescriptions that govern transitions from one status to another. Nevertheless, there are rituals that can be a reference point throughout a person's life. For example, getting married and going on a honeymoon, or having a party for a significant birthday. People will have significant experiences in common but a wider range of possibilities and times to make decisions. We can engage in the 'ongoing creation of narratives of self-identity relating to our perceptions of the past, present and hoped-for future' (Barker 2003: 442).

> The idea of liminality is also broadened to refer to a state or a category that is outside the conventional ways of doing things (Keesing and Strathern 1998: 507) and therefore can be applied to the outsiders in this chapter. It might be hypothesized that, as well as engaging in rituals, outsiders want to experience a special state apart from normal life, on a regular basis. They want to live life with a special intensity, not be found it is assumed, in conventional ways of living or working.

These transgressive practices find sustenance from friends, from the body modification subculture, and from the media in terms of books and magazines. Often, a body modification artist is involved, as in the case of one respondent, Karen, who had nipple piercings, permanent tattoos and scarifications. She also had support from a women's sado-masochist group and was further sustained by conscious references to practices in non-industrial societies.

Subculture

The women interviewed saw themselves as outsiders and the subculture was important in maintaining this perception, but the implications for individuals in their daily lives varied. Those whose markings were visible, could create a strong reaction in everyday situations, while those who did not display them might pass as normal. Jane, one interviewee, had a 6-inch by 6-inch dreamcatcher symbol across her chest, but she ensured that this was not visible on her social work placement or revealed to her mother. For Jane and others, display would only take place in a subcultural setting. Yet other body modifiers reduced the possibilities of negative reactions at work by providing services for deviant groups, a factor that made them less visible to the general population. However, a more serious long-term problem for the women was maintaining a boundary between themselves and others. The boundaries are pervious as the meanings of body markings are negotiated and changed. Tattoos and piercings have become more commonplace and fashionable, and female body modifications have featured in videos designed to appeal to a male gaze. The availability of these different meanings results in the outsider stance being harder to maintain and damage is done to the concept of reclaiming the body.

Gay subculture

Body modification has a long history in gay subcultures. It is a way of declaring an outsider status: it draws attention to the body as queer and 'in the face of pressures to be closeted, mainstream, or assimilationist, the use of spectacular body marks by leather people, radical gays and lesbians, and the transgendered can reflect a defiant aesthetics of deviance' (Pitts 2003: 87). As with the women interviewed, though, the interpersonal implications are varied. Two respondents with visible markings, Matthew and Shawn, owned a body-piercing studio and therefore could operate under the canopy of the subculture and exhibit a strong rejection of mainstream society. Others might not be perceived as outsiders and would only display their markings in a subcultural setting. They were able to pass in everyday activities and jobs. One interviewee, Bob, relished his hidden identity, 'If I cover my body, people will not type me as somebody who would be branded. I like that. I break some of the stereotypes. I enjoy fooling people that way. I've got stuff all over my body but I can choose to not let people know that' (Pitts 2003: 109).

Bob had been a mental health counsellor but, when interviewed, was the manager of a gay sex club. He had left his former job because of the hostility directed at him when it became public knowledge that he had undergone a scarification ritual. He had left his place of residence and gone to California, where he could find the support of a subculture. The importance of the subculture to such outsiders resides in its supportive role and its provision of services. This is especially the case with regard to the rituals involved in body marking. The audience affirms the practices involved, and they have to be carried out with the skill of a body modification artist, as they involve piercing, scarring and branding. The rituals are painful but they are experienced as erotic and, as an expression of masochistic sexuality, challenge conventional ideas. At the same time they increase the solidarity of the group.

The meanings of body modification

As with the female modifiers, however, the gay and lesbian modifiers find it difficult to maintain an exclusive interpretation of body modification. Pitts states that the 'problem of relying on bodily representation for signifying queer political claims is that the meanings of its signs are contested, positioned in a shifting cultural landscape in which queer communities have only limited influence' (2003: 116). This shifting 'cultural landscape' involves medical experts searching for causes; other groups who adopt some of the practices, as in college hazing rituals that use branding; and cultural commentators who are sceptical about the use of non-industrial tribal practices that are abstracted from their original societal context. The body functions as an indexical sign – the body means something – but what it means is shifting and so the body projects of body modifiers can have different symbolic meanings. The meanings of body modifications are anchored by liminal rituals but boundaries, between themselves and others, are more permeable than the participants would like.

Disability: becoming disabled

Disabled people, like body modifiers, depart from the norm but, unlike them, they have not chosen their fate, so they cannot be regarded as wilfully deviant. Robert Murphy was a professor of anthropology who became disabled as a result of a tumour on his spinal cord. He places disability in the context of a culture that celebrates youthfulness and a 'slim, well-muscled body' which 'is not only an aesthetic matter but also a moral imperative' (Murphy 1995: 141). He was able to comment directly from his own experiences of crossing the boundary from being able-bodied to being disabled:

> The recently disabled paralytic faces the world with a changed body and an altered identity – which even by itself would make reentry into society a delicate and chancy matter. But his future is made even more perilous by the way he is treated by the nondisabled, including some of his oldest friends and associates and even family members. Although this varies considerably from one situation to another, there is a clear pattern in the United States, and in many other countries, of a prejudice toward the disabled and debasement of their social status.
>
> (Murphy 1995: 140)

To become disabled is, then, to be pushed to the margins. Murphy refers to the way people look away or keep their physical distance; the way in which the disabled are patronized or have deference removed. As a result interpersonal communication is taxing for the disabled person, especially as they have to try very hard to put people at their ease. On the other hand new alliances can be formed:

> I used to be invisible to black campus policemen, who often greeted a black colleague with whom I was walking by saying deliberately and clearly in the singular, 'Hello, Professor, how are you today?' They now know who I am and say hello. I am now a white man who is worse off than they are, and my subtle loss of public standing brings me closer to their own status. We share a common position on the periphery of society – we are fellow outsiders.
>
> (Murphy 1995: 150–1)

Murphy also enjoyed the egalitarian ethos of his fellow disabled and the ease of his relationships with women.

Liminality, nature and culture

As an anthropologist, Murphy was able to bring the concepts and insights from his own profession to the analysis of the disabled. He notes that being disabled involves an indeterminacy that is both physical and social. First, the disabled person enters a liminal state, but a crucial difference is that this is not a transitional stage. The disabled person remains permanently outside of everyday social life. Second, light is thrown on the indeterminancy of the disabled by referring to the key distinction that Claude Lévi-Strauss makes between nature and culture. Disability throws into doubt the separation of these spheres because

> physical impairment is an infringement by nature, an intrusion that undercuts one's status as a bearer of culture and [T]this, finally, is what makes disability so different from other kinds of 'deviance'. It is not just a departure from the moral code, but a distortion of conventional classification and understanding.
>
> (Murphy 1995: 154)

Finally, another anthropologist, Mary Douglas, argued that societies construct classifications of reality, and phenomena that do not fit into the categories cause a disturbance. As the disabled depart from the normal human form they can introduce a measure of indeterminacy into interpersonal communication.

The sense of disturbance or destabilization will vary according to the 'severity and type of disability. At the bottom of the scale are persons with facial disfigurement or marked body distortion; wheelchairs are somewhere in the middle. The main criterion seems to be based on the extent to which one differs from the standard human form' (Murphy 1995: 154). Variations are important and so are the ways in which physical disabilities are mediated by the culture. For example, in the UK and around the world, the public value of inclusion has developed, and this has led to the possibility of greater participation in everyday activities by disabled people.

Cash study: interview with a disabled man

Bob broke his neck between the fifth and fourth vertebrae in an accident in 1972, when he was 18. Consequently, he is paralyzed in all four limbs and from the chest down. He has some limited use of both arms but his hands are paralyzed. He is doubly incontinent. He has to take care of sudden movements because he has to breathe through his diaphragm, and his internal thermostat can malfunction in hot or cold temperatures. His waking hours are spent in a wheelchair.

He sees himself as belonging to a group, in the sense of an aggregate, of disabled people and can empathize 'immediately' with media reports of anyone who has broken their neck or back. However, if anyone enquires, he does not find the idea of attending a day centre, that is restricted to disabled people, appealing:

'I just don't want to do it as a disabled person. I am quite happy going where there are able-bodied and disabled people, there because they like doing a particular activity....' He has two or three friends in the same situation who provide a supportive network for each other. He cannot say however whether he is typical or not 'because I don't stay in contact with that many disabled people, quite deliberately, because you could easily get set in your ways of thinking.' Although his life is dominated by his quadriplegia, he resists being marginalized as a disabled person.

Liminality

Following Turner it seems appropriate to use the idea of a liminal state. Bob thinks of his life as 'a very unnatural existence.' His life is 'humdrum' and predominantly housebound and he is aware that he has not been able to follow a similar life course to those around him. 'I haven't really done much, compared to other people. All my friends have gone out to work, and had families.' In addition, he lives with his mother and has never left home, whereas his sister left home at 16. As a result, he regards the situation that he is in with his mother as 'highly unnatural' and his relationship with his sister as probably more distant than it might have been.

Bob knows lots of people, especially nurses, but conversation is often restricted. Less often he meets people on a more sociable basis and is at ease sitting around a table talking but even so 'that's not quite so easy because you haven't actually done the same things as a lot of other people...'.

Bob laments the inflexibility that his disability demands, 'What you eat, what you drink, when you do it, it's pretty basic stuff. It's bloody annoying actually; the spontaneity in your life just goes out the window.'

All these aspects of his life suggest a liminal state and one that is permanent. Bob comments, 'You do feel like life has ground to a halt a bit, compared to the mainstream.' He is totally reliant on others and says, 'I don't feel like an independent body anymore.'

Interactions

In his interactions with others, Bob distinguishes between his friends, of whom he has quite a large circle and the other people he meets outside of the home. With the former he interacts 'totally normally' whereas with the latter it is not always so easy and 'things don't flow'. Bob suggests that 'a lot of people do not like to be confronted with disabled people, and anything to do with it is just a reminder of the fragility, of how close you could come yourself to that experience.' He remembers that he himself used to recoil from disabled children from a local school before his accident only to to see them later as 'crazy and wonderful people', when he found himself next to them in hospital. In other contexts people will address the person accompanying Bob or a 'lot of people will talk over your head'. Bob sees this as a product of lack of contact and familiarity with disability and thinks that younger people are definitely less prone to such behaviour.

To an extent Bob lives in a state of suspension, he values his friends as a 'huge cushion' against feeling 'bitter and twisted with the whole damn situation' and offered the following reflection on whether he regards himself as an outsider:

> In relation to the pretty basic things that you have to do in life, just to function, I am an outsider, a total outsider physically, and just the way that you have to come at things because of what's happened ... But I don't wake up every morning and think, 'God, I'm an outsider.' You just know that your life's different and that you have to put a lot more thought into things that should happen in a few seconds or a few minutes; things take so bloody long!

The discussion above has considered the importance of the body and appearance; the importance of subcultures; and the utility of the concept of liminality. The following section looks at the phenomenon of adapting to a new culture.

Becoming an insider

> The 'intercultural person' projects the fundamental outlook of a person who has achieved a high level of identity transformation through a prolonged process of stress, adaptation, and growth experiences through intercultural encounters.
>
> (Gudykunst and Kim 2003: 383–4)

This final section of the chapter examines the experience of migrants and incorporates interviews with six people. The aim is to explore how they are adapting to a new culture and the role of interpersonal communication in this adaptation.

In the novel, *Harbor*, Lorraine Adams presents the harsh circumstances of Aziz, an illegal, Algerian, immigrant to the USA:

He saw that he was unseen. Days – no, weeks – went by without a person speaking to him, and longer still, without someone's eyes meeting his own. His place in the order of things was not a place; maybe, as he came to think of it, it was an insert, a scooping out, into which he belonged, but if he were to die or to quit or not be there for some reason, another, not like him but adequate to his function, would be fitted in and, like the tab in a cereal box, would keep it neat and closed.

(Adams 2006: 62–3)

The stranger

The fictional Aziz is an outsider and an extreme example of what Gudykunst and Kim call the stranger, a central concept in their approach to intercultural communication. They do not restrict the use of the concept of the stranger to migrants, however, because they assume that, in essence, communicating with people from other cultures is the same as communicating with people from our own cultures. The underlying process is the same and, therefore, it follows that a person can be a stranger in their own culture, on entry to an unfamiliar situation. 'In general', they say, 'we include anyone entering a relatively unknown or unfamiliar environment under the rubric of *stranger*' (Gudykunst and Kim 2003: 24). In this sense anyone can be a stranger but there will tend to be a higher degree of strangeness and a lower degree of familiarity in encounters between migrants and natives, as opposed to encounters between people from the same society. Because my respondents had moved into a new country they had become strangers and I wanted to explore the extent to which they had made the transition from cultural outsiders to cultural insiders, in much less harsh circumstances than Aziz.

The six migrants identified themselves as temporary visitors or sojourners who, in Ting-Toomey's definition, 'are typically individuals who have a transitional stay in a new culture as they try to achieve their instrumental goals (e.g. an international student wanting to achieve her or his MBA degree) and/or socioemotional goals (e.g. making friends with US students)' (1999: 235). Five of the interviewees had come to England to study:

- Two female, third-year BA students, Susanne from Germany (aged 23) and Faiza from Turkey (aged 23);
- A male, first-year BA student, Folami from Nigeria (aged 24);
- A male, A level student, Lyuben from Bulgaria (aged 17);
- A female, postgraduate trainee teacher, Faith from Zimbabwe (aged 34).

The sixth interviewee was a young, female graduate, Mari (aged 21), who went from England to work for a charity, in a school in rural Malawi.

Enculturation, acculturation and deculturation

To enter a new society instigates a learning process for an individual. Kim has identified a number of processes involved in cross-cultural adaptation. Initially, an individual has to adapt to the society into which they are born, and a process of enculturation takes place that establishes their place in a familiar world. They become, as a result, cultural insiders. When an individual enters another culture their original cultural adaptation may well be thrown into doubt and Kim theorizes that two new processes are set in motion. New learning, acculturation, has to take place and, at the same time, unlearning or deculturation. As these processes continue over time, the individual, initially a stranger, will experience an internal transformation that will, in the long term, result in the assimilation of the individual into the new society, thereby completing the journey from cultural outsider to cultural insider.

Adaptation to a new culture is an active process involving communication. Kim states that: 'Adaptation occurs in and through communication. Just as natives have acquired their cultural patterns through interaction with others, strangers over time acquire the new cultural patterns by participating in the host communication activities' (Gudykunst and Kim 2003: 361). Strangers have to learn a new etiquette for everyday situations. Mari learned that

> greetings are very important in Malawi. We learnt to say, 'How are you?' and 'I'm fine' in Chichewa. We addressed every person. The phrases were never plural and therefore it was quite time-consuming. You would greet and shake hands, even if you knew the person well. So at school, every morning, we'd have this long drawn-out process, for about ten minutes: shaking hands and curtseying to the women.

During her stay Mari attended a funeral. Everyone had to be greeted individually and she found that Malawians also used handclaps as a greeting, 'They would clap their hands at you. If they are at a little distance, instead of shaking your hand and curtseying they'll just clap at you, twice. We learnt to do that back.' Similarly, on his arrival from Nigeria to England, Folami encountered English etiquette, which requires the extensive use of 'please' and 'thank you'. Like many foreigners Folami was bemused by this unfamiliar practice, 'I have to be more polite and say, "Can I have that, please?" or "No, thank you." At first, when people said you have to say "please" I thought they were taking the mickey, because I did not grow up having to say "please" in this way. But I have to be British to fit in.' In her study of English behaviour, Kate Fox points out that in economic transactions the 'generic rule is that every request (by either staff or customer) must end with "please" and every fulfillment of a request (ditto) requires a "thank-you"' (2004: 94). Strangers have to learn these rules that the host population take for granted.

Intrapersonal and interpersonal communication

At the intrapersonal level Kim argues that individuals have to achieve host communication competence which involves cognitive, affective and operational dimensions:

- Strangers will have to gain a cognitive understanding of how the host population makes sense of their world. Folami was wary of the existence of racist attitudes but was gratified that he could share his interests in music, dress and football with new friends, all of whom were white.
- Strangers will have to gain an insight into the host population's emotional and aesthetic life. Faith was raised in the anglicized culture of Zimbabwe but had to adjust to the grey English weather and, although she experienced a great sense of freedom in England, she found social life more inhibited.
- Strangers will have to grasp how things are done and be able to act appropriately. Susanne had to adjust to British patterns of sociability, especially going out more and drinking more than she would in Germany. 'It's the whole culture of, "Come on, I'll buy you a drink." In Germany, everybody buys their own drink, whereas here you get a round in and you get lots of people buying drinks for you.'

Intrapersonal communication will enhance and be enhanced by interpersonal communication and researchers have noted that the more contacts migrants have with the native population the better as far as adaptation is concerned, although an individual's ethnic group may assist adaptation initially. Folami benefitted from the knowledge and experience of Nigerian/British contacts to tell him 'what's up', 'what they've been through' and how to interpret situations. On the other hand, Faiza said that she did not want contact with Turkish people during the first few years because it would have stopped her from learning another language, and given her a greater feeling of being abroad rather than being integrated into British life. Now she is more confident about living and communicating in England and has many friends, including many Turkish ones. Interpersonal communication will be facilitated if an individual's original culture is close to the new culture and more difficult if a stranger exhibits obvious physical, behavioural or ethnic differences. Susanne found life in England was not that different to life in Germany whereas Mari found herself in a very different culture in terms of gender expectations. Of all the respondents, Mari experienced the greatest sense of constraint, 'I was conscious of being a woman in a way that I am not at home. I was not as confident out by myself. Our organization wanted us to fit into the rural community and this affected how I behaved and dressed, which for me implied a lack of independence and power.' As a result Mari found the unsolicited attention of males difficult to respond to in the same way that she would have done in England, where she did not feel the need to have a male friend with her, in order to feel safe.

The adaptive personality

Kim also identifies personality as an important variable in adapting to a new culture and the interviewees provided evidence for her concept of the adaptive personality (Kim 2001: 172). Such a personality is characterized by openness, strength, and positivity and these aspects tend to mutually reinforce one another. 'Openness', in Kim's view, 'allows strangers to examine themselves and the environment with a genuine willingness to be transformed as they incorporate new experiences and new learning' (2001: 174). Strength is the quality that allows a person to be steadfast and at the same time flexible. Positivity is the belief that it is possible to change and that the change itself can be rewarding. The importance of this mental outlook is that it can render insiders more receptive to strangers who exhibit it and, crucially, it may help to undermine stereotypical categorizations of strangers. In addition, if the institutions that migrants participate in are receptive, then the whole process of becoming a cultural insider is eased. It was an important fact, for example, that the students interviewed were very positive about their educational experiences in Britain.

Case study: the adaptive personality

Faith: 'I wanted to explore the world before I got too old to try. I'm glad I came because I'm learning new things everyday. I'm learning about policies that help support the nation as a whole: the NHS, the benefit system, disability and equal opportunity in the workplace, free education. I would like to use this knowledge back home.'

Faiza: 'It is nice to be studying in another country. It's a very good opportunity: a different culture, different people, and a different language. I really enjoy it.'

Folami: 'I grew up in a big family house. I wanted to see what I could do on my own without my family helping me, just to feel like a man.'

Lyuben: 'I've got a few English friends and a few Indian and Arabic friends. I consider myself an open person. I try and experience

different realities. I compare experiences to mine to see what sort of things they go through, to get into their situation and see what sort of life they are living.'

Mari: 'I prepared myself to be open-minded, because I think it's an effective way of dealing with new cultures. Before I left I went to a lot of effort to ensure that I took the right clothes (covering the knees and shoulders). It was effective in that many Malawians complimented us on our "Malawian" dress, and it set us apart from tourists. I think people appreciated our efforts to fit in.'

Susanne: 'I found it exciting to explore a foreign culture, seeing a different country. I've always been quite independent. I never had problems, even when I was younger, to go on holiday and not see my parents for a month. I always liked to go travelling and experience new things.'

Intercultural personhood

Gudykunst and Kim refer to the 'continuous interplay of deculturation and acculturation that brings about change in strangers in the direction of assimilation, the highest degree of adaptation theoretically conceivable' (2003: 360). They call this final state 'intercultural personhood' and offer the following endorsement:

> In becoming intercultural, we rise above the hidden forces of culture and discover that there are many ways to be 'good', 'true', and 'beautiful'. In this developmental process, we acquire a greater capacity to overcome cultural parochialism and develop *a wider circle of identification*, approaching the limits of many cultures and ultimately of humanity itself. The process of becoming intercultural, then, is like climbing a high mountain. As we reach the mountaintop, we see that all paths below ultimately lead to the same summit and that each path presents unique scenery. Becoming intercultural is a gradual process of liberating ourselves from our limited and exclusive interests and viewpoints and striving to attain a perspective in which we see ourselves as a part of a larger, more inclusive whole.
>
> (Gudykunst and Kim 2003: 385, original emphasis)

Intercultural personhood is regarded as a desirable and an appropriate goal in a world in which individuals are increasingly likely to become strangers or to interact with strangers. However, it is not effortlessly achieved and is the outcome of a long process involving stress as well as adaptation and growth.

First contacts can be demanding for the stranger. Gudykunst and Kim (2003: 380) state that:

> Because strangers' cultural identities and habits are placed against the systematic forces of the host culture, the strangers are at least temporarily in an unsettling state of 'disequilibrium' manifested in many emotional 'lows' of uncertainty and confusion. Indeed, the challenges of handling daily activities are most severe during the initial phases, as has been shown in studies of culture shock.

Lyuben commented that, initially, he had 'a sense of isolation because people don't know who you are, or what you are capable of. It would be the same in my country. If I don't know who a foreigner is, I need time to get to know him, then to be close to him and let him into my personal space.' In the beginning particularly, both the host group and the strangers may interact on the basis of generalizations about one another. Gudykunst and Kim (2003: 24) summarize the consequences for the host group of operating in terms of limited information in the following way:

> Further, members of the host group do not possess information regarding individual strangers, even though they may have some information about the groups or cultures from which the strangers come. Since we do not have information regarding individual strangers, our initial impression of them must, therefore, be an abstract or categoric one (i.e. a stereotypic one). Strangers are classified on the basis of whatever information we can obtain. If the only information we have is their cultures, we base our initial impression on this information. If we have additional information (their ethnicities, genders, classes), we use that as well.

Contact tends to break down stereotypes. English people, for example, did not know what country Faiza came from and were uncertain of her religion, Islam, because she does not wear black clothing and headwear. People would ask her, 'Are you a Muslim?' and they would compliment her on her colourful headscarf: 'It's so nice, you look beautiful. The headscarf looks very nice on you.' To her amused delight some British non-Muslims, greeted her with, 'Assalumu alaikum'. Her experience was that 'it doesn't matter what your religion is'. More important is 'who you are, your respect, your attitude, your success, your mind, what you can do'. She was also able to observe the differences between London and a town in Kent. In the latter when she was out shopping, people initially looked at her as if she were 'an alien rather than a person', especially as she rode a bicycle. 'I think this is because the population of the town is mainly native. It's not mixed like London, where everyone is

different.' Eventually people got used to her as, in her words, 'a different Muslim concept'.

Adaptation takes place over time and no one person's experience will be exactly the same as another's. As the learning occurs changes will take place in the person. Kim argues that the changes will not be experienced as a loss but as a positive change. The analogy is made between learning to adapt to a new culture and learning a second language: when a person learns another language it is not at the expense of their first language; it enhances their ability to communicate and contributes to their growth (Kim 2001: 67). In summary, '[I] intercultural learning and growth are, in this view, the core or essence of the sojourn experience. Strangers are capable not only of adapting to new cultures but also, and more important, of undertaking modifications within themselves' (Gudykunst and Kim 2003: 379). The resultant transformation enables the individual to function more effectively in a strange place and become a better human being. Mari put it this way:

> I have become a more confident person due to my experience in Malawi. I am not so afraid of facing new situations, and I found I was able to travel and teach alone. I was worried about language barriers but I was able to establish amazing relationships with the staff and pupils at my school, and other local people whom I came into contact with. I do not feel so hostile to religion because I have seen how it helps people in times of difficulty in Malawi. I will always remember the warmth and friendliness of people there, and their courage in times of hardship.

Exercise 1

This can be carried out as an individual or as a group.

Entering a new group or situation can produce a culture shock or crisis. Geoff Dyer imaginatively constructs the experience of the famous jazz saxophonist, Lester Young's (1909–1959) entry to the army:

> Jazz was about making your own sound, finding a way to be different from everybody else, never playing the same thing two nights running. The army wanted everyone to be the same, identical, indistinguishable, looking alike, everything remaining the same day after day, nothing changing. Everything had to form right angles and sharp edges. The sheets of his bed were folded hard as the metal angles of his locker. They shaved your head like a carpenter planing a block of wood, trying to make it absolutely square. Even the uniforms were designed to remould the body, to make square people. Nothing curved or soft, no

colors, no silence. It seemed almost unbelievable that in the space of a fortnight the same person could suddenly find himself in so totally different a world.

He had a slack, drawling walk and here he was expected to march, to tramp up and down the parade ground in boots heavy as a ball and chain. Marching until his head felt brittle as glass.[4]

(Dyer 1998: 10–11)

Can you recall being in a situation where you found yourself in a totally different world from any one that you had experienced before?

Discuss the factors that led to your success or failure to adapt to the new situation.

Exercise 2

This can be carried out as an individual or as a group.

a) A young man, aged 20, made an enquiry about a job in a shop, which is one of a high street photography chain. He was asked by the manager, 'Do you always wear those things in your ear?' He was wearing an ear bar as well as a small stud below the lip.

b) It was reported (Sunday Times, 4.3.2007) that, in an attempt to cut the welfare bill, the government was considering a scheme to help the jobless that would make available free haircuts, suits and tattoo removal.

c) February 2007: BBC Radio 1 listeners were invited to comment on the widely-reported event that the singer, Britney Spears, had shaved off her hair after allegedly leaving a rehab clinic after one day. They were asked, 'Does Britney need help? Why do you think she cut her hair off? Does she need to spend some time away from the spotlight? Or is she just a girl having fun?'

d) Shabina Begum's school in Luton refused to let her, as a Muslim, wear a full-length dress or jilbab. She left the school in 2002 and won a case against the school in the Court of Appeal in 2005. In 2006, however, the House of Lords upheld Denbigh High School's decision to prevent Shabina Begum from wearing the jilbab.

Examine, in the light of the cases listed above, the extent to which we are free to choose our own appearance styles, if we wish to be 'insiders'.

Key points

- Identity as an outsider can be a product of choice as in the cases of the musicians, the Gypsies and the body modifiers, or a product of marginalization as in the case of the disabled.
- A distinctive identity, based on aesthetic, moral or political criteria, is sustained by group or subcultural activity. The boundaries between the outsider group and others can, however, be difficult to maintain.
- Outsiders who wish to be insiders start out as strangers and have to be prepared for an intensive and extensive learning process. Their original learning, enculturation, is enhanced and challenged by new learning, acculturation and unlearning, deculturation.
- Interviews supported the usefulness of Kim's concept of the adaptive personality.
- The interviewees can be seen as embarking on a journey towards intercultural personhood.

Notes

1   The aim of the interviews in this chapter was not to present typical individuals but to explore the ideas raised by the other researchers and, in the case of the musicians, to look at a more contemporary example.
2   For reasons of confidentiality different first names have been attributed to interviewees.
3   See Pitts 2000. Media treatments of body modifiers are examined, especially the tendency to set subcultural interpretations against those of mental health experts who tend to see body modification as a social or mental problem.

References

Adams, L. (2006) *Harbor*. London: Portobello Books.

Allport, G.W. (1954) *The Nature of Prejudice*. New York: Macmillan.

Andersch, E.G., Staats, L.C. and Bostrom, R.N. (1969) *Communication in Everyday Use*. Austin, TX: Holt, Rinehart & Winston.

Antaki, C. and Widdicombe, S. (1998) *Identities in Talk*. London: Sage.

Argyle, M. (1983) *The Psychology of Interpersonal Behaviour*. Harmondsworth: Penguin.

Argyle, M. (1988) *Bodily Communication*, 2nd edn. London/New York: Methuen.

Argyle, M. (1994) *The Psychology of Interpersonal Behaviour*. London: Penguin.

Asch, S.E. (1951) 'Effects of group pressure upon the modification and distortion of judgements' in H. Guetzkow (ed.) *Groups, Leadership and Men*. Pittsburgh, PA: Carnegie Press.

Atkinson, R.L., Atkinson, R.C., Smith, E.E., Bem, D.J. and Nolen-Hoeksema, S. (1996) *Hilgard's Introduction to Psychology*, 12th edn. Orlando, Florida: Harcourt Brace.

Axel, R. (1998) *Gestures: The Do's and Taboos of Body Language Around the World*. New York: John Wiley & Sons Inc.

Babb, P., Butcher, H., Church, J., and Zealy, L. (eds) (2006) *Social Trends No. 36*. Basingstoke: Palgrave Macmillan.

Bales, R.F. (1950) *Interaction Process Analysis: A Method for the Study of Small Groups*. Chicago: University of Chicago Press.

Bales, R.F. (1953) 'The equilibrium problem in small groups' in T. Parsons, R.F. Bales and E.A. Shils (eds) *Working Papers in the Theory of Action*. New York: The Free Press.

Bales, R.F. and Slater, P.E. (1956) 'Role differentiation in small decision-making groups' in T. Parsons and R.F. Bales (eds) *Family, Socialization and Interaction*. London: Routledge.

Bannister & Agnew, (1976) discussed in Gross, R.D. (2005) *Psychology: The Science of Mind and Behaviour*. Abingdon: Hodder Arnold.

Barker, C. (2003) *Cultural Studies: Theory and Practice*. London: Sage.

Barnlund, D.C. (1970) 'A transactional model of communication' in K.K. Sereno and C.D. Mortensen (eds) *Foundations of Communications Theory*. New York: Harper Row.

Baron, R.A. and Byrne, D. (1994) *Social Psychology*. Boston: Allyn and Bacon.

Baron, R.A. and Byrne, D. (1997) *Social Psychology*. London: Allyn and Bacon.

Baron, R.A., Byrne, D. and Branscombe, N.R. (2006) *Social Psychology*. Boston: Pearson Education Inc.

Baron, R.A. and Greenberg, J. (1990) *Behaviour in Organizations*. New Jersey: Allyn and Bacon.

Baron, R.S., Kerr, N. and Miller, N. (1992) *Group Process, Group Decision, Group Action*. Buckingham: Open University Press.

Barrett, R. (1997) 'The "Homo-genius" speech community' in A. Livia and K. Hall (eds) *Queerly Phrased: Language, Gender and Sexuality*. New York/Oxford: Oxford University Press.

Becker, H.S. (1966) *Outsiders: Studies in the Sociology of Deviance*. London: Collier-Macmillan Limited.

Becker, S.L. (1968) What rhetoric (communication theory) is relevant for contemporary speech communication? Paper presented at the University of Minnesota Spring Symposium in Speech Communication.

Belbin, R.M. (1996) *The Coming Shape of Organizations*. London: Butterworth-Heinemann.

Bennett, M. (1993) 'Towards ethnorelativism: a developmental model of intercultural sensitivity' in R.M. Paige (ed.) *Education for the Intercultural Experience*. Yarmouth, ME: Intercultural Press.

Berger, A.A. (2005) *Shop 'Til You Drop? Consumer Behavior and American Culture*. Lanham, MD: Rowman & Littlefield Publishers.

Berlo, D.K. (1960) *The Process of Communication: An Introduction to Theory and Practice*. New York: Holt, Rinehart and Winston.

Berne, E. (1964) *Games People Play*. London: Penguin.

Berne, E. (1975) *What Do You Say After You've Said Hello?* UK: Corgi Books.

Blumer, H. (1986) *The Symbolic Interactionism: Perspective and Method*. Los Angeles, CA: University of California Press.

Bocock, R. (1993) *Consumption*. London: Routledge.

Bodi, F. (2006) The racists are driven by envy of Asian success, *Guardian*, 26 July.

Bourdieu, P. (1986) *Distinction: A Social Critique of the Judgement of Taste*. London: Routledge.

Bowie, F. (1997) 'Wales from within: conflicting interpretations of Welsh identity' in S. Macdonald (ed.) *Inside European Identities: Ethnography in Western Europe*. Oxford/New York: Berg Publishers.

Brislin, R. (1993) *Understanding Culture's Influence on Behavior*. Fort Worth, TX: Harcourt Brace Jovanovich.

Brockriede, W.E. (1968) Demonstrations of the concept of rhetoric, *Quarterly Journal* 54.

Brown, R. (1988) *Group Processes*. Oxford/Massachusetts: Blackwell.

Brown, R. (2000) *Group Processes*. Oxford/Massachusetts: Blackwell.

Bryson, B. (1990) *Mother Tongue: The English Language*. London: Penguin Books.

Burston, P. and Richardson, C. (1995) *A Queer Romance: Lesbians, Gay Men and Popular Culture*. New York/London: Routledge.

Butler, J. (1990) *Gender Trouble: Feminism and the Subversion of Identity*. NewYork/ London: Routledge.

Butler, J. (1999) *Gender Trouble: Feminism and the Subversion of Identity*. New York/ London: Routledge.

Cameron, D. (1985) 'Beyond alienation: an integrational approach to women and language' in J. Corner and J. Hawthorn (1993) *Communication Studies: An Introductory Reader*. London: Edward Arnold.

Cameron, D. (1992) *Feminism and Linguistic Theory*. London: Macmillan.

Cameron, D. (2006) 'Gender and language ideologies' in J. Holmes and M. Meyerhoff (eds) *The Handbook of Language and Gender*. Oxford: Blackwell.

Cathcart, R.S., Samovar, L.A. and Henman, L. (1996) *Small Group Communication: Theory and Practice*. Madison, WI: Brown & Benchmark.

Coates, J. (2004) *Women, Men and Language*. Harlow: Pearson Education.

Cochrane, K. (2006) column in the *New Statesman*, 29 May, p. 31.

Coggle, P. (1997) quoted in 'It's not what you say, it's the way that you say it' by E. Houghton, *Independent*, 15 October.

Cook, M. (1970) Experiments on orientation and proxemics, *Human Relations* 23: 61–76.

Cooley, C. (1909) *Social Organization*. US: Scribner.

Cooley, C.H. (1902) *Human Nature and Social Order*. New York: Shocken.

Crawford, M. and Unger, R. (2004) *Women and Gender: A Feminist Psychology*. New York: McGraw-Hill.

Crutchfield, R.S. (1955) Conformity and character, *American Psychologist*, 10: 191–8.

Dance, F.E.X. (1970) 'A helical model of communication' in K.K. Sereno and C.D. Mortensen (eds) *Foundations of Communication Theory*. New York: Harper & Row.

Davis, H. (1989) What makes bad language bad? *Language & Communication*, 9: 1–9.

De Mooij, M. (1998) *Global Marketing and Advertising: Understanding Cultural Paradoxes*. Thousand Oaks, CA: Sage.

Deaux, K. (1991) 'Social identities' in R. Curtis (ed.) *The Relational Self*. New York: Guildford.

Dyer, G. (1998) *But Beautiful: A Book about Jazz*. London: Abacus.

Earley, P.C. (1993) East meets West meets Mideast: further explorations of collectivistic and individualistic work groups, *Academy of Management Journal*, 36: 319–48.

Eco, U. ([1967] 1995) 'Towards a semiological guerrilla warfare' in U. Eco, *Faith in Fakes: Travels in Hyperreality*. London: Minerva.

Edwards, D. (1998) 'The relevant thing about her: social identity categories in use' in C. Antaki and S. Widdecombe (1998) *Identities in Talk*. London: Sage.

Edwards, J.R. (1997) 'Social class differences and the identification of sex in children' in N. Coupland and A. Jaworski (eds) *Sociolinguistics*. Basingstoke: Palgrave.

Eisenberg, E.M. (2001) Building a mystery: towards a new theory of communication and identity, *Journal of Communication*, September: 534–52.

Ekman, P. (1982) *Emotion in the Human Face*, 2nd edn. Cambridge: Cambridge University Press.

Ekman, P. and Friesen, W.V. (1982) Felt, false, and miserable smiles, *Journal of Nonverbal Behaviour*, 6: 238–52.

Ellis, A. and Beattie, G. (1986) *The Psychology of Language and Communication*. New York: Guildford Press.

Elmes, S. (2005) *Talking for Britain: A Journey through the Nation's Dialects*. London: Penguin Books.

Featherstone, M. (1991) *Consumer Culture & Postmodernism*. London: Sage.

Ferraro, G. (1990) *The Cultural Dimension of International Business*. Englewood Cliffs, NJ: Prentice Hall.

Festinger, L. (1957) *A Theory of Cognitive Dissonance*. US: Stanford University Press.

Fiske, J. (1989) *Reading the Popular*. London: Routledge.

Fiske, S.T. (2004) *Social Beings: A Core Motives Approach to Social Psychology*. New York: John Wiley & Sons.

Flocker, M. (2003) *The Metrosexual Guide to Style*. Cambridge, MA: DeCapo Press.

Fowles, J. (1996) *Advertising and Popular Culture*. Thousand Oaks, CA: Sage Publications.

Fox, K. (2004) *Watching the English: The Hidden Rules of English Behaviour*. London: Hodder and Stoughton.

Gahagan, J. (1984) *Social Interaction and its Management*. London: Methuen.

Gay Y. and Blasco, P. (1999) *Gypsies in Madrid: Sex, Gender and the Performance of Identity*. Oxford: Berg.

Gerbner, G. (1956) Towards a general model of communication, *Audio Visual Communication Review*, 4.

Giddens, A. (1991) *Modernity and Self-identity: Self and Society in the Late Modern Age*. Cambridge: Polity Press.

Giles, H. and Trudgill, P. (1983) 'Sociolinguistics and linguistic value judgements' in P. Trudgill (ed.) *On Dialect*. Oxford: Basil Blackwell.

Goffman, E. (1959) *The Presentation of Self in Everyday Life*. Allen Lane: Penguin.

Goleman, D. (2000) Leadership that gets results, *Harvard Business Review*, 78(2): 78–90.

Goleman, D. (2004) *Emotional Intelligence and Working with Emotional Intelligence*. London: Bloomsbury.

Griffin, E. (2003) *A First Look at Communication*, 5th edn. New York: McGraw-Hill.

Gross, L. (1998) 'Minorities, majorities and the media' in T. Liebes and J. Curran (eds) *Media, Ritual and Identity*. London/New York: Routledge.

Gross, R.D. (2005) *Psychology: The Science of Mind and Behaviour*. Abingdon: Hodder Arnold.

Gudykunst, W.B. and Kim, Y.Y. (1997) *Communicating With Strangers: An Approach to Intercultural Communication*, 3rd edn. Boston: McGraw-Hill.

Gudykunst, W.B. and Kim, Y.Y. (2003) *Communicating with Strangers: An Approach to Intercultural Communication,* 4th edn. Boston: McGraw-Hill.

Gudykunst, W.B. and Ting-Toomey, S. (1988) *Culture and Interpersonal Communication.* Newbury Park, CA: Sage.

Haggard, E.A. and Isaacs, F.S. (1966) 'Micromomentary facial expressions as indicators of ego mechanisms in psychotherapy' in L.A. Gottschalk and A.A. Auerbach (eds) *Methods of Research in Psychotherapy.* New York: Appleton-Century-Crofts.

Hall, E. ([1977]1981) *Beyond Culture.* New York: Doubleday.

Hall, E. (1983) *The Dance of Life: Other Dimensions of Time.* New York: Doubleday.

Hall, E.T. (1966) *The Hidden Dimension.* New York: Doubleday.

Hall, K. (2006) 'Exceptional speakers: contested and problematized gender identities' in J. Holmes and M. Meyerhoff (2006) *The Handbook of Language and Gender.* Oxford: Blackwell.

Hall, S. (1996) 'New ethnicities' in D. Morley and C. Kuan-Hsing (eds) *Stuart Hall: Critical Dialogues.* London: Routledge.

Handy, C.B. (1993) *Understanding Organizations.* London: Penguin.

Harris, T. (1969) *I'm OK – You're OK.* New York: Harper & Row.

Harris, T. and Harris, A. B. (1995) *Staying OK.* London: Arrow Books.

Harding, N. (2003) *The Social Construction of Management: Texts and Identities.* London: Routledge.

Harris, R. and Rampton, B. (eds) (2003) *The Language, Ethnicity and Race Reader.* London: Routledge.

Hebdige, D. (1979) *Subculture: The Meaning of Style.* London: Methuen.

Hersey, P. and Blanchard, K.H. (1988) *Management of Organizational Behavior: Utilizing Human Resources.* Englewood Cliffs, NJ: Prentice Hall International.

Hofstede, G. (1980) *Culture's Consequences: International Differences in Work-related Values*: Beverly Hills, CA: Sage.

Hofstede, G. (1984) *Culture's Consequences: International Differences in Work-related Values* (abridged edn). Beverly Hills, CA: Sage.

Hofstede, G. (2001) *Culture's Consequences: Comparing Values, Behaviors, Institutions and Organisations across Nations.* Thousand Oaks, CA: Sage.

Holmes, J. and Meyerhoff, M. (2006) *The Handbook of Language and Gender.* Oxford: Blackwell.

Huczynski, A. and Buchanan, D. (2004) *Organizational Behaviour.* Harlow: Financial Times/Prentice Hall.

Hughes, S. (1992) Expletives of lower working-class women, *Language in Society,* 21: 291–303.

Huq, R. (2004) 'Global youth cultures in localized spaces: the case of the UK new Asian dance music and French rap' in D. Muggleton and R. Weinzierl (2004) *The Post-subcultures Reader.* Oxford: Berg.

Jagose, A. (1996) *Queer Theory: An Introduction.* New York: University Press.

Jakobson, R. (1960) 'Closing statements: linguistics and poetics' in T.A. Sebeok (ed.) *Style in Language*. Cambridge, MA: MIT Press.

Janis, I.L. (1972) *Victims of Groupthink*. Boston: Houghton Mifflin.

Jourard, S.M. (1971) *Self-disclosure: An Experimental Analysis of the Transparent Self*. New York: Wiley Interscience.

Karau, S. and Williams, K.D. (1993) Social loafing: a meta-analytic review and theoretical integration, *Journal of Personality and Social Psychology*, 65: 681–706.

Katz, E. and Lazarsfeld, P.F. (1955) *Personal Influence*. Glencoe, IL: Free Press.

Keesing, R.M. and Strathern, A.J. (1998) *Cultural Anthropology: A Contemporary Perspective*, 3rd edn. London: Harcourt.

Kendall, S. (2006) 'Creating gendered demeanors of authority at work and at home' in J. Holmes and M. Meyerhoff (2006) *The Handbook of Language and Gender*. Oxford: Blackwell.

Kim, Y.Y. (1997) 'Adapting to a new culture' in L.A. Samovar and R.E. Porter (eds) *Intercultural Communication: A Reader*. Belmont, CA: Wadsworth/Thomson.

Kim, Y.Y. (2001) *Becoming Intercultural: An Integrative Theory of Communication and Cross-cultural Adaptation*. London: Sage.

Kuhn, H.H. (1960) Self attitudes by age, sex and professional training, *Sociology Quarterly*, 1: 39–55.

Lasswell, H. (1948) 'The structure and function of communication in society' in L. Bryson (ed.) *The Communication of Ideas*. New York: Harper & Row.

Latane, B., Williams, K. and Harkins, S. (1979) Many hands make light the work: the causes and consequences of social loafing, *Journal of Personality and Social Psychology*, 37: 822–32.

Leary, M.R. and Kowalski, R.M. (1990) Impression management: a literature review and two-component model, *Psychological Bulletin*, 107: 34–47.

Leavitt, H.J. (1951) Some effects of certain communication patterns on group performance, *Journal of Abnormal and Social Psychology*, 46: 38–50.

Leiss, W., Kline, S. and Jhally, S. (1997) *Social Communication in Advertising: Persons, Products and Images of Well-being*, 2nd edn. London: Routledge.

Levine, R. and Campbell, D. (1972) *Ethnocentrism*. New York: Wiley.

Lewin, K. (1948) *Resolving Social Conflicts*. New York: Harper & Row.

Lewis, R. (2006) *When Cultures Collide: Leading Across Cultures*. London: Nicholas Brealey International.

Likert, R. (1961) *New Patterns of Management*. New York: McGraw-Hill.

Lippmann, W. (1922) *Public Opinion*. New York: Harcourt.

Lucas, I. (1997) 'The color of his eyes: Polari and the Sisters of Perpetual Indulgence' in A. Livia and K. Hall (eds) *Queerly Phrased: Language, Gender and Sexuality*. New York/Oxford: Oxford University Press.

Luft, J. (1969) *Of Human Interaction*. US: National Press Books.

Lukens, J. (1978) Ethnocentric speech, *Ethnic Groups*, 2: 35–53.

Lury, C. (1996) *Consumer Culture*. Cambridge: Polity Press.

Lustig, M.W. and Cassotta, L.L. (1996) 'Comparing group communication across cultures: leadership, conformity, and discussion processes' in R.S. Cathcart, L.A. Samovar and L. Henman (eds) *Small Group Communication: Theory & Practice*. Madison, WI: Brown & Benchmark.

McCracken, G. (1986) Culture and consumption: a theoretical account of the structure and movement of the cultural meaning of consumer goods, *Journal of Consumer Research*, 13: 71–81.

McQuail, D. (1984) *Communication*. Harlow: Longman.

McQuail, D. (2005) *Mass Communication Theory: An Introduction*. London: Sage.

McQuail, D. and Windahl, S. (1996) *Communication Models for the Study of Mass Communication*. London: Longman.

Marcus, H. and Kitayama, S. (1991) Culture and the self, *Psychological Review*, 98: 224–53.

Maslow, A. (1954) *Motivation and Personality*. New York: Harper & Row.

Mead, G.H. (1934) *Mind, Self and Society*. Chicago: University of Chicago Press.

Mehrabian, A. (1971) *Silent Messages*. Belmont, CA: Wadsworth.

Mercer, K. (2005) 'Black hair/style politics' in K. Gelder (ed.) *The Subcultures Reader*. Abingdon: Hodder Arnold.

Merton, R.K. (1957) *Social Theory and Social Structure*. New York: Free Press.

Mills, J. (2004) 'Mothers and mother tongue: perspectives on self-construction by mothers of Pakistani heritage' in A. Pavlenko and A. Blackledge (eds) *Negotiation of Identities in Multilingual Contexts*. Clevedon: Multilingual matters Ltd.

Millwood Hargrave, A. (ed.) (1991) *A Matter of Manners? – The Limits of Broadcasting Language*. Broadcasting Standards Council, Research Monograph Series: 3, John Libbey.

Milroy, L. (1980) *Language and Social Networks*. Oxford: Basil Blackwell.

Mitchell, A. (1983) *Nine American Lifestyles: Who We Are and Where We're Going*. New York: Macmillan.

Montgomery, M. (1995) *An Introduction to Language and Society*, 2nd edn. London: Routledge.

Moorhead, G., Ference, R. and Neck, C.P. (1996) 'Group decision fiascos continue: Space Shuttle Challenger and a groupthink framework' in R.S. Cathcart, L.A. Samovar and L. Henman (eds) *Small Group Communication: Theory & Practice*. Madison, WI: Brown & Benchmark.

Moreno, J.L. (1953) *Who Shall Survive?* New York: Beacon Press.

Morgan, G. (1997) *Images of Organization*. London: Sage.

Morley, D. and Robins, K. (1995) *Spaces of Identity*. London: Routledge.

Morris, D. (2002) *People Watching*. Vintage: London.

Mortensen, C.D. and Ayres, C.M. (1997) *Miscommunication*. London: Sage.

Mortensen, D. (1972) *Communication: The Study of Human Interaction*. New York: McGraw-Hill.

Muggleton, D. and Weinzierl, R. (2004) *The Post-subcultures Reader*. Oxford: Berg.

Murphy, R. (1995) 'Encounters: the body silent in America' in B. Ingstad and S.R. Whyte (eds) *Disability and Culture*. Berkeley, CA: University of California Press.

Myers, G. and Myers, M. (1985) *The Dynamics of Human Communication*. New York: McGraw-Hill.

Newcomb, T.H. (1953) An approach to the study of communicative acts, *Psychological Review*, 60.

Noelle-Neumann, E. (1974) The spiral of silence: a theory of public opinion, *Journal of Communication*, 24: 24–51.

Omaar, R. (2006) *Only Half of Me: Being a Muslim in Britain*. London: Viking, Penguin Books.

Palahniuk, C. (2006) *Fight Club*. London: Vintage Books.

Paterson, M. (2006) *Consumption and Everyday Life*. London: Routledge.

Paxman, J. (1998) *The English: A Portrait of a People*. London: Michael Joseph.

Petty, R.E. and Cacioppo, J.T. (1996) *Attitudes and Persuasion: Classic and Contemporary Approaches*. Boulder, CO/Oxford: Westview Press.

Pittock, M.G.H. (1999) *Celtic Identity and the British Image*. Manchester: Manchester University Press.

Pitts, V.L. (2000) 'Body modification, self-mutilation and agency in media accounts of a subculture' in M. Featherstone (ed.) *Body Modification*. New York: Sage.

Pitts, V.L. (2003) *In the Flesh: The Cultural Politics of Body Modification*. New York: Palgrave MacMillan.

Polhemus, T. (1994) *Streetstyle*. London: Thames & Hudson.

Polhemus, T. and Uzi Part, B. (2004) *Hot Bodies Cool Styles*. London: Thames and Hudson.

Rogers, C. (1961) *On Becoming a Person*. New York: Houghton Mifflin.

Romaine, S. (2000) *Language and Society*. Oxford: Oxford University Press.

Rundell, M. (1995) The word on the street, *English Today*, 11(3), July.

Said, E. (1978) *Orientalism*. London: Routledge and Kegan Paul.

Salzman, M., Matathia, I. and O'Reilly, A. (2005) *The Future of Men*. New York: Palgrave Macmillan.

Samovar, L. and Porter, R. (2004) *Communication Between Cultures*. Belmont, CA: Wadsworth/Thomson Learning.

Sardar, Z. (2002) Nothing left to belong to, *New Statesman*, 25 February.

Savage, M., Bagnall, G. and Longhurst, B. (2005) *Globalisation and Belonging*. London: Sage.

Schachter, S. (1951) Deviation, rejection and communication, *Journal of Abnormal and Social Psychology*, 46: 190–207.

Schramm, W. (ed.) (1954) *The Process and Effects of Mass Communication*. Champaign, ILL: University of Illinois Press.

Shannon, C. and Weaver, W. (1949) *Mathematical Theory of Communication*. Champaign, ILL: University of Illinois Press.

Sherif, M., Harvey, O.J., White, B., Hood, W.R. and Sherif, C.W. (1961) *Intergroup Conflict and Cooperation: The Robbers Cave Experiment*. Norman, OK: University of Oklahoma Institute of Intergroup Relations.

Slater, D. (1997) *Consumer Culture and Modernity*. Cambridge: Polity Press.

Smith, K. and Berg, D. (1997) Cross cultural groups at work, *European Management Journal*, 15(1): 8–15.

Smith, P.B. and Bond, M.H. (1998) *Social Psychology Across Cultures: Analysis and Perspectives*. Hemel Hempstead: Prentice Hall Europe.

Snyder, M. (1979) 'Self-monitoring' in Berkowitz (ed.) *Advances in Experimental Social Psychology*, vol 12. New York: Academic Press.

Spender, D. (1985) *Man Made Language*, 2nd edn. London/New York: Routledge & Kegan Paul.

Storry, M. and Childs, P. (eds) (2002) *British Cultural Identities*, 2nd edn. London: Routledge.

Sullivan, N. (2003) *A Critical Introduction to Queer Theory*. Edinburgh: Edinburgh University Press.

Tajfel, H. and Turner, J.C. (1986) discussed in Brown, R. (2000) *Group Processes*. Oxford: Blackwell.

Tannen, D. (1992) *You Just Don't Understand: Men and Women in Conversation*. London: Virago.

Tannen, D. (2006) 'Gender and family interaction' in J. Holmes and M. Meyerhoff (eds) *The Handbook of Language and Gender*. Oxford: Blackwell.

Ting-Toomey, S. (1999) *Communicating Across Cultures*. New York: Guildford Press.

Traugott, E.C. and Pratt, M.L. (1980) *Linguistics*. San Diego, CA: Harcourt Brace Jovanovich Inc.

Triandis, H.C. (1988) 'Collectivism vs. individualism' in G. Verma and C. Bagley (eds) *Cross-cultural Studies of Personality, Attitudes, and Cognition*. London: Macmillan.

Triandis, H.C., Bontempo, R., Villareal, M., Asai, M. and Lucca, N. (1988) Individualism-collectivism: cross-cultural studies of self-ingroup relationships, *Journal of Personality and Social Psychology*, 54: 323–38.

Triandis, H.C., Leung, K., Villareal, M. and Clack, F. (1985) Allocentric versus Idiocentric tendencies, *Journal of Research in Personality*, 19: 395–415.

Trompenaars, F. and Hampden-Turner, C. (2004) *Managing People across Cultures*. Chichester: John Wiley & Sons.

Trompenaars, F. and Woolliams, P. (2004) *Marketing Across Cultures*. Chichester: John Wiley & Sons.

Trudgill, P. (1983) *Sociolinguistics: An Introduction to Language and Society*. London: Penguin.

Trudgill, P. (2000) *Sociolinguistics: An Introduction to Language and Society*. London: Penguin.

Tuckman, B.C. and Jensen, M.A.C. (1977) Stages of small group development revisited, *Group and Organization Studies*, 2(4): 419–27.

Veblen, T. (1998) *The Theory of the Leisure Class*. Amherst, NY: Prometheus Books.

Watson, J. and Hill, A. (2006) *The Dictionary of Media and Communication Studies*, 7th edn. Abingdon: Hodder Arnold.

Wesley, B.H. and MacLean Jr, M.S. (1957) A conceptual model for communications research, *Journalism Quarterly*, 34.

White, R.K. and Lippitt, R. (1960) *Autocracy and Democracy*. New York: Harper.

Widdicombe, S. and Wooffitt, R. (1995) *The Language of Youth Subcultures: Social Identity in Action*. Hemel Hampstead: Harvester Wheatsheaf.

Williams, K.D. and Karau, S.J. (1991) Social loafing and social compensation: the effects of expectations of co-worker performance, *Journal of Personality and Social Psychology*, 61: 570–81.

Winge, T.M. (2004) 'Constructing "Neo-Tribal" identities through dress: modern primitives and body modifications' in D. Muggleton and R. Weinzierl (eds) *The Post-subcultures Reader*. Oxford: Berg.

Woodwood, K. (2002) *Understanding Identity*. London: Arnold.

Yeomans, L. (2006) Women in public relations and emotional labour. Paper presented to the 8th Annual Conference of the European Public Relations Education and Research Association, 6–9 September.

Yip, A. (2004) Negotiating space within family and kin in identity construction: the narratives of British non-heterosexual Muslims, *The Sociological Review*, 52(3): 336–50.

Index

s?

Education... Media, Film & Cultural Studies

Health, Nursing & Social Welfare... Higher Education

Psychology, Counselling & Psychotherapy... Study Skills

Keep up with what's buzzing
at Open University Press
by signing up to receive
regular title information at
www.openup.co.uk/elert

Sociology

OPEN UNIVERSITY PRESS

cation